Baudrillard

Baudrillard is widely recognised as a powerful new force in cultural and social criticism, and is often referred to as the 'High Priest of Postmodernism'. This study presents a detached assessment of his social thought and his reputation, challenging the way his work has been received in postmodernism and proposing a new reading of his contribution to social theory.

Using many sources currently available only in French, Mike Gane provides the keys to understanding Baudrillard's project and reveals the extent and scope of Baudrillard's challenge to modern social theory and cultural criticism. He looks at the sources of Baudrillard's ideas, analysing how Baudrillard has turned these sources against themselves. He describes Baudrillard's dramatic encounter with critical Marxist theory and psychoanalysis, showing how Baudrillard's post-Marxist writings define, through the exploration of fatal theory, a new episode in cultural history: a period of cultural implosion.

This balanced account of Baudrillard's social theory emphasises the originality of his work and argues that his significance can only be understood by grasping the paradoxes of his project – Baudrillard's work is poetic yet, at the same time, critical and fatal.

Mike Gane is Senior Lecturer in the Department of Social Sciences, Loughborough University. His previous books include *On Durkheim's Rules of Sociological Method* and (as editor) *Towards a Critique of Foucault* and *Ideological Representations and Power in Social Relations*.

Baudrillard
Critical and Fatal Theory

Mike Gane

London and New York

First published 1991
by Routledge
11 New Fetter Lane, London EC4P 4EE

Simultaneously published in the USA and Canada
by Routledge
a division of Routledge, Chapman and Hall Inc.
29 West 35th Street, New York, NY 10001

© 1991 Mike Gane

Printed and bound in Great Britain by Mackays of Chatham PLC, Kent

British Library Cataloguing in Publication Data
Gane, Michael, *1943–*
  Baudrillard: critical and fatal theory
  1. French Philosophy. Baudrillard, Jean
  I. Title
  194

Library of Congress Cataloging in Publication Data
Gane, Mike.
  Baudrillard: critical and fatal theory / by Mike Gane.
  p. cm.
  Includes bibliographical references and index.
  1. Baudrillard, Jean. 2. Sociology–France–History.
  3. Postmodernism. I. Title.
  HM22. F8B383 1991
  301'. 0944–dc20
                                                 90–49946
                                                   CIP

ISBN 0–415–03774–3
ISBN 0–415–03775–1 pbk

For N.B.G.

Contents

Acknowledgements

I would like to thank all the many people with whom I have discussed and argued issues raised in this book, but especially Chris Rojek of Routledge who initially pursuaded me of the importance of the project and who offered encouragement throughout; also friends and colleagues at Loughborough University, in the Department of Social Sciences and the Department of European Studies, who have provided expert opinion and critical commentary.

I have also given a paper on Baudrillard to seminars at Essex University and Edinburgh University, and to the Discourse and Rhetoric Group at Loughborough University and would like to thank these seminars for their debates. I have also discussed these issues with colleagues on the editorial board of the journal *Economy and Society*, especially Beverley Brown and Ali Rattansi. I would like to thank Monique Arnaud, not only for help with French translations, but also with essential critical discussion on all aspects of this project. Finally, I would like to thank Jean Baudrillard for generously responding to my queries.

As is customary and essential, it is necessary to stress that responsibility for any error of fact or interpretation is entirely mine.

Part I

The tangled web of hatreds, of complicities, of rivalries between different schools of thought and of changes in mood causes each atom in the intellectual world . . . to prefer itself, while all the atoms detest each other. . . . The fact that certain disconcerting effects of beauty and truth may spring forth from time to time . . . remains a miraculous paradox.

(Baudrillard, 1990c: 88)

1 Introduction: reading Baudrillard

To whoever embarks on terrible seas.
                    Nietzsche (1969:264)

Baudrillard's writings vary enormously in range, register, style, complexity.
His writing seems to differ markedly from his spoken interviews (which
seem in comparison, less forceful, less logical – steps of arguments are
often passed over, and most noticeably, he often makes concessions which
he probably would not make if writing. If an interviewer is corrected yet
continues to follow a disputed interpretation, Baudrillard is not likely to
put up any determined resistance.) His written work, however, appears
to follow lines of argument without concession to their limit. There are,
perhaps, two Baudrillards. I became aware of this watching Baudrillard
responding to questions from Bernard Pivot on the French television
programme *Apostrophe*, but it is also apparent in Baudrillard's interviews
(for example, in the recent interview (Baudrillard, 1988), where Baudrillard
becomes less assured and will often appear to be pushed into a position he
really does not accept, even to the point of putting his own position into
question. But a more confident Baudrillard appears in the written texts,
when the writing is pushed to the limit and there appear to be no limits to
expression or position.)

It is instructive to compare the experience of reading Baudrillard with
that of reading the texts of Marshall McLuhan. George Steiner once wrote:

> This is not an easy thing to do. (They) are so compounded of novelty,
> force of suggestion, vulgarity of mind and sheer carelessness that one
> is quickly tempted to put them aside, . . . the question of how to read
> McLuhan, of whether reading him is an obsolescent mode of contact,
> is implicit in McLuhan's own work. . . . He sets his readers a perpetual
> problem: that of reading any further.
>
>   (Steiner, 1969:261)

Something of the same feeling occurs to the reader of Baudrillard. It would
be possible to argue that Baudrillard is the French McLuhan, or simply is

the McLuhan of today (his most recent book is still decisively influenced by him). But who reads McLuhan now? Perhaps Baudrillard will force people to reread a number of writers – McLuhan, Nietzsche – who are often thought to be unreadable. It is certainly striking that a number of recent writers have disguised their dependence on Baudrillard's work as if he were not quite respectable in academic discourse proper (see, for instance, Rundell, 1987; Richman, 1982; Bauman, 1990a).

But how to read Baudrillard? The problem here is that Baudrillard's works, as many commentators have noted, have a remarkable unity. There is tension, and out of this there is development. Yet one possible failing in his total project is an abstraction due to the lack of backgrounding, or contextualisation from work to work. As for the English reader, key Baudrillard texts are as yet unavailable in translation and confusion and misinterpretation are high probabilities. In this perspective it is essential that the overall structure of the trajectory of Baudrillard's work is established, so that the changes in style, which alter as the strategic dynamic changes, are recognised as an essential element of the message of the project. Baudrillard himself has outlined the nature of this project in his 'Habilitation' statement which is available in English (1988c). And I shall use this as a first guide to the construction of an account of his work.

I shall also use it as a guide to the essential context of his writing, as a way of locating important influences and debates in which Baudrillard is situated. Some of this context is clearly available, and has been available in English for a long period of time. There are other essential components of the rhetorical context of Baudrillard's work, which is only at this moment coming into English, and there are other influences which can only be reached through French sources. All of this necessary effort of establishing the intellectual networks which render Baudrillard's project meaningful is also, in a sense, passive if it remains purely at the level of classification, for Baudrillard's work is also posed as a challenge, both to the world at large and to the reader as such. Baudrillard himself has often made the distinction between the two types of analysis: structural ranking or ordering, and analysis of a strategic kind which is part of a struggle.[1] As I shall show, Baudrillard's work has contained a very basic internal tension between two very different theoretical positions: his intellectual biography can be understood as a process of the effects of these positions on each other, and as the process of the radical displacement of the dominance of one over the other.

These two positions are fundamentally those of Marx (radicalised, though in different ways, through Nietzsche, Althusser and Adorno), and Durkheim (radicalised through Mauss and Bataille). The latter influence has gone almost completely unnoticed in the accounts of Baudrillard's works in English. Both of these basic 'paradigms' (Baudrillard) will be examined at some length, but here a brief outline conspectus of Baudrillard's works is essential: a first period was dominated by structural theory (Marx, semiology and sociology). The principal works of this period (1968–72) were studies of the affluent societies (*Le Système des Objets* and *La Societé de Consommation*, followed by a collection of essays, *For a Critique of the Political Economy of the Sign*). These works continued Marxist analyses into commodity consumerism in advanced capitalist societies, as patterns increasingly dominated by semiological relations. Indeed semiological characteristics had become so predominant that consumption could only be explained as a process involving the consumption of signs themselves (use values being a term which came under increasing criticism from Baudrillard). But latent was another, potentially more radical, critique of capitalist consumption as corrosive not of human relations (to Baudrillard a notion tinged with essentialist implications) but of more fundamental symbolic exchange relations articulated around ritual, gift, initiation, reversibility. At the crucial juncture (*The Mirror of Production*, 1973, trans. 1975a), Baudrillard pilloried Marxist theory (and indeed sociological structuralism) as being caught up in the very code of capitalist reproduction itself. After this critique Baudrillard wanted to retain little of Marxist theory except for the analysis of the process of exchange value and the law of value which was extended dramatically into a wider theory, not of exploitation, but of the dynamic of capitalist culture itself. The critique of this culture was no longer based principally on the formation of class opposition, or on revolutionary proletarian principles. It was based on the principles of those cultures outside and beyond capitalism and rationalism: symbolic cultures. The general theory of these cultures was elaborated in Baudrillard's major work (*L'Echange Symbolique et la Mort*, 1976). His subsequent essays have been attempts to move from critical theory, associated with Marxist theory, to what he calls fatal theory (in three major essays (*De La Séduction* (1979), *Les Strategies Fatales* (1983b) and *La Transparence du Mal* (1990b)). I have said that these are close to a Durkheimian paradigm, but this is my (not Baudrillard's) judgement, and it has to be qualified, for Durkheim could not have foreseen these particular analyses, nor would he have agreed with them in the form in which they have been written. For Durkheim remained essentially a rationalist and a social scientist, and was sceptical of the effectiveness of an aesthetic mode of investigation. The remarkable project Baudrillard has set himself has been to use the Durkheimian paradigm but to place himself in it as a primitive, as a pre- or anti-rationalist, and to evolve a poetic theoretical analysis of the effects of the most advanced technical transformations in our culture. Yet Baudrillard only very rarely refers to Durkheim, preferring to adopt his paradigm as already modified in the work of Bataille and others.

Alongside the works I have noted here as the most significant of Baudrillard's writings, there are other essays and publications which are important. The first group is a large number of articles contributed to journals, particularly the journal *Traverses*, on which Baudrillard was a contributing editor (between 1976 and 1989). Many of these essays have been collected in volumes called *Simulacra and Simulation* (1981a) and *La Transparence du Mal* (1990). A second group consist of political writing, centred on a critique of Communist and Socialist Party debates in France in the 1970s and 1980s (collected in *La Gauche Divine*, 1985a). The third group are two volumes of a journal called *Cool Memories* (1987b, 1990d) which are closer to notebooks than diaries, and a companion volume, *America* (1988), in which heterogeneous reflections are unified into a voyage. The fourth is single volume of poetry, *L'Ange de Stuc* published in 1978, but written as early as twenty years before in the 1950s. These latter two groups reveal Baudrillard's effort to maintain a link with poetic language and with the lived everyday world, especially after the development of the new position from 1973. In the end, he has said, his intention has been to write in two modes, the theoretical and the poetic. This can be seen in his theoretical work where sections of the theoretical writing make their appearance on the page in a form close to the poetic. Thus it is clear that, for Baudrillard, the theoretical is the mode in which the poetic can still have force, and, in its close proximity to the journal can make contact with lived experience.

We again return to the question: how to read Baudrillard? Evidently we are faced with a considerable body of work, of very different kinds of writing, yet produced with a high degree of integrity and unity of purpose. It seems clear that there are dangers in thinking that this body of work is indeed the outcome of a single homogeneous authorial project and time. It is inevitably tempting to apply, say, Baudrillard's own theoretical elaboration of the anagrammatic nature of poetry to his own poetry, since they were both published at about the same time (1976–8) – indeed it is natural to assume that the poetry is an application of the theory. I have, presumably, like many others, attempted to unravel this, only to be informed by Baudrillard himself that as the poetry was written long before the theory of the anagram, there is no direct relation. This, however, leads to the possibility that much of the basic theoretical and propositional framework of Baudrillard's mature position was established at a fairly early stage, and was overlaid as it were with a different superstructure of semiological Marxism from 1968 to 1972, only then to emerge in the form of the theory of symbolic exchange. There is then the possibility of internal discrepancies and the emergence of the complex whole as a unity of such diffraction. It must also be remembered that Baudrillard's educational background is in languages, that he taught German in a French lycée before moving into sociology, and that he was a prolific translator of important theoretical and literary works from German into French (including Marx, Brecht, Weiss, Muhlmann). In this perspective it is likely that the important, even decisive influence, of Hölderlin, Marx, Nietzsche, Heidegger and the Frankfurt school (especially Benjamin, Marcuse, Adorno) was established very early on. One of the key questions in Baudrillard is the assessment of the relative balance of literature (fiction), theory, philosophy and sociology. This is essential to any attempt to define the nature of Baudrillard's theoretical objectives.

The essential point to make with respect to Baudrillard's work is that it has remained remarkably well focused on the problem of the object, of the cultural object (generally the fusion of sign and object). Thus, all his various means of approaching these questions are unified by the intransigence of this insistence. It is vital, then, to consider Baudrillard's construction of his notion of the 'object' in relation to his conception of social and cultural evolution: obviously his work is inspired by Marxist analysis of the commodity (but he rarely refers to Lukacs or the problematic of reification, even during his most intense involvement with Marxism), yet the term 'object' is much broader, and this is for a good theoretical reason which lies at the base of Baudrillard's theoretical project.[2] The commodity is one form of the object, its exchange-value form. The commodity can be used as a model for the analysis of other forms, but in general it the freeing of the object as such which dominates the configurations of western culture from the Renaissance, and perhaps earlier. Thus Baudrillard's analyses concern, to speak in Weberian terms, the enchanted world (in which there are no objects, no social relations, no process of production and no consumption – as we understand it), and the descent into 'disenchantment'.

Baudrillard must be read in this context. His project must be regarded as an assault on the 'disenchanted' world from the point of view of a militant of the symbolic (enchanted but cruel) cultures. In this he is prepared to appear in theory as a terrorist, as seducer, as devil's incubus. His latest essay (*La Transparence du Mal* (1990b)) has as its epigraph (in English): 'since the world drives to a delirious state of things, we must drive to a delirious point of view' (1990b:9). He adds: 'Il vaut mieux perir par les extrêmes que par les extremités.' This can be taken as a basic Baudrillardian maxim; better to perish by extremes than by extremities. Baudrillard is a cruel, theoretical extremist, and must be read accordingly. He follows the logic of his own position without allowing convention (or intellectual blackmail) to set up artificial barriers: wherever it leads, without reserve, what counts is total commitment to the divided logic of his investigations. In relation to one of his books he wrote: 'It must laugh in its sleep. It must turn in its grave!' (1990c:116). At the back of this, no doubt, there is an elaborate doctrine (probably inspired by Dostoyevsky, Hölderlin and Nietzsche, as well as Kafka, Bataille, Borges and McLuhan), which will have to be reconstructed as far as possible from the fragments Baudrillard gives us. It is important, however, not to reduce Baudrillard to fanaticism or to a notion of individualistic anarchism.[3] At this stage it is necessary only to pose the question of reading an ultra, that is, not to close the borders too soon (which would reduce Baudrillard immediately to outlaw status, as has been done in previous periods to Spinoza, Marx, Nietzsche and others). If Baudrillard accuses the west of hypocritical attitudes of tolerance, he will no doubt be expected to be misunderstood. In the reading to be adopted here the challenge is to follow through the logic of Baudrillard's position wherever it may lead, in the belief that this logic itself contains its own principle. Baudrillard has sought to follow a subversive strategy against the temptations of banal or sentimental opposition to the present system, a revolutionary who has sought to find a line of continuation of revolutionary possibilities after the collapse of the revolutionary movement. In this he provides a measure for the extent to which all others have been reconciled to 'the object system'. If his work is not dangerous, then, it is nothing. A reading must be prepared for this.

But what I propose here is, partly but not completely for the sake of exposition, to reverse something of the order of Baudrillard's investigations. I propose to work from Baudrillard's basic framework as the most direct way of coming to terms with his theoretical ingenuity and repositionings. In this way the reading will work from an initial framework in order to assess the way Baudrillard's individual essays move towards or away from it.

In fact this procedure has the added advantage of allowing more general theoretical considerations to come to the fore. What it suggests is the possibility in the French sociological tradition for there to be a working compromise between the Marxist and the Durkheimian problematics (just as in Germany there has been the same possibility between Marx and Weber). Let us say then that Baudrillard in effect thinks about world history in terms of three distinct social formations:

1 primitive symbolic cultures (no element of signs);[4]
2 societies in which symbolic cultures are found, in combination with hierarchies (a limited, circulation of signs);
3 mass societies (dominated by the circulation of signs).

In this framework there is evidently the possibility of analysis of a Marxist kind, since societies of type (1) are non-historical primitive communist societies, and type (2) are class societies. For Durkheim, type -1- are segmental societies, and type -2- are en route to the societies based on organic solidarity.[5] Baudrillard attempts to develop a new theory of symbolic cultures, and a new theory of mass societies. But the latter has not appeared without a long gestation period: his first analyses of it are predominantly written in the form of a Marxist semiology, of a society dominated by affluence and new disciplines of consumption, and in which class struggle was still important. After the collapse of the revolt in Paris in 1968 his position changed to take account of his view that revolutionary class struggle was from then on no longer possible. In fact, therefore, his conception of these societies was one based on the dominance of a new phase of capitalism and mass culture, but without a class which could negate the system. As class struggle was effectively eliminated, history, in the Marxist sense, had come to an end: the inner contradictions of capitalist society had in a sense been (negatively) resolved.[6] There was still the possibility of working within a Durkheimian perspective and to elaborate an analysis of the abnormal forms of the new society. In a highly disguised form, this is perhaps Baudrillard's project.

As I have presented it, it is clear that this theoretical programme in general is not unique to Baudrillard (it can be found in say Lefebvre, Lévi-Strauss or in writings of the Frankfurt school). What is interesting is the particular way in which Baudrillard has developed these ideas as a curious mixture of old, even 'lumpen' notions, and ultra-modern, high-tech terminology. He has also sought to elaborate curious new epistemological notions to underpin his analyses. Many of his ideas are presented in a fairly casual and unsystematic manner, but it is clear that his basic framework is highly logical, indeed, some writers have noted its obsessive consistency.[7] However, in order to come to grips with this body of literature it is essential only to note that Baudrillard provides:

1 a theory of symbolic exchange;
2 a theory, genealogy and pathology of modern western culture since the Renaissance.

His project is an astonishing critique, a fatal critique, of the latter from the former.[8] As he reinvokes the principle of evil it is necessary to recall Durkheim's remark:

> religious forces are of two kinds. Some are beneficient. On the other hand, there are evil and impure powers, productive of disorders, causes of death and sickness, instigators of sacrilege. . . . (but) the pure and the impure are not two separate classes, but varieties of the same class, which includes all sacred things.
>
> (Durkheim, 1961:455–58)

Thus, in the end, it is possible to suggest that Baudrillard has made, however bizarre it may at first appear, a contribution to the sociology of the sacred as well as to the critique of contemporary culture.[9]

But it is necessary to return to the question of how to read this form of writing. The basic protocols of reading, at first coming to terms with the work, are those appropriate for a kind of voyage: a first phase is, as far as possible, that of drift as it were, a kind of suspension of critical thought in order to enter the flow of Baudrillard's (dis)course. This has its own rationale. It is often the case that theoretical critiques miss their target by applying the censor of critical consciousness too early. A provocative element of a doctrine, once visible, can seem an irresistible offence. It becomes the occasion which allows the critic the enormous pleasure of converting, immediately, a phrase into a doctrine and a doctrine into a category which can be rejected. It is often rejected on grounds that the author belongs to a particular political grouping, and therefore, by circular reasoning, the offence of the discourse is doubled in the offence of the political position. Thus the recent debate on the statement 'there is no such thing as society' (Margaret Thatcher) can be reduced immediately to a doctrine and accepted or rejected according to the political affiliation of the critic. But the suspension of criticism also has merit, just as it does in the case of Baudrillard's notion of the recent death of the social, or even of the fact that primitive societies are neither primitive nor societies. Such propositions can be theoretically radical: they challenge the view society has of itself, and point to other forms of analysis which may be subversive of conventional wisdom. If sociology and social analysis depend on notions of the social, it is essential even so, to question the definition which arises out of the institutional conceptions or presentations of their own constitution, as if individuals either did not exist, or somehow existed in a form of diminished responsibility in relation to their institutions (Baudrillard puts this in the strongest and most offensive form: with the modern social we have all become physically and mentally deficient).

Nevertheless, this phase of suspension, or of minimal criticism and maximal seduction, has as its function the facilitation of total familiarisation. This phase must depend in part on the acceptance of a positive ritual attitude to the author (in terms of Durkheim and Goffman),[10] or an acceptance of the progressive metaphysical research programme or the author (in terms close to that of Karl Popper);[11] it is to read as if the author were in possession of a secret omniscience. But this must give way to a phase in which the former is reversed, and in a severe manner. The reading becomes critical and searches for the slightest error and pushes the negative relation to the text to the limit: everything must be regarded as suspect, in relation to the author, everything must be regarded as having been cynically manipulated. The mistakes of the author are the key, and they must be exposed.

In the end, however, there must be further readings which restore some balance or order to this delirium if it is not to destroy itself. A further reading can aim to be more relaxed, urbane, sophisticated, subtle: it asks the question – what is the author ultimately up to?[12] It does not seek to establish behind the various dubious practices of the text, a conspiracy of evil. It may be that these are minor aberrations in a project that is fundamentally wise. To some extent this reading has as its context the current light of knowledge and opinion on the issues in hand. It also looks to the effects of new or novel ideas and creative theory, and to the extent to which possible novelty has given rise to a problem of the reader's unfamiliarity with the issues; and to the important implications of new positions on current problems in the balance of their effects, both banal and extreme. This is not really simply a question of treating the text in good will, or trying to arrive at a final balance sheet. It is a reading which tries to avoid the pitfalls of naiveté and of cynicism.

But even this reading is superficial, for it ignores completely the question of how the reading is accomplished in relation to the specific text. It moves from total acceptance, to total criticism, to balance. The problems have to move to the level of the activity of reading, to the conflict between hermeneutics and reading in depth (symptomatic reading) or as deconstruction. Douglas Kellner has already claimed to have performed a symptomatic reading on parts of Baudrillard's work (*America*, 1988a). But what is meant by this is that Kellner has rejected the book on moral and political grounds (Baudrillard has symptomatically failed to tackle the social issues from the point of view of Marxism). Others, notably Arthur Kroker, have tried to develop a form of reading inspired by Baudrillard himself: panic reading. Panic being, for Baudrillard, an ecstatic form of catastrophe.[13]

Although the results of these readings are derisory, and may be meant to be derisory, they nevertheless draw attention to an important point: the possibility that there is a sphere of Baudrillard's thought which embraces a conception and a practice of reading and writing. This is certainly implicit in any relation the author might envisage with his readers. Is a panic reading of Baudrillard the correct mode of reading? Is it the correct way to read McLuhan? Baudrillard has given clues here. He has, for example, explicitly objected to the notion of symptomatic reading which implies reading in depth, just as it implies the existence of the unconscious, or repression. He has also criticised naive hermeneutic reading as if the subject was completely masterful. The reasons for these harsh comments are historical, theoretical and political. Theoretically they are related to Baudrillard's own idea of the stages of evolution of western culture itself. The major stages have already been indicated, but it is clear that the genealogy of simulation is vital here, especially the phases two and three, of production and hyperreal phases of simulation, opposed in principle to the notion of symbolic exchange itself.

Baudrillard's project has been marked by the attempt to engage in a critique of the order of simulation from the point of view of symbolic cultures. But, this being said, it is clear that in each period of simulation he has found ways of responding to the dominant order through forms of criticism which can throw the dominant ones into relief, either through criticism or derision. Marxism itself appears as a critique appropriate to the period of simulation based on production. Baudrillard's eventual conclusion about Marxism is that it was unable to provide a transcendental critique, only a poor simulation of capitalism itself (it did not grasp the semiological code of capitalism, only one of its derived forms – the commodity). Freud's conception of the individual unconscious was likewise a version of a particular phase of the repression of the individual in the period of simulation in depth and separation, a very specific form of simulation and unique to a particular period in the evolution of western culture. Whereas Marx was caught in the mirror of production, Freud was caught in the mirror of desire (as a productive force in a separated structure). But this phase of western culture has passed, and capitalism itself has been modified, triumphantly in its own terms. For Baudrillard it is essential to keep pace with these developments and not allow a critique evolved to cope (well or badly) with one phase to maintain itself through inertia, into a subsequent one. It is necessary for a successful strategy to be one step ahead of its adversary. The symptomatic reading cannot be applied successfully to phenomena which lie outside its domain of possible objects (and these include primitive as well as ultra-modern cultures which have no depth).

Baudrillard's analytical matrix is not a series of homogeneous cultural blocs, however. The analysis specifies the leading, the hegemonic forms of the epoch in question.[14] Within each period there are indeed powerful oppositions, some violent, which can be triumphant for a time. The process of modernity and modernisation, itself reawakens old forms, it reactivates earlier structures which often contain constrasting principles and values. But the very process of modernity also induces criticism, in part based on previous values, adopting techniques of derision, irony, parody, in order to challenge the pretensions of a new order of reality. These include literary and poetic forms, scientific and rational criticism, political challenge, art, theatre, and ways of living. There are different modalities here: some of this opposition adopts a banal strategy of attempting to manipulate its object, or develops forms of pastiche which simply enter into a complicity with the dominant forms (in Baudrillard's terms most of what passes for modern art); they do not rise to the level at which a negative field is revealed. Baudrillard, as someone who wishes to maintain the value of revolutionary criticism, tries to combine strategies based on the symbolic orders with those which attain the greatest ironic force of criticism of the dominant cultural simulations.[15]

This implies, for Baudrillard, that in relation to each period his own project would have to change, to adopt the appropriate mode of writing, the most effective alliance of symbolic challenge and ironic form. This means Baudrillard's project is certainly a divided one, a double project. He relates, after 1973, to the symbolic order as a basic term, and to the forms of critique arising within simulation as auxiliaries. There is, in other words, a doubling up of the repertoires of criticism: one based on a radical alterity to the modern system, the other based on radical difference within the system (terms used by Baudrillard, 1990b). Marxists, evidently, but perhaps unconsciously, have been working with this principle for some time, for their analyses are undertaken both from the point of view of the oppressed groups but also from that of science, and from that of communist principles (a version of symbolic exchange).[16] Marx's own formula specifies two kinds of dialectic: one which is revolutionary and seeks the negation of the present order, the other ends up glorifying it (Marx, 1963:20). The most remarkable aspect of Baudrillard's project is the way in which the attempt to hold onto a critical position on modern society is accomplished in the face of his own acknowledgement that transcendental internal criticism is no longer a possibility (if it ever was).

It is certain that the majority of Baudrillard's readers and indeed his critics will be either situated in a productivist or even a pre-productivist style of reading. It is quite natural for us to ask how Baudrillard works as an author, and how his texts work as signifying practices, how they can be used as a critique of the existing order, and so on. This is the reason why Baudrillard's main critic, Douglas Kellner, finds Baudrillard's works up to 1973 fairly congenial; these are the texts which appear to belong most of all to the second phase of simulation, where Baudrillard himself appears to develop a symptomatic reading of the objects of consumer capitalism and indeed, of the discourses which are engendered by them. After 1976, for Kellner, Baudrillard become something of an aristocrat of Nietzschean inspiration who indulges in the 'post-modern carnival'. Clearly there is more than a hint of a recognition here of the asynchrony of writing: pre-capitalist (aristocratic) forms of critique–indulgence of postmodernism (mass culture, or shall we say the affluent society?).

For Baudrillard, however, the world itself, the capitalist order, has changed so fundamentally as to make the productivist critique counter-productive. Production is no longer determinant, and it is no longer adequate to talk of the economic mode of production as an infrastructure which can 'overdetermine' the other social practices.[17] A higher code is in operation, and has been from the beginning, in effect, (and this has yet to be grasped in its full ramifications). Thus to read Baudrillard is to begin to question the effectiveness of a purely political reading, or the reading even of the symptomatic type, or indeed of the reading which assumes the homogeneous subject and the homogeneous text as if the project was under the control of a single thought or unified process of decision making. If we apply a reading of the symptomatic type to Baudrillard up to about 1972 we will certainly not be out of line with Baudrillard's own conceptions, but even here the writing is in fact divided in a more fundamental sense (what is raised is the issue of just how profound this division is in the early works, what precisely is the status of the basic and the auxiliary terms as already outlined?).

Perhaps the key problem is that the symbolic order, in so far as it can be thought or practised in Baudrillard's work inevitably appears through the form of representation adopted in a simulation order, unless there is a mode of establishing in writing a symbolic practice of a new type (we can assume that the simple adoption of a term from a primitive culture, such as 'mana' or 'potlatch', by itself is insufficient). As Baudrillard adopts the full force of McLuhan's notion that the medium is the message, it is to be expected that the medium of the writing style is considered tactically and strategically. Baudrillard is surprisingly persistent here, and has sought to find appropriate modes of thinking and modes of epistemology for this project (if it is still conceivable to Baudrillard as a project with its implication of individual rational will). The question for the reader is to become aware, then, of the complexities of the alliances established in this writing.

But at base there is a coherent and stable framework, which is to be found in Baudrillard's partisanship: his adherence to the superiority of the symbolic cultures and the inevitable frailty and vulnerability of the orders of simulation found in the west. The relation of the symbolic orders to western culture is irreconcilable in principle. The symbolic orders have a primordial nature which ultimately, according to Baudrillard, will be revealed as a higher order. It is Baudrillard's notion of communism as the Other not to capitalism, but to western cultures (yet the term communism has been decisively mystified by bourgeois notions of formal equality and contract, just as primitive society is a term mystified by notions of bourgeois civil society). What Baudrillard develops is a series of contrasts between the two irreconcilable orders, across many dimensions. Sometimes this is done through a brief juxtaposition, but in other cases it is established at great length. It develops in relation to the specific investigation undertaken, and it develops in relation to new materials which can be used to reconstruct it. In reading Baudrillard, therefore, specific attention has to be paid to the way in which this basic contradiction is reproduced. This, then, has to be read in conjunction with the mode of irony belonging to the secondary line of critical work (at least in its formal objectives). In this way it is possible to situate an analysis of the first phases of simulation with the attempt to criticise it poetically (in *L'Ange de Stuc*), a poetic form which certainly belongs to the period of Malarmé (a response belonging to the second order of simulation). The idea of a pataphysical critique of the third order of simulation, is evidently an application of an ironic response (pataphysics) to a second-order simulation (bourgeois industrial society), in the third order (the hyperreal) (contemporary mass society). These weapons are in the service of the basic term, and they do not appear simply as the effort to apply the latest, or highest means of critique. Another order of calculation is at work here. It is this problem, and its adequate assessment which forms the central issue of this work: Baudrillard – from critical to fatal theory.

2 Essential background and context

you know that in the German Ideology (Marx and Engels) there are chapter headings like 'Saint Bruno', 'Saint Max' which parody the great ideologues of the time – well we could write a similar work (for Parisian intellectuals)
(Pierre Macherey, 1977:8)

'*The Intellectual has no future',*
    Baudrillard (1989a:55)

One of the central objectives of this work is to reflect on the relationship of Baudrillard's writings to critical theory particularly (but not exclusively), French Marxism and some of the important strands of French theory which has been aligned with it in recent years. Very possibly Baudrillard's current work represents the ending of an exceptional period, often thought of as a period which began with a surge of existential humanism and passed, in the mid-1960s into structuralism and then post-structuralism. Baudrillard's work is often thought to have followed this trajectory culminating in a triumphant 'postmodernism' in the 1980s. Even some of Baudrillard's own recent comments have hinted that there is some sort of cultural ending in France, not necessarily the end of Marxism, rather the end of a certain kind of critical intellectualism. Here is the irony of 'The French Ideology'.

INTELLECTUALS

This thesis, important and plausible as it is, is not the central point here, which is rather the way in which Baudrillard himself has presented it. Given that Baudrillard is a very abstract and unconventional social theorist, it is interesting and significant to be able to find, amongst his many pronouncements, one or two in a straightforward idiom free from jargon, which indicate something of the unpretentious sociological framework of his thought. Interviews tend to achieve this. One such interview of 1984–5, conducted by Maria Shevtsova, solicited some essential reflections on French intellectuals and their situation. Baudrillard's contribution suggested that whatever impression might be given by his other writings (where strong theses are rarely qualified) some of his basic propositions remain surprisingly 'materialist' and sociological.[1]

Essentially, he suggested, it is an illusion to think that intellectuals create social ideas and values, it is even a spontaneous illusion held by intellectuals themselves. What really happens when a society develops a differentiation between the social masses and intellectuals is that a specific kind of energy from social movements is imparted to intellectuals who are in a position critically to elaborate alternative ideas and values. The eventual balance sheet of the effectiveness and importance of intellectual work is always ambiguous, however. It might well be very important. But the possibility exists that its significance could be nothing. This imparts a certain suspended character to intellectuals: they remain marginal and are never sure that their work has the slightest political or social effectiveness (Baudrillard, 1984–5).

Indeed, intellectuals in the French sense, are not, he suggests, simply those who occupy and develop 'mental' labour of a distinctive and skilled type.[2] French intellectuals have come, in the post-war period, to occupy a relatively independent position from both right-wing governments, and from the French Communist Party. Part of the current crisis is due to the very fact that the Socialist Party has, with no great success, tried to co-opt intellectuals into positions of power. The instance of Michel Foucault was symptomatic: 'he would have liked to have been a political consultant at the highest governmental level. And he was offered this kind of position. If anyone could have done it, it was Foucault. Anyway, when he risked it, he discovered he couldn't do it: it was a failure' (Baudrillard, 1984–5). It is clear that this indicates another basic demarcation line in Baudrillard's thought: that between intellectual and political power. However much the intellectuals believe their work is significant, it is essential to remember the crucial centres of power are beyond them, and in order to remain intellectuals (in the French sense) it must be so, since the critical function is diminished to the extent that the intellectual becomes the representative of a group or organisation.

But the current problem goes beyond this. The intellectual is only capable of developing critical analyses of any true significance if alternative values and ideas are already current in society itself. One of the crucial characteristics of the post-war period was the strength, not only of genuine social movements but also of genuine alternative values circulating in French society. Intellectuals were nourished by these and indeed were borne along by their energies, in a kind of dialectic between intellectuals and masses. Today, Baudrillard suggests, the very existence of these alternatives is questionable, placing the intellectual in a new position, indeed threatening the very existence of intellectuals as an elite, marginalised and privileged, yet exercising possibly a vital, if fundamentally ambiguous, critical function. Intellectuals as such, are defined not by their effect on political power, but by their 'use of discourse, by the rhetorical use of discourse, by its reflexive, critical use' (Baudrillard, 1984–5). There are many other factors which today are tending to erase this as a possibility.

One of the most central of these is the emergence of the mass media. It is certainly a paradox that with the increasing penetration of the media and its worldwide development the associated increased circulation of ideas has crucially diminished the role of intellectuals as such. What has happened, he suggests, is that the immense circulation of contradictory ideas has abolished the specific negativity of criticism. 'Mass media . . . are not vehicles for negativity' (Baudrillard, 1984–5). Indeed the situation is precisely the reverse, 'they carry a kind of neutralising positivity' (ibid). Intellectuals instinctively distrust the media, for they recognise the potential levelling of criticism where all ideas mediated in these structures lose their specific character and merge into a generalised flux of ideas. But some intellectuals, for example, the French 'New Philosophers' of the 1970s, attempted to use the media opportunistically. They were rightly criticised and lost credibility for so doing. Indeed, Baudrillard remarks, it was precisely this unserious aspect of their practice which for him 'disqualified' them.

Curiously, then, Baudrillard's conception of French intellectuals is surprisingly materialistic, but moralistic and elitist. He is ultimately sceptical as to the effectiveness of ideas. But the position is sufficiently complex to allow the emergence of tension: his adherence to the possibly vital function of the intellectual is associated with the necessity of the intellectuals' autonomy from party, yet the intellectual is not the fundamental creative source of values and ideas.

Intellectuals take up materials which already exist, he 'gets something from his culture and speaks from it' (Baudrillard, 1984–5) Yet he imparts something and negates something. And this critical, negative act, sets up an energy between sections of society itself. Intellectuals are completely dependent on intellectual resources within society, for what they do has 'something of a relation to their social interests and even to the classes to which they belong' (ibid). Ultimately, then, the position of the intellectual is highly conditional, and today in danger. In a sense, it would be quite appropriate to understand Baudrillard as suggesting that he himself is one of the last:

> (the) theory of commitment through Sartre in the 60s . . . had been more or less the point of departure for intellectuals. There was the debate with Marxism. It didn't matter if you were Marxist or not: you were nonetheless in the same sphere of discussion. Argument was possible. Then all this slowly fell away.
>
> (ibid:168)

SARTRE: *SAINT JEAN-PAUL*

It is clear, then, that Baudrillard supports a well-established, even conventional view that, as far as the modern situation is concerned, at least in France, it is Sartre who forms the model and 'point of departure' for intellectuals. It is certainly Sartre, and more recently, Foucault, who corresponds to the idea of the relatively autonomous social critic, oppositional to both the central political authority and to the organised opposition (the French Communist Party) of the left, while at the same time trying to develop a dialogue with Marxism. There can be little doubt that Sartre exercised an enormous influence, and attempts to begin the story of modern French philosophy and Marxism with Sartre (in the sequence: existentialism, structuralism, post-structuralism) have wide currency, and Baudrillard's own version certainly reflects an important element of his own intellectual biography. Yet Baudrillard does not often refer to Sartre's work, and certainly by the time Baudrillard began publishing in earnest (the late 1960s), the existentialist current in France was on the wane. There are, however, many signs in his earlier work of the impact of existential Marxism, and it is certainly convenient to begin with a consideration of this important kind of social theory against which 'structuralism' developed. This is not in order to reduce Baudrillard to existentialism but in order to try to identify some of the critical differences between the two.

Of course, as is well known, Sartre's critique of modern society, asserts that it is above all else a society which produces specific kinds of inauthentic relations between its members. It is essential, in the Sartrean vision, to engage in a committed struggle for the recovery of essential human qualities in social relations. To begin to understand this problem Sartre developed a specifically humanist methodology and social theory, which was centred on the idea of the vital recognition of the irreducible significance of individual and group action (praxis), and Sartre had no difficulty in trying to link this idea with a version of humanistic Marxism based on an interpretation of the early works of Marx. This conception was then used to develop both specific analyses of individual projects (e.g. Flaubert, Genet), and on political and social processes. It also developed a specific kind of conception of dialectical processes which had implications for what could pass as genuine knowledge. It also gave rise to a particular critique of the character of everyday life and its objects based on a development of phenomenology (of Husserlian inspiration). This had a wide impact on sociological work in France and beyond. Above all Sartre asserted the dignity of philosophical theory in the practical critique of modern forms of individual and social alienation, as well as developing critical writing in many other genres (as demonstrated in the journal he founded, *Les Temps Modernes*).

As Foucault has pointed out it is remarkable that Sartre's first essay was a discussion of Nietzsche, since much of post-Sartrean philosophy has been a return to Nietzsche. Nevertheless Sartre's project is certainly marked by the insistence on the importance of the human subject as an irreducible centre of free praxis, and his writings are witness to a stream of criticism of all philosophy and theory which seek to deny it. The basic motto of existentialism, that explanation of human action can never be found in a resort to a given human tendency as 'essence' but only through practical, lived and experienced 'existence', was used as a critique of ideology itself, i.e. of 'false consciousness' underpinned by 'bad faith' (*mauvais fois*).

It can be seen that this orientation readily lends itself to development as an existential psychology or phenomenological psychoanalysis, since the opposition between the true and false consciousness can be extended to include relations to the body and to the self more generally. Sartre's famous effort to do this in terms of relations between self and Other, on various levels of reflexivity, was taken up by social psychologists such as Laing and Cooper in Britain in the 1960s. This complemented the attempt by Perry Anderson to develop not only a journal like *Les Temps Modernes* in Britain (*New Left Review*) but also to apply Sartrean ideas to an analysis of socialism in Britain. This attempt marked an important moment since it introduced the sequence (existentialism, structuralism, post-structuralism) in a most condensed form into the debate in Britain (1965–75). It can thus be claimed that even in Britain the contemporary developments in Marxist theory (i.e. of the new left), also have Sartrean existentialism as their point of departure.[3]

One of the central texts of Sartre's high Marxism is his *Problem of Method* written in 1957. It is an attempt to reconstruct a dialectical method for Marxism. It did this by positing human praxis as a primordial phenomenon, and drawing on, and indeed synthesising contributions from, such writers as Weber, Lukacs, Husserl, etc., formed a conception of praxis as having the shape of a transcendental project dominated by situated intentionality. All human action, in principle, could be analysed by reconstruction of the forward and backward movement of praxes. In order to understand an action, then, it was necessary to know the starting conditions, the objective, and the synthetic processes of creating the end result, whether it be a material object or a meaningful gesture. Thought or analysis which deviated from this, which denied the necessity of the 'progressive–regressive method' could be identified as reductionist (that is, missing out an essential step specific to the analysis of any human historical act). Thus Stalinist thought, which could explain historical events purely by reference to socioeconomic, or class conditions, was a prime example of analysis in an alienated mode.

Of course such ideas had been developed by very many other writers as diverse as William James (pragmatism as a term is derived from the same root as praxis) and Talcott Parsons (whose formulation of action theory is also derived from Husserlian influences). What made Sartre's efforts attractive to Marxists was the attempt to link alienation to Marx's conception of the capitalist process and the communist movement against it (now understood as a recovery of human authenticity). Crucial to this effort was to take up a critical ontology of the capitalist process to show that it rested not simply on appropriation (via property relations) of the social product by an exploiting class, but that human relations themselves are profoundly influenced. Sartre here continued the theme developed in the early works of Marx, that production under capitalist relations are not mere objectifications of human intentions, but that in an alienated mode human relations are themselves reduced to pseudo-relations between things, that is they are 'reified'. The worker's labour power is transformed into a market commodity. This forms the basis of a whole series of processes which are said to be the action of forces beyond human control. Sartre elaborates on a theme of the end of the third volume of Marx's *Capital* which describes the world as a ghostly world where 'Rent, Interest, Profit,' seem to be the active agents.[4]

But Sartre's genius was not content merely to render Marx's enterprise simply into an existential register. He was also a thinker of great theoretical originality. Sartre's social ontology provided a basically very simple model of social structures as arising out of the lived praxes of individuals and groups. Although he was prepared to begin, abstractly, with the idea of an isolated individual, this individual quickly became the centre of social action through the fundamental internalisation of the individual's association and membership of groups seen from without by others. From this Sartre elaborated a whole spectrum of group forms and modes whose internal structures could alter rapidly according to the kinds of interactions which were engendered in facing problems in different situations. With the skill and imagination of a formidable writer of fiction, many of his examples were imaginatively conjured, *ad hoc*, to suit the particular argumentative purpose to hand. These examples undoubtedly had an impact all of their own, and they seem to bring the animation of everyday life into the theoretical text.

His objection to Marxism was not that it was erroneous, but that no one knew, any longer, how to use it. In a memorable phrase, Marxists 'insist on standing in their own light' (Sartre, 1963:38). In other words they simply applied already available formulas in a way which guaranteed a certain conclusion irrespective of the particular evidence. It is interesting that Sartre should pick up Lukacs' criticism of the modern novel as the 'permanent carnival of fetishised interiority', since these are almost exactly the terms a Marxist critic like Douglas Kellner today uses against Baudrillard. Sartre's response was interesting: 'the addition of one violent and concrete word "carnival" which suggests colour, agitation, noise, is for the purpose of covering up the poverty of the concept and its gratuity' (ibid). Indeed, talking of Lukacs' pigeonholing of Heidegger as fascist, Sartre claimed that he seemed incapable of reading a word without a constant stream of already formed judgements intervening. In order to understand what had happened, for example in the case of Heidegger:

> Lukacs would have to read him, to grasp the meaning of sentences one by one. And there is no longer any Marxist, to my knowledge, who is capable of doing this. They literally do not understand a word of what they read.
>
> (ibid:38–9)

This view he extended to the whole of the relation to social and political life: Marxism had become a fossilised schematic system, albeit possibly the best available, but one in dire need of fresh contact with lived experience. Making a bridge between Marxism and existential philosophical orientations which stressed the significance of individual human intentions were the best way of achieving this.

ALTHUSSER: *SAINT LOUIS*

The stimulus of Sartre's attack, which both stressed the vital importance but also the failure of Marxist theory in the 1940s and 1950s produced an enormous critical response. One of the most incisive was that of Louis Althusser from within the French Communist Party itself. Althusser's own development forms a crucial part of the background to Baudrillard's evolution.[5] The relationship between Althusser and Sartre can be seen indirectly through the confrontation of the English philosopher John Lewis, who wrote a Sartrean critique of Althusser in the journal *Marxism Today* (1972) to which Althusser replied.

The elements of the reply attempt to differentiate between humanist and structural Marxism. The crucial points concern agency and historical process for in the Sartrian reading it is man who makes history, it is the individual human subject that transcends the situation and in so doing creates historical events. For Althusser this:

> 'man' is a little lay god. Like every living being he is 'up to his neck' in reality, but endowed with the prodigious power of being able at any moment to step outside of that reality, of being able to change its character.
>
> (Althusser, 1972:314)

Marx effectively attacked the rather gross notion of 'man' as agent (with already given essential attributes) and replaced it with the idea that class struggle is the motor of historical processes, claimed Althusser. This change should not be underestimated in its philosophical and its political implications. It has serious import above all for the idea of dialectical 'transcendence', and for the role of intentionality in history, since history is no longer something which is 'made', in the strong sense, by a subject. If a carpenter makes a table it is evidently absurd to say the table 'transcends' the wood. The difference between the carpenter and the idea of 'man' as maker of history seems to be, says Althusser, that in the latter case the 'raw material of history is already history . . . man produces everything'. Thus the powers of God (man) become transcendental and omnipotent. At the heart of this argument is a critique of the ideological notion of the essential attributes of things and beings, a demonstration of the irony of existentialism which began itself as a critique of the essentialist notions of action.[6]

This kind of critique had already made its appearance in Britain, in Nicos

Poulantzas's critique of the Sartrean-inspired historical writings of Perry Anderson and Tom Nairn in the *New Left Review* in the mid-1960s. This was in part a process of self-criticism since Poulantzas himself was en route between existentialism and structuralism. Generalised into a sociology, by Anderson, said Poulantzas, the 'unity of a determinate social formation is attributed to a class-subject, and hence to its class "consciousness"', clearly stigmatising its idealist leanings. Poulantzas in this article of 1967 had already developed a way of linking most of the epistemological problems of social theory to the function of the category of the subject:

> This conception of class which becomes the subject of society and history to the extent that it constitutes, by its conception of the world, the consciousness-will of the 'totality' of men . . . thus presupposes precisely the Hegelian type of circular and unilinear totality. Here we should not forget the direct descent of Lukacs from Weber, for it is this filiation which allows us to elucidate the relationship between Lukacs's Hegelian 'totality' and the functionalist totality which in large part predominates in contemporary political science. What links Weber's theories to contemporary functionalism as Parsons has noted, is that the global social structure is, in the last analysis, considered as the product of a society-subject which creates in its teleological development certain social values or ends.
>
> (Poulantzas, 1967:61)

This is obviously a theme of very great theoretical significance which has many important ramifications.[7] It is on the one hand, a grave irony that Althusser's own attempts to elaborate a theory of the state ideological apparatuses (ISAs) should fall dramatically into this structure of teleological reasoning (see my article (Gane, 1983)). On the other hand, Althusser continued to make a vital clarification on the difference between Marx and Hegel. In his autocritique he pointed to the necessary intellectual defence of the Marxist notion of the social topography (base and superstructure) in order to prevent the dialectic becoming absolutely delirious:

> a dialectic, which 'starting' from Being = Nothingness, itself produces, by the negation of the negation, all the figures in which it operates, of which it is the dialectic; it is a dialectic which produces its own 'spheres' of existence; it is, to put it bluntly – a dialectic which produces its own material substance.
>
> (Althusser, 1976:139–40)

The problem with this formulation, of course, like most considerations of the dialectic, is that although materialist, it, too, appears dogmatic. The problem becomes acute for a thinker like Baudrillard who believes the world to have become delirious. Nevertheless, as Baudrillard shows later in his career, perhaps the world become delirious will require the dialectic itself to be transcended.

Althusser's basic critical work, however, even now remains an important force in social theory. Not only can its influence be detected as something which important currents now actively continue to debate with, including Baudrillard's, but much contemporary social theory seems to have been constituted at a time when Althusser's influence was direct with the result that, both in France and the English-speaking orbit, its very terminology is still marked with Althusser's stamp (take, for example, concepts like 'social formation', 'social practice', 'genealogy', 'social reproduction' and 'ideological state apparatus').

The first and very striking characteristic of this work is that it is not made up of huge treatises; in fact the corpus is not substantial at all.[8] All of the works in English are collections of essays, the longest being 'The Object of Capital' (in Althusser and Balibar, 1970:73–198). Apart from some published notes towards an investigation of the state, which are theoretical notes, and letters on May 68, and interventions in the discussions of the French Communist Party, there are no pieces of 'empirical' or 'concrete' analyses either. Yet the influence of these articles, reviews, seminar papers, lectures, letters, introductions, has been felt as if it were, taken together, as substantial as if they were all treatises. This illusion is, I think, easily explained: Althusser not only did what Sartre claimed Marxists could not do – read – he also made other people read.

But curiously Althusser remained firmly within a limited number of stated objectives concerned with the reading of Marxist texts. It is very difficult to avoid the impression that in the 1970s, even Althusser felt caught in a closed claustrophic theoretical net: a catastrophic disintegration of Marxism. As a philosopher, Althusser's projects all circled around an effort of clarification and development of Marxist theory. This gave his writing, inevitably, an anti-critical defence edge; this only at the last moment began to soften (in the direction of open democratic struggles and new social movements (Althusser, 1978)). At the same time this concentration entailed an extreme specialisation, quite unlike that of any other major Marxist. It was as if Althusser was happy to accept a strict, rigorous division between Marxist practices. And his specifically philosophical specialisation effectively modernised Marxist theory without giving it any new social analyses or objects. Might Althusser's own judgement on Feuerbach, that his philosophy represented an enormous theoretical 'contraction' (1982:180), which was part of a theoretical crisis which 'exploded' (1971:116) be applied to his own? Is it true, as Paul Hirst has suggested, that 'In failing, Althusser did something which is theoretically more progressive and more significant than virtually any other Marxist thinker . . . he pushed forms of Marxist theorisation to the limits where their problematic nature became evident' (Hirst, 1985:134)? Other writers, notably Laclau and Mouffe (1985:97) have argued that Althusser's conceptualisations do not lead of themselves to this result. To reach a revolutionary dissolution it is necessary to proceed 'by radicalizing some of its themes in a way that will explode its basic concepts'.

But there is no doubt that most interpreters have concluded that at the end of his project Althusser had reached a point of intense, profound, involuted, implosive theoretical crisis.

Althusser was not only aware of this, but in the end openly admitted it. His basic project involved attempts to work out in an explicit and adequate manner the principles Marxist practices contained in the practical state. Even this conception of the problem was adopted from Canguilhem. What is of interest here is to attempt to examine how this extremely inward-looking series of projects could have had such important effects. In order to do this I will outline the two basic projects and examine their methodological configurations. Althusser's work reveals in an exceptional clear manner the theoretical effects of changes in 'position' from which arguments are elaborated. And this is particularly relevant in the examination of the development of other writers like Baudrillard. But more than this. It is also possible to see that sociological theories contain arguments that are developed from the standpoint of a number of possible points of view, and that differences which stem from the arguments developed can play a fundamental role in the progressive, or regressive, development in the theory as a whole. It was not perhaps so much Althusser's opening up of the question of reading theoretical texts which can now be seen as just as significant as placing the activity of theory itself in question. This is one of the aspects of his work which makes his writings directly relevant to the contemporary context of the debate on modernisms and postmodernisms. The parallels between the work of Althusser and Baudrillard make it necessary to examine Althusser in some detail.

Althusser's major project of the early 1960s consisted in an attempt to read the Marxist classics and to reflect on Marxist practices in order to produce Marxist philosophy itself. The development of Marxism depended on this, since the conjuncture was one in which a theoretical contradiction had become the dominant one. The specific nature of this struggle was identified to be one in which Marxist philosophy was being invaded by humanist, historicist and evolutionist conceptions. It was essential therefore to define and defend theoretical Marxism against them. The strategy adopted was to stress the scientific character of Marxist theory and to provide a philosophy which would be adequate to this theory. Thus against the dominant trends in the 1950s and early 1960s, he argued that Marx's own theoretical development involved a decisive break with all humanist critiques of capitalism of the Sartrean type, which simply reproduced the mirror structure of individualistic ideology, and that Marx's theory was much more than a historical explanation of the development of capitalism, and finally that Marx's philosophy was not a simple extension, or inversion, of Hegel's, but was a scientific breakthrough.

Theory in this period was dominated by the idea that the principal work to be read was Marx's *Capital*, understood to be scientific in its very form, as Marx himself claimed. Althusser stressed its fundamental principle:

practices were determined not by their goals, but by their means. Societies are social formations in which determinant practices (economic) coexist with dominant ones (politics, economics); in this theory all reductionisms of levels (epiphenomenalism, expressionism, structuralism, essentialism, functionalism) are made redundant. The key idea here were the formulas, taken from Freud, of 'overdetermined complexity', and the ideological system as society's imaginary.

So concerned was Althusser to defend the scientificity of *Capital* that he reflected the claim of scientificity into his own philosophy itself. It was not simply a theoretical practice, it was Theory with a capital T. It was scientific because it installed the same critique of essences as science, reflecting the scientificity of its objects (in the practical state) and transforming them into the theoretical state. Philosophy was itself a practice not a praxis (a term for Althusser always stigmatised by hints of teleology and essentialism). Given the internal nature of this reflection to Marxism itself, Althusser complemented it with the Spinozist notion that each science established its own internal criteria of truth, thus reinforcing all efforts to defend Marxism against ideological and hence empiricist reduction. He countered the suggestion that this simply led to theoretical closure with the claim that, to the contrary, it led to a forceful break with ideological closure.[9]

Actually, despite some acute epistemological analyses, no new philosophy, Theory as such, emerged. Indeed, even in Althusser's longest essay, on the object of *Capital*, it is the polemical force of the argument that is noticeable, the definition of the object is difficult to discover – it has even been suggested that Althusser never did arrive at it, having got lost in so many digressions. Indeed the paper is marked by a whole series of theoretical 'detours' to establish Marxism as an a-humanism, not a historicism, etc. This is true also of the paper which went most explicitly in this direction, 'From Capital to Marx's philosophy' (1970:14–69), the direction of the idea of immanent structural causation. Some of these moves are essential to the understanding of a writer apparently remote, like Baudrillard, who explicitly theorises the important transformation of the neutral a-humanism into the far more challenging Althusserian form of theoretical anti-humanism. He also provides an amazing continuation of the concept of structural causality by turning causality into the dynamic strategy of the object.

Characteristically, Althusser, throughout this period, continually reflected on his own methods. This perhaps can be seen to be related to a specifically French intellectual milieu where an established 'Cartesian' tradition emphasising clarity of method is seen as paramount; and, in complete consistency with his own theory of practice, he pressed the idea that mode of practice, even in theory and philosophy, determines the product. Not only, in so doing, did he really establish the theoretical significance of reading practices, and this has become central to modern social theory, but also linked this with the Marxist emphasis on the materialist basis of dialectical principles which led Marx in the first place to examine mode of production in the economic system as primary. Fundamentally, the notions of production and practice were keys used to unlock the barriers within Marxist theory itself.

In an important paper of early 1967, on theoretical work, he described his method as one of theoretical involution, by which the most developed parts of theory could be made to work on the least. Indeed, this is an extension of the idea of transforming notions in the practical state into adequate concepts. Responding to the question of how it is possible to arrive at the basic principles of Marxism, he said: first of all Marxist works and practices have to be identified, but then as these are uneven, a work of 'critical correction' has to be made:

> this operation of critical correction is not imposed . . . from the outside, but results from the application, the involution, of these works to themselves: from the application of their more elaborated forms to their less elaborated concepts, or again of their theoretical system to certain terms of their discourse, etc.
>
> (Althusser, 1990:61, trans. mod.)

Althusser gives examples: working from the principles of *Capital* it is possible to identify the ideological nature of some of Marx's own earlier formulations, e.g. those of 1844. And of course, by working from the principles of the analysis of the mode of production, Althusser elaborated a whole theory of knowledge as a theory of the mode of production of knowledge. This practice, was at first, remarkably fruitful and has had lasting effects. It was achieved, even more remarkably, through no further analysis of anything 'outside' of Marx's writing. But what kind of knowledge was this?

It is this body of theory which can be seen to have directly influenced Baudrillard's sociology in the period 1968–70, for it is in this period that Baudrillard began to situate his analysis of consumer society within the framework of an overdetermined social totality, with the mode of production as ultimately determinant. But neither Baudrillard's nor Althusser's theoretical positions remained constant.

After 1967 things began to change dramatically in Althusser's conception of philosophy as he began to reflect on Leninism, and particularly Lenin's conception of practice. This was very decisively influenced during this period by Mao. Fundamentally, a number of related changes were effected and these circled around the increasing significance in Althusser's thought, of the class struggle. In place of the primacy of production, there was a marked shift of interest towards the principle of reproduction, especially the problem of the state. Associated with this was the gradual abandonment of the conception of philosophy as theoretical practice, as Theory. Now was introduced the idea that with Marxist philosophy was begun a new kind of philosophical practice, and this did not entail the production of a new philosophy as such.

At first it seems that Althusser remained convinced that the principal objective of philosophy was to defend and to open Marxist science. As work continued, however, there seemed to be a perceptible shift from this position, to one in which the principal objectives were connected with the goals and aims of the proletariat in the class struggle itself. When Althusser announced, in 1978, the opening of the crisis of Marxism itself, it was to suggest that *Capital* had in part hindered the class struggle in crucial respects. More and more, Marx's works were seen primarily as works of struggle, of critique, rather than the standard by which 'critical corrections' could be made. Indeed, critical corrections of *Capital* itself were called for from the point of view of proletarian struggle.

Again there are curious elements in this period. For example, it is during the analysis of Lenin's philosophical practice that Althusser came close to deconstruction terminology. The practice (of philosophy, and it is here that the promise of a content for philosophical practice was diverted) is one of a struggle of demarcations, in which 'nothing' is at issue; yet the analysis is founded on the principle of the defence of a doctrine. There is an analysis of the state which attempts, in part successfully, to develop a new theory, yet the analysis runs into epistemological difficulties, and underplays class struggle. In political terms, Althusser seemed hostile to the May 68 movement, and was unable to find unambiguous links with it, and therefore to express it; but he was able to find significance in the new popular alliance in France in the early 1970s, and fought in vain to keep the PCF to it. Althusser's writings come to an end with another involution, this time his target was the PCF leadership itself. Baudrillard by this time had moved decisively to the left of Marxism and the communists and wrote a stinging critique of the naiveté of Althusser's efforts. His basic argument was that Althusser in criticising the party as Stalinist in relation to a potential base of militant workers was playing the same role as those philosophers who focused on the gulag: the essential social structures were mystified in these analyses since the crucial relations were now quite different and that to pose the problems in these terms was a diversion (Baudrillard, 1985a:56–66).

In the 1970s Althusser continued to reflect on practice, and on the correction of practice, and in some of these texts emerges a new conception of struggle. It is discussed as a strategy which had been adopted many times, and indeed seems to be consistent with the idea of 'detours' indicated earlier. Against the rationalist principle of the importance of arriving directly at the truth through the application of rational methods, Althusser argued that to arrive at the truth, or truthful practice, involves more than reason. It involves social struggle. In these circumstances, it is not enough to state the truth for truth to have its effect in practice. In order to be effective it is essential to exaggerate, to bend the stick in the opposite

direction in order to straighten it. In this perspective if there is such a thing
as true practice, it seems (to express this in terms developed by Baudrillard
who made this a key practice) to be the result of work in the more-than-true,
of effects at a distance, with the aim of positional displacement. Althusser
acknowledges here the influences of Lenin and Machiavelli:

> Machiavelli, whose rule of method, rarely stated but always practised,
> was that one must think in extremes which means within a position from
> which one states borderline theses, or, to make thought possible, one
> occupies the place of the impossible.
>
> (Althusser, 1976:170; 1990:209)

> in a written text like 'What is to be done?' the only form which this relation
> of forces can take is its presence, its recognition and its anticipation in
> certain radical formulae, which cause the relation of force between the
> new ideas and the dominant ideas to be felt in the very statement of the
> theses themselves.
>
> (Althusser, 1976:171; 1990:210)

If these ideas are right, he suggests, the determination of the effectiveness
of thought cannot be gauged from thought itself: the effects themselves in
the others towards which the thought is aimed must reveal themselves.

Here emerges a quite different idea of 'truth' from the traditional
enlightenment commitment to reason and rationalism,[10] since no relation
of linear approximation to an absolute is invoked, nor is there an appeal
to the lifting of illusions by true knowledge. But yet there is a determinant
resonance in theory itself in which the tensions can themselves be 'felt',
since 'ideas have a historical existence only insofar as they are taken up and
incorporated in the materiality of social relations' (Althusser, 1990:210).

With quite unforeseen displacements these ideas were adopted and
practised in the most radical manner conceivable (perhaps even totally
inconceivable to the Althusserians themselves), yet they form the
absolutely indispensible background to the development of fatal theory
elaborated by Baudrillard in the 1980s. Baudrillard is one of the very few
thinkers to have taken Althusser's own new conception of philosophy at all
seriously.[11] In fact for Althusser: 'this relation of force, counterbending and
bending, this extremism in the formulation of theses, belongs quite properly
to philosophy, and . . . even if they did not admit as much . . . the great
philosophers always practised it' (Althusser 1990:211).

LÉVI-STRAUSS: *SAINT CLAUDE*

Althusser has, by and large, been read and understood as a 'structuralist'.
Like Foucault he always denied it. But other important thinkers who also
in various ways debated with Sartrean philosophy embraced the idea and
developed structuralism as a specific orientation. One of the most important

of these was Claude Lévi-Strauss, whose work was mainly in the field of anthropology and who pioneered a specifically structuralist methodology, which after a first emphasis on applications to the study of kinship was later turned to the study of mythology. Unlike Sartre or Althusser Lévi-Strauss was much more of an academic intellectual who rarely engaged with political issues of the modern state, except (aligning himself with Baudrillard) in a famous defence of 'primitive' societies against the industrial powers. Yet (unlike Baudrillard) on many occasions he claimed a continuing objective was to make a contribution to and to be working on the ground of Marxist theory.

When we pass from Sartre, to Althusser, to Lévi-Strauss we pass from an extreme emphasis on the historical agent on the one hand, to the extreme elimination of the agent in favour of structural processes on the other. Lévi-Strauss's own formulation didn't actually expunge individual praxis altogether for what he wanted was to make a contribution to the theory of superstructures 'scarcely touched upon by Marx':

> if . . . the conceptual scheme governs and defines practices, it is because these, which the ethnologist studies as discrete realities . . ., are not to be confused with praxis, which – and here I agree with Sartre – constitutes the fundamental totality for the sciences of man. Marxism, if not Marx himself, has too commonly reasoned as though practices followed directly from praxis. I believe there is always a mediator between praxis and practices, namely the conceptual scheme by the operation of which matter and form, neither with any independent existence, are realized as structures, that is as entities which are both empirical and intelligible.
>
> (Lévi-Strauss, 1972:130)

In the end his objective seemed to be to want to establish, out of Marxism a specific object, the relations of infrastructure and superstructure, in societies specifically identified by Marx as societies without class struggles (i.e. primitive stateless societies). Marx had also called these societies, societies without history, since he wished to define history as the processes produced in class struggle. In fact Lévi-Strauss's work began to show that in these societies kinship formations did effectively act like infrastructures, and as such they, too, were subject to internal contradictions. Mythical superstructures could be analysed by suitable methods to reveal that they contain complicated forms of contradiction resolution in the ideological lives of these societies.

One of the most influential 'works' of Lévi-Strauss, however, was a series of broadcast conversations, made in 1959, and published soon after. These conversations with Georges Charbonnier focused mainly on the question of painting and art. They seemed to have had a remarkable impact on Baudrillard in terms of establishing an overall perspective. Lévi-Strauss developed a number of theses. The first was an elaboration of the distinction between small-scale primitive societies, which he likened to clocks, they were cold, and without historical dynamic, and modern civilised societies, which were more like steam engines – dynamic, historical, hot. The former minimised disorder and entropy, and tended to remain in their initial state, whereas the latter maintained a certain disorder and hierarchy, and therefore entropy. He noted, circumspectly, that all societies do have a history; the point here is that primitive societies: 'are surrounded by the substance of history and try to remain impervious to it, modern societies interiorise history as it were, and turn it into the motive power of their development' (Lévi-Strauss, 1969:39). This formed the background for a number of observations on art.

First, the art of a primitive society functions as the language of a social group. It is created and consumed collectively. With social differentiation and the break-up of the community, art becomes associated with writing, privilege and the possession of objects. The original language of signs is broken up and art tends to become figurative. This can be seen in the evolution of statuary from Egyptian, through Greek to Renaissance art. It is also the case in pre-Columbian Mexico. The 'outstandingly original feature' in western art is this attempt by the artist and the spectator to possess the object. In order to analyse these relations further, Lévi-Strauss drew up what he calls three differences: first the difference between collective and individual creation, second the difference between art as a language of. signs as opposed to practice of representation and possession and third, in the tradition of western art, the difference between 'traditional' art which focuses on the signified and modern art which focuses on the style of art (its signifiers).

In the western tradition, the academicism of the signified leads to the representation of sublime landscapes, for instance. When this is attacked by Impressionism the objects become more humble, commonplace, but there is not a radical overhaul of the project itself. The revolution, in fact, is superficial, even reactionary. Cubism, however, addresses deeper problems, the semantics of the object (and thus it approaches primitive art). But this art remains individualistic, and cannot overcome the third difference. What happens is that novelty for its own sake becomes a pressure and results in an immense proliferation of individual styles, indeed each artist moves quickly from one style to another (Picasso, Masson, Picabia). What we observe 'is an almost obsessional consumption of all the sign-systems which have been, or still are, in use . . ., since the conditions of artistic production remain individualistic, there no possibility whatever of a true language being established' (Lévi-Strauss, 1969:75). The tendency is unmistakable, there is no real 'assimilation of foreign idioms so much as a sort of gratuitous playing about with artistic languages' (ibid: 77). Thus, the modern problem is that such a profusion of styles never adds up to a formal sign system, or language in which communication can occur. The pressure to abstract experimentation only ends up by 'emptying art of any signifying function' (Lévi-Strauss, 1969: 78). And the artist as such in the face of a social structure of this kind is powerless to transform art into a language however persistent the attempts.

Thus there is a striking contrast between primitive societies and modern societies: in the former the world is enchanted, supernatural, and the art itself is never representative or figurative:

> either through deficiency or excess the model is always wide of the representation, and the exigence of art always exceeded the means at the artist's disposal. . . . The object is much more important, objects are heavier, denser, imbued with . . . things we have eliminated from them.

(ibid: 85)

In the latter, in modern societies, there is only an exacerbation of an inherent contradiction, modern art is 'left with nothing but a system of signs, but "outside language", since the sign system is created by a single individual, and he is liable to change his system fairly frequently' (ibid: 87).

Baudrillard's version of these theses retains the overall framework and also takes the position of the superiority of the primitive. But his terms, after 1971, are different. The language of signs is rethought in terms of the concept of symbolic exchange, and the notion of the sign is brought in as appropriate to a society which distinguishes between the signifier, signified and referent (real world). In between the two ends of the historical process appear a limited number of 'pure signs', but as the number and the circulation of signs increases they also lose density and as they enter into modernity.[12] Notice that Baudrillard takes these theses of Lévi-Strauss on art *against* his structuralist analysis of myth.

DEBORD: *SAINT GUY*

Baudrillard's later works, especially those designated 'postmodern' have, very largely, at least in the English-speaking world, assumed that these apparently undomesticated, untamed styles, must have been characteristic of Baudrillard's work in the 1960s. Possibly thinking also that as this period was one of great social upheaval, and that he was installed as university teacher at Nanterre, a prime site of student revolt, and that further, he was associated with a journal called *Utopie*, and books on alienation in mass consumer societies, he must have been some sort of intellectual anarchist, possibly of the situationist type, or ultra of the communist movement. Indeed his works have been translated by American interlocutors who themselves have emerged from radical existentialist or Marxist backgrounds, and have claimed that his work is centrally concerned with a critique of the commodity under advanced capitalism. Mark Poster, for example, has himself been largely influenced by existential Marxism, and Douglas Kellner has written a major work on Marcuse and Marxism (Kellner, 1984).

This view is also reinforced, if by default, by the strange distance or neglect shown to Baudrillard's work by other schools of Marxism, especially structural Marxism. In the surveys of structuralism, and of Marxism, or in works on the leading Marxists of that period, his name is conspicuously absent. However, if one also seeks to find how Baudrillard has been received in writing on the situationists and the Marxist humanists, his name is also absent. As he himself later said:

> The University was a very warm, effervescent place in the years around '68, but my level of integration in the University wasn't very high . . . I remember *Utopie*, which was a small review and sold very little. . . . But we felt we were writing for someone.
>
> (Baudrillard, 1984–5:166)

It is then important not to treat his book *The Object System* (1968) in isolation from his efforts in *Utopie*, for although the writings in the latter do not make his work seem part of the world of Raoul Vaneighem, they certainly do not make it part of a detached academic world of the university.

But it would be wrong to dismiss altogether the connection between Baudrillard and the situationists even if there is little actual cross-referencing between the two, for Baudrillard has always maintained that he was close to them if not actually a member.[13] This affinity is evident in the theses argued in the key situationist text *Society of the Spectacle* by Guy Debord (1987, orig. 1967). The general thesis is that modern forms of alienation isolate the worker producer in a lonely crowd faced with the spectacle of alienated powers which are the creations of such producers. Affluence creates 'false choice' in spectaclar abundance. Against this cannot be any appeal to the authentic needs or genuine choice as an absolute: 'pseudo-need imposed by modern consumption clearly cannot be opposed by any genuine need or desire that is not itself shaped by society and its history . . . mechnical accumulation liberates unlimited artificiality, in the face of which living desire is helpless'. (Debord, 1987: Chapter 3). The major differences in political orientations on the left are those for whom the worker is a passive spectator and those for whom the worker was an active agency. Debord cites the account of the Leninist party by Lukacs as a description of 'everything the Bolshevik party was not'. And bemoans the the fact that all revolutionary theory has become reactionary, as the workers' initiatives themselves have been usurped by political organisations. Debord's political position supports that of sovereign workers councils, an 'anti-statist dictatorship of the proletariat'.

Debord at this juncture turns in a surprising direction, to a discussion of time (Debord, 1987: Chapters 5 and 6). Debord attempts to draw up a general account of the fall of reversible time and the appearance and triumph of irreversible time with commodity production. Communism entails the reappearance of playful reversible time once more. Nomadic societies are dominated by time as repetition, sedentary agrarian societies are dominated by cyclical rhythms of the seasons. With social differentiation elites become masters of cyclical time and attempt to establish 'events' in another dimension, an irreversible time for those who rule. With writing, it becomes possible for the first time to possess history. Monotheistic religions perched between cyclical and irreversible time: they placed eternity on the other side of history's countdown. In the middle ages reversible time was gradually 'chewed away', as life became conceived as journey, and a new obsession with death arose. Peasant millenarian movements were a response, a challenge to history, with which the church had compromised. But these movements were irrational and had to lose, since they still believed in alienated forces guiding their actions ('like taking orders from a chief outside their ranks'). The tendency was completed joyfully in the Renaissance, with the conquest of history as the accumulation of knowledge. With bourgeois production, labour time – work – is conceived as transformational of historical conditions; it represents the victory of progressive over traditional time. History becomes movement; capital is accumulated. But as the bourgeoisie imposes irreversible time on society it retains its control over it (and as it becomes specialised in the possession of things it, too, becomes possessed by them). On the other hand, the proletariat attempts to live in historical time 'the simple unforgettable centre of its revolutionary project' (ibid, para. 144). This is framed in the context of a bourgeoisie which has established its revolutionary Year One, and world time.

Capitalism reproduces its time of production in equivalent, exchangeable units. The effect on labour, is as Marx demonstrated, to reduce human existence to a mere shell of time. On the surface of society there develops a new pseudo-cyclical time, which degrades everyday qualities of existence as it expropriates what is left of natural cycles ('day and night, work and weekly rest, recurrence of vacations') but in the mode of spectacular time, the time of the commodity, now dominated by the consumption of images: society has become the spectacular society. But its recycling of reversibility comes in the form of parody: the gift, festival, ceremony, are dominated by presentation as commercial. And there remains a contradiction between the real irreversibility of labour time in production and the pseudo-cycles of fashion. The latter, in fact, is the false consciousness of time in the commodity system, that is, of the time which has already been expropriated from labour. One of the ironies is that as the fashion system becomes a dominant system it even begins to forbid people to grow old, and, to die: but the absence of death in the culture is only a reflection of the real absence of life. The revolutionary project, then, for a classless, communist society, entails the 'withering away of the social measure of time to the benefit of a playful model or irreversible time . . . a model in which independent federated times are simultaneously present' (Debord, 1987: para. 163).

Something of the decisive duality of Baudrillard's own position can be seen in Debord. On the one hand, a conception of historical development largely influenced by Marx, leading to a conception of modern society as alienated, characterised by commodity production and which gives rise to a proletariat, itself living in the form of commodity alienation and irreversible time. On the other hand, Debord's project envisages the recovery of reversible time, a characteristic of primitive societies – as if he can find no principle of time within contemporary society which be used as a basis of critique.

BARTHES: *SAINT ROLAND*

However, certainly in Baudrillard's early writings, the writings of 1968–72, the influence of the situationists and of Guy Debord is not the essential one. These works, no longer free political, polemical or critical literary pieces, are works of social science. They appear to adhere to Marxist theory, even indeed to move towards it more closely from 1968–70, and then to react very violently against it. However, in the first of these works, the decisive influence, and this is made explicit by Baudrillard, is that of Roland Barthes. Barthes not only provides the general methodological guidelines but also the model for this kind of analysis. Indeed Barthes probably even provided the problem, the identification of the subject of study itself: not the commodity or the 'thing' (as opposed to the word), but the system of 'objects'.

Almost all of Roland Barthes' essays have been translated into English and his influence has been enormous (particularly his early essays which influenced Marcuse's conception of one-dimension societies). His corpus of works also includes a number of auto-referential essays which give clues to the significance that he himself gave to his works and how he saw them as falling into distinct periods. This makes it possible to identify the elements of Barthes' own intellectual career. One such statement can be taken here as especially helpful (though it omits to present Barthes' very early period of *Writing Degree Zero* of 1953 (Barthes, 1967b) in which he developed a powerful version of a thesis later to be known, through Marcuse – on whom Barthes exercised a considerable impact, as one-dimensionalism). This statement, which appeared in *Le Monde* in 1974, said that Barthes' famous critical review essays on consumer society, collected in 1956, and published in the collection called *Mythologies* (1972), had been written before he had read the theories of Saussure, the founder of structural linguistics. Barthes describes the project which grew in his mind at this time, as one intended:

to give my denunciation of the self-proclaimed petit-bourgeois myths the
means of developing scientifically; this means was semiology or the close
analysis of the process of meaning by which the bourgeoisie converts its
historical class-culture into universal nature; semiology appeared to me,
then, in its programme and its tasks, as the fundamental method of an
ideological critique.

(Barthes, 1988:5)

The general statement of this position was presented in well known essay
'Myth today' in the (1957) edition of *Mythologies* (Barthes, 1972), which he
describes as euphoric: 'since it reassured intellectual commitment by giving
it the instrument of analysis, and responsibilized the study of meaning by
giving it political range' (Barthes, 1988:5). However, Barthes, indicates that
the fundamental characteristic was that this was the time in his career when
scientificity had become the primary modality.

After 1957 he concentrated on developing a structural and semiological
study of fashion in clothes, indeed to 'reconstitute the grammar of a known
language which had not yet been analysed'; and, at the same time 'to
conceive a certain way of teaching semiology'. These efforts resulted in *The
Fashion System* (1985), and *Elements of Semiology* (1967a) and other essays.
In this period, he remarked, his dominant concern was 'less the project of
instituting semiology as science than the pleasure of exercising a systematics'
(Barthes, 1988:6). Semiology, he said, had become a kind of 'intoxication'.

The third phase (from about 1966) was the moment of the Text (which
developed under the influences of Kristeva, Derrida, Foucault, Lacan and
the Tel Quel project) to situate these together in a new dialectic of a
Marxist type (Barthes, 1988:6). He suggested that this dialectic be thought
in Althusserian terms of an overdetermined totality (Barthes, 1977:169,
orig. 1971).

There can be little doubt that Baudrillard was also to follow an intellectual
trajectory of a similar type, not so much as instigator or originator, but
as a disciple. His project also was not identical to that of Barthes. I
suggest very schematically and provisionally that his own trajectory is
best understood as involving a (Marxist) semiology of domestic objects
(1968) and a more general (Marxist) sociology of consumer society (1970),
possibly a brief flirtation with the Text (in the Barthean sense), before
entering a (self-)critical period in order to find a way out of or beyond
Marxism. This interpretation could be derived from a literal reading of
his essays, and it places Baudrillard only at a distance with the anarchic
ultra-left situationists. His more obvious affinities, at least officially, are
with more cautious structuralist and Marxist intellectuals. Indeed he often
cites Veblen, but not Debord.[14]

Baudrillard himself made no secret of the fact that Barthes had not only
furnished the method but also the problem for his first book *The Object
System* (Baudrillard, 1968). In the introduction he cited a key passage

from Barthes *The Elements of Semiology* (Barthes, 1967a) on the relation between levels of analysis. But it is clear, however, that Barthes elsewhere (also Barthes, 1964, in French) had also indicated the idea of studying 'the object' as such: in this essay ('The semantics of the object') he had sketched out the analysis of objects simply as a result of technological forces, but, since they carry information, as a 'system of signs' (Barthes, 1988:180). Barthes noted carefully the problem of defining the 'object': it is indeed 'something' but a something with two different groups of connotations. A first group, suggesting in the manner of Sartre or Ionescu, the radical, non-human qualities of objects which might be seen to threaten the existence of man, or which might be seen as absurd or meaningless. These relations to the object are, said Barthes, essentially subjective ones. Other orientations are technologically focused: objects are interesting because they are fabricated and consumed in mass society. This definition is essentially sociological, but it breaks down into two aspects: the object appears to have a use, and so there is a kind of 'transitivity of the object' (ibid:81), but on top of this the technology and functionality are never pure, since the object is also a vehicle for the transmission of meaning, and so can also be seen as a bearer of signs. The telephone, for example, fulfils an obvious function as a medium of communication, but its appearance can be independent of this function, either signifying luxury, or femininity, or some previous stylistic fashion.

In considering these signs, there are, he suggests, two basic co-ordinates: a metaphorical order in depth (the lamp suggests the time in the advert is evening); and a classificatory order (for example, objects are classified in the department store into different groups of consumer items). So:

> When objects are put together, we cannot attribute to them co-ordinations as complicated as in human language. In reality the objects – whether these are the objects of the image or the real objects of a room, or of a street – are linked only by a single form of connection, which is parataxis, ie, the pure and simple juxtaposition of elements. This kind of parataxis of objects is extremely frequent in life: it is the system to which are subject, for example all the pieces of furniture in a room. The furnishing of a room achieves a final meaning (a 'style') solely by the juxtaposition of elements.
>
> (ibid:187)

The problem of understanding the significance of objects is thus one of establishing function, of meaning; or, in other words, there is in the object a struggle between function and a meaning which 'renders it intransitive, assigns it a place in what might be called a tableau vivant of the human image-repertoire' (ibid: 189). And then there is a third element, a restoration of the sign to function, into the 'spectacle of function', just as it is possible that a sign be transformed into an 'unreal function' (e.g. a raincoat that could not function as such). Herein we encounter, says

Barthes, the conversion of 'nature into pseudo-nature' (Barthes, 1988: 190). In this way we arrive at the specifically Barthean conception of modern alienation.

Barthes' work after 1974 forms the focus of a recent essay by Jacques Leenhardt (1986) who attempts to outline the dominant phases of the French intelligentsia since the war. Dominated in the period up to 1956 by the notion of truth, he claims, this gave way in a subsequent period to the demand for knowledge, especially sociological knowledge, as transcendental values were eclipsed. In this phase it was logical that structuralism became obsessed with the notion of mirrors and reproduction, and the death of the subject. Baudrillard was one of the most 'desperate' expressions of this attitude with his notion of the death of the social itself. Roland Barthes' last works move against this trend, says Leenhardt, as can be seen especially in *Camera Lucida* (Barthes, 1984). This marks the beginning of the attempt to rethink rationalism as can be seen in its concluding words: 'It is up to me to choose whether to subject the spectacle (a given photograph) to the civilized code of perfect illusion, or to confront in it the rise of an unbearable reality' (cited in Leenhardt, 1986:65).[15]

Leenhardt sees in this conclusion a new awakening from the mode of scientism that dominated intellectuals in the phase of structuralism:

> The man of knowledge faces a choice that he must make: either he barricades himself behind the discourse of pure knowledge and translates the spectacle before his eyes in the 'civilized codes of perfect illusion' . . . or else, he initiates a deeper relationship with the species which appears in him under the 'obsolete name of pity', as Barthes terms it, and therefore faces the 'rise of an unbearable reality'.
>
> (ibid:65)

Something of the 'reversal' as Leenhardt calls this move, can perhaps be glimpsed in the fact that *Camera Lucida* is dedicated to Sartre.[16]

BATAILLE, DERRIDA AND FOUCAULT: *SAINTS GEORGES, JACQUES, MICHEL*

From Barthes, who is well known in English translation, it is necessary to examine the influence of Georges Bataille, who is relatively unknown but whose writings are now beginning to be translated. Bataille is perhaps, for English readers, the strange missing link, the bizarre, and for English readers of French rationalism, virtually unthinkable phenomenon of a (Marxist) Nietzschean, surrealist Durkheimian. His impact on the writing of Baudrillard has been absolutely decisive, especially his conception of the nature of primitive cultures and his notion of *la part maudite* (the devil's share, or as the translation of the book by that name has it *The Accursed Share* (1988, orig. 1949, not 1967 as is stated in the English version): as this seems a difficult notion to translate, with its powerful implication of evil, lost in the translation, but so important to Baudrillard, I propose to keep the term in French in this book). Bataille was a librarian but wrote of transgression and sacrifice. One commentator recently called him a 'pyromaniac in slippers' (Merquior, 1986a:113).

There are many aspects to Bataille's – at heart, contradictory – work. For the purposes of this book it is necessary to point to his corrosive attack on the projection of the principle of utility back onto previous history and particularly onto primitive culture. Following Marcel Mauss, he took up the concept of potlatch and generated a whole new theory of expenditure, sacrifice, destruction, as a fundamental cultural complex. Negativity is not connected directly with the dialectic (and transcendence) but with the destructive moment of potlatch (a principle of loss (Bataille, 1985:118–20)). Destruction is a more fundamental principle than that of production, it is the need for destruction which generates production. A theme developed in Baudrillard in a much modified form in terms of the primacy of seduction (perhaps by *la part maudite*) over production.

Bataille's influence has been enormous on post-war philosophy and social theory in France. Sartre condemned Bataille as a mystic and idealist, but Derrida took quite the opposite line and launched a consideration of what materialism might mean in deconstructive thought from Bataille's work. Talking of his own programme, Derrida said (1981):

> (Marxist) texts are not to be read according to a hermeneutical or exegetical method which would seek out a finished signified beneath a textual surface. Reading is transformational . . . I will have to analyze what I consider a heterogeneity, conceptualizing both its necessity and the rules for deciphering it; and do so by taking into account the decisive progress simultaneously accomplished by Althusser and those following him. All this poses questions. . . . Above all they refer to the general economy whose traits I have attempted to outline based on a reading of Bataille. . .
>
> Rigorously reinscribed in the general economy (Bataille) and in . . . double writing, the insistence on matter as the absolute exterior of opposition, the materialist insistence . . . seems to me necessary.
>
> (ibid:64–6)

A footnote adds that key texts of Derrida 'are situated explicitly in relation to Bataille, and also explicitly propose a reading of Bataille' (ibid: 106).

Very briefly Derrida's argument can be summed up as an attempt to reveal certain fundamental contradictions in Bataille's reading of Hegel which are only half recognised in Bataille. Derrida argues that the very principle of destruction and loss in Bataille seems to explode the restricted economy of the dialectic in Hegelianism, because they are so irreversible:

The blind spot of Hegelianism, around which can be organised the representation of meaning, is the point at which destruction, suppression, death and sacrifice constitute so irreversible an expenditure, so radical a negativity – here we would have to say an expenditure and a negativity without reserve – that they can no longer be determined as negativity in a process or system.

(Derrida, 1978:259)

Derrida attempts to work out this interpretation against Bataille's own account, as a challenge of the idea of transgression against transcendence (*Aufheben*), since the latter can only, in the Hegelian system represent the victory of the slave. (Here we glimpse also the difference between Nietzsche and Marx.) For Hegel, says Derrida, transcendence is included in the process or circle of absolute knowledge, and never passes beyond it, it is thus restricted in its absolute scope (to discourse, the 'system or work of signification'). Thus Bataille uses only an empty form 'in an analogical fashion, in order to designate, as was never done before, the transgressive relationship which links the world of meaning to the world of nonmeaning. This displacement is paradigmatic' (Derrida 1978:275).

Derrida thus contrasts transcendence in its Hegelian and dialectical sense (presumably in the Marxist sense it is still within not the framework of discourse but of matter), and the concept of transgression which moves towards neutralisation (neutrality 'has a negative essence (ne-uter), is the negative side of transgression' (ibid: 274)).[17]

But a very different emphasis is drawn out of Bataille's work by Michel Foucault, who found in it not the radical alterity of materialism, but the explosive function of transgression. This is done through taking Bataille's link of the death of God with sexuality conceived as transgression of limit (here as law). In Bataille this approach to the concept of limit displaces the idea of totality, and of the philosophical subject:

The works of Bataille define the situation in far greater detail: in the constant movement to different levels of speech and a systematic disengagement from the 'I' who has begun to speak and is already on the verge of deploying his language and installing himself in it. . . . And it is at the centre of the subject's disappearance that philosophical language proceeds as if through a labyrinth, not to recapture him, but to test (and through language itself) the extremity of its loss.

(Foucault, 1977:43)

For Foucault this conception of transgression breaks out of the temptations of a dialectic of mystic transcendence, and marks a point where sexuality ('decisive for our culture as spoken') becomes a 'dark domain' where liberation takes the form of a liberation from dialectical language: Bataille, there, looses his language 'in the dead of night'. The crisis, then, is precisely that the experience of the limit 'is realized in language and the movement where it says what cannot be said' (Foucault, 1977:51).

But let us look now at the way that Foucault himself reflected on the stages of his thought and his specific opposition to philosophical existentialism:

Since 1945 . . . Marxism was a kind of horizon which Sartre thought for a time was impossible to surpass. At that time it was definitely a very closed horizon, and a very imposing one . . . throughout the period from 1945 to 1955 in France – the young French university . . . was very much preoccupied with the task of building . . . the phenomenology–Marxism relation. ( ) . . . later, once a kind of structural thinking – structural method – had begun to develop . . . we saw structuralism replace phenomenology and become coupled with Marxism. . . . So the problem of language appeared and it was clear that phenomenology was no match for structuralism . . . (and) psychoanalysis – in large part under the influence of Lacan – also raised a problem . . . the unconscious could not feature in any discussion of a phenomenological kind.

(Foucault, 1983:197–8)

In sum:

everything which took place in the 'sixties arose from a dissatisfaction with the phenomenological theory of the subject, and involved different escapades, subterfuges, breakthroughs . . . in the direction of linguistics, psychoanalysis or Nietzsche . . . ( ) I read him because of Bataille . . . (Nietzsche) appeared in 1972 for people who were Marxists during the 'sixties and who emerged from Marxism by way of Nietzsche. But the first people who had recourse to Nietzsche were not looking for a way out of Marxism. They wanted a way out of phenomenology.

(ibid:198)

As for Foucault's own trajectory, he points to the fact that there was another possibility, this time via the influence of the epistemologist Georges Canguilhem: 'many of his students were neither Marxists nor Freudians nor structuralists. And here I am speaking of myself' (ibid)

The interviewer, Gerard Raulet, seemed quite surprised by this line of presentation, and pressed Foucault to elaborate, and Foucault replied that:

reading Nietzsche was the the point of rupture for me. There is a history of the subject just as there is a history of reason; but we can never demand that the history of reason unfold as a first and founding act of the rationalist subject.

(Foucault, 1983:199)

So for Foucault at least Bataille represented not only the principle of transgression, but was also an essential stepping stone to the radical work of Nietzsche, whose ideas were one of the many bases from which the attack on phenomenology was launched. Raulet then asked Foucault if his work could be said to belong to the current called post-modernism. Foucault replied: 'What are we calling post-modernity? I'm not up to date' (Foucault, 1983:204).

What indeed would have been Foucault's general response to the debate on postmodernism? But what is clear is that Foucault's relation to Bataille was always partly ambivalent just as it was to Canguilhem's influential studies of scientific epistemology, and to Lévi-Strauss: he admitted that he never completely resolved the conflicting attractions of literature (e.g. Blanchot and Bataille) and the traditions of the positive social sciences (e.g. Dumezil) (see Caruso, 1969:120–1).

This may be true of Foucault as an intellectual personality, but his writings fall decisively into the positive tradition; the situation is altogether more complex for a personality like Baudrillard, who lives on the tension between the two. The relation between Baudrillard and Foucault was, however, decisive. Not only was Baudrillard indebted to Foucault for the way he thought about genealogical series, he was also indebted to certain series as exemplars for his own work (clearly Baudrillard's genealogy of death attempts to follow Foucault's genealogy of madness, and perhaps even more important, his genealogy of simulation follows Foucault's genealogy of epistemes of western knowledge). Certainly the major divergence and break between the two came with Foucault's analysis of power and discipline, which from Baudrillard's point of view marked the complete abandonment of Foucault's major project, and received the sharp critique: 'Forget Foucault!'

KRISTEVA: *SAINT JULIA*

One of the most important influences, or more accurately, resources, for Baudrillard's conceptions, is the work of Julia Kristeva. In an important article of 1966 and one of 1974 she devoted space to the development of an idea of transfinite and translinguistic phenomena. These terms play an important tole in the later theory developed by Baudrillard, but they may also be used in the interpretation of Baudrillard's own work.

In a discussion of 'the novel as polylogue' Kristeva examines the possibility of identifying the specific form of ambiguity in the novel as arising out of the interpenetration of two kinds of discourse: monological and dialogical. The latter structure is defined as involving the transfinite. At first the idea was taken, she notes, from set theory; it must be understood metaphorically. The transfinite is the analog of the difference between the logical and the poetic, the quantitative and the infinite. The transfinite is the 'next larger than' (see Kristeva, 1980:90, 167–87), and therefore is that which broadens out from the sentence itself, into the poetic. There is, then, a clear difference in Kristeva's thought, between what might be called the semiotic operation which occurs in a finite field, and the symbolic operation which opens onto unlimited or potentially interminable or transfinite polylogue. The specific field of ambivalence in language is a resultant of the confluence of monological and dialogical discourse thus conceived. Linked to this in Kristeva's work is an attempt to document the passage from writing dominated by the symbol to that dominated by the sign, which she sees occurring between the end of the middle ages and the Renaissance, a movement which parallels that in Greece after the fourth century BC. It is marked by the gradual disappearance of the epic system (Kristeva, 1986:63).

These are taken up in modified versions by Baudrillard. The notion of ambivalence is inflected with Freudian notions and lies specifically in the field of the symbolic itself, as opposed to that of the monological or the outcome of the meeting of the dialogic (developed by Kristeva along lines first indicated by Bakhtin) and the monologic. It is possible to see via Kristeva, that Baudrillard's language is a divided one: he cannot dispense with a semiotic register and although he seeks transfinite order in the poetic range his purely poetic writings are never sufficient for his purposes. His attempt to reach the transfinite as such in his later works is always through the meeting of the semiological and the symbolic, that is as the action of the poetic register in the semiological, and it is in this way that his writing doubles itself into a mode that is ambivalent. The aim of Baudrillard's transfinite writing is that of self-annulment, or the gift and its cancellation. A form of writing that is non-accumulative (that is deconstructive) is never, however, really the principal aim of Baudrillard, and certainly not a form of writing that is dialogic, and in this respect his work is like that of Kristeva who tends to establish a theoretical corpus.[18]

LEFEBVRE: *SAINT HENRI*

Finally, it is necessary to examine the work of Henri Lefebvre, often simply conflated with that of Sartre, but who developed a distinctive social theory which had a decisive effect on Baudrillard in its content, and against which in certain respects Baudrillard reacted violently.

Lefebvre's book, *Everyday Life in the Modern World* (originally published in 1968), is a summation of a long period of work which in the post-war years took Lefebvre's Marxism into the one-dimensional triumph of capitalist society. His version of this succinctly follows the evolution of capitalist cultures in the 1950s and 1960s, against the background of a theory of the gradual effacement of the symbol, the emergence and dominance of the sign and then the dominance of the signal (Lefebvre, 1971:38–9).[19] His book begins with a long search for the correct concept of this new society: he discusses and rejects the notions of technological society, affluent society, leisure society, and in the end chooses the concept of 'Bureaucratic society of controlled consumption' (ibid:60), making the decisive move away from production as the decisive theoretical moment, and away from the domination of the subject in consumption: 'in the modern world everyday life has ceased to be a "subject" rich in subjectivity; it has become an "object" of social organisation' (Lefebvre, 1971:59–60).

The picture which emerges is of a society which in the 1960s saw an intensification of the fashion cycle, a rapid transformation of the semantic field from the domination of the symbol to the sign, the transformation of the world of the art object with the emergence of television the drama had moved to pure display, with subsequent loss of depth and substance, and the simultaneous loss of the heavy material culture of the past (the symbolic craft objects like the grandfather clock (Lefebvre, 1971: 64)). The new culture after 1960 was articulated around programming, functionalism, a new cyberneticism: its dominant tone was cool, robotic.

This whole progression was a witness to the 'loss of referentials', the increasing flattening of cultures into the consumption of signs themselves for their own sake, a process difficult to distinguish from madness, he argues (Lefebvre, 1971: 108). In relation to language itself there is evidently three stages: the first period of modernity, of Baudelaire to Joyce, in which the poet attempts to establish an alchemy of speech over everyday life; in a second phase language itself attempts in surrealism and futurism to establish a second reality against everyday life; and third, form becomes reality in the new novel, which is stark, cool, a neo-formalism (ibid: 125–6). In relation to these later phases it is not a question any more of a new false consciousness (as it might be in the thought of existential writers) but here there is a remarkable, a 'true' consciousness but in the form of a terrorism of everyday life: this new truth is a consumer society as itself normal, the norm, it is a reality 'isolated from possibility, virtuality' (ibid: 179): a pure (formal) space defines this new world. His analysis approaches the Barthean formula:

> the neutralisation and disappearance of symbols, the attenuation of pertinence (contrast) and the prevalence of associations of words and sentences, associations seen as evidence of 'what goes without saying'. . . . Zero point is a neutral state (not an act or a situation) characterised by a pseudo-presence, that of a simple witness, and therefore a pseudo-absence.
>
> (Lefebvre, 1971:184)

There are zero points of objects (their splitting and recombining), of space (the new desert spaces of the cities), of need (the imaginary satisfaction in advance of needs), and of time in its total programming. A zero point in communication is the irruption of a complete transparency, so that there is nothing to communicate (ibid: 184). There is the appearance of the neutral space throughout society: the hygiene of the DIY ghetto, the ghetto of the feminine, of youth. Ironically it is 'a society . . . obsessed with dialogue, communication, participation, integration and coherence, all the things it lacks' (ibid: 184). It is a social totality made up only of zero points. It marks the decline of the festival, of style, of art as society and its culture enter the plane of unreality and transparency (as against that of praxis (ibid: 189)).

Lefebvre's response to this is to ask whether a counter-terrorism is possible (1971: 188). His answers bring him both close to and away from Baudrillard. His first response is to argue for a radical analysis of modern culture by turning the tools of modern analysis against themselves: 'our radical analysis turns formalism, structuralism and functionalism against themselves, attacks obsessional classifications with a classification of forms and exposes their general content, which is everyday life maintained by terror' (ibid: 180). This is evidently taken up by Baudrillard who uses the tools of structuralism to denounce the new ambience of modern culture as itself structuralist.

But Lefebvre's second response is to argue for a new cultural revolution, not as Baudrillard tries later in 1973 in relation to the symbolic order, but here it is expressed as a call for the renaissance of urban festivals and sexual revolution. This is specifically not a straightforward aesthetic demand, but it is a demand for a transformation of everyday life into art, and for technology to serve and transform everyday life in its turn (this latter formulation is the subject of a direct critique (Baudrillard, 1969b)). The sexual revolution is not a call he notes for a rejection of all 'controls' on sexuality, but for the passing of these controls over to those who wish to engage in sexual relations, not institutions. The source of energy for this revolution is the city itself, which can be liberated in a renewal of the festival so that a new harmony between everyday life and the urban form can be achieved: the concept of adaptation is higher than that of mastery or praxis, he argues. (Lefebvre, 1971:206).

BAUDRILLARD: *SAINT JEAN*

Thus if we now return to Baudrillard, some of the major elements of the intellectual field with which he engages have become visible (I have deliberately omitted writers such as Bourdieu, Lyotard, even Deleuze, who though interesting in this context are not essential to the understanding of the context of Baudrillard). It is also clear that there are other writers whose intellectual biographies have specific features which parallel his in remarkable ways without being identical. Baudrillard is certainly among those whose intellectual career reveals considerable development (like Althusser and Foucault), but in this case from 'critical' structuralism to post-structuralism (as a form of pre-structuralism in effect) and beyond. But there are a number of other interesting elements. His work represents a shift also from literary to sociological concerns, where the literary aspect, however, remains very marked and not simply in terms of style. Baudrillard followed and himself developed new variations on old epistemological and political arguments, but the main threads of his development remain strictly rooted to the theme of cultural analysis and focus directly on the processes of consumption in capitalist societies and the changing nature of the object. His analyses have sometimes approached formal structural, and sociological ambitions, yet there is an element (drawn perhaps from Bataille, or Debord or some other source) which has led to transgressive or transfinite analyses, to *la part maudite* and the principle of evil.

There is an undeniabie difference which arises in the acute ambiguity of Baudrillard's attitudes to modernity and postmodernity: whereas for Foucault, and the post-structuralists, there is absolutely no doubt that the attack on the conception of the homogeneous and transcendental subject is seen as an essential and progressive step, for Baudrillard, this is often tinged with apparent nostalgia for something which is posited as a genuine (symbolic) culture[20] (he himself says this ends with his book, *Seduction* (1979), though this is far from being self-evident). It is true that Baudrillard himself engaged with post-structuralism, but whereas others directed post-structuralist critiques at humanism, Baudrillard launches ironic critiques at postmodern society (itself become post-structuralist) arguing that these critiques are most appropriate to this particular object: a society in which internal transcendence is no longer a possibility. One of the crucial questions, in the light of this very brief and highly selective survey, is to ask whether Baudrillard's development of these problems moves towards a conception and a practice of theoretical transgression in the sense identified by Derrida in Bataille, or ironically to an older tradition (though obscure in detail) of Durkheim's forgotten analysis of social teratology, with its implication that there might be after all something which might be defined as a norm.[21]

3 Baudrillard, postmodernism, Marxism and feminism

I have nothing to do with post modernism.
  Baudrillard (in Gane, 1990:331)

In Britain, at least, Baudrillard is a latecomer to sociology and cultural theory. It is highly significant that his work has been influential in Canada, the US and Australia, long before it began to emerge in Britain, where it did so only on the shoulders of these other developments, and then first on the margins, in art journals, before being promoted in turn by journals like *Theory, Culture and Society, Screen, Marxism Today* and *New Left Review*. In restrospect, the story of this exclusion and late embracement and the ironies it entails on each side is a remarkable one.

In the first instance, it may be explained simply because Baudrillard's work is difficult to classify – or perhaps it is unclassifiable – that his work got not the slightest mention in an encyclopaedic survey such as Joan Miller's *French Structuralism* (1981), or a theoretical survey such as John Thompson's *Studies in the Theory of Ideology* (1984), or the highly critical attack on structuralism in J. Merquior's *From Prague to Paris* (1986), or Peter Dews' *Logics of Disintegration* (1987); even important surveys of French philosophy seem to find no place for it, for example V. Descombes *Modern French Philosophy* (1979) or A.P. Griffith's edited collection, *Contemporary French Philosophy* (1988).[1]

Since the mid-1980s, however, things have begun to change, and Baudrillard has even become theoretically fashionable in some quarters. This sudden take-up was undoubtedly connected with the emergence and promotion of the themes around the concept of 'postmodernism'. Baudrillard, for obscure reasons, was associated with this promotion almost from the beginning. Perhaps a key point was the influential article by Fredric Jameson in 1984, called 'Postmodernism, or the cultural logic of late capitalism' (Jameson, 1984a), at about the same time as the publication of Hal Foster's (1986) collection, *Postmodern Culture* (first published two years earlier in the US under the title *The Anti-aesthetic*: some would say that change of title was indeed a shrewd operation). The ball was rolling and within the space of a couple of years there were conferences, seminars, meetings, collections, taking up the search for the postmodern. Lash and Urry tried to integrate Baudrillard's notions into the culture of late capitalism in *The End of Organised Capitalism* (1987), as did D. Hebdige in terms of popular culture in *Hiding in the Light* (1988).[2] But these were now part of the torrent: *The Postmodern Scene: Excremental Culture and Hyper-aesthetics* (Kroker and Cook, 1988), *Life After Postmodernism* (Fekete, 1988), *Body Invaders, Sexuality and the Postmodern Condition* (Kroker and Kroker 1988), *Panic Encyclopaedia* (Kroker, Kroker and Cook, 1989) from a group lead by Arthur Kroker at Concordia University in Canada. Many discussions of this new phenomenon began to appear, notably those by Douglas Kellner in *Theory, Culture and Society*, leading up to the first book on Baudrillard (Kellner, 1989a). Kellner's articles presented Baudrillard as the most important postmodern social theorist, but his book paradoxically altered course and concluded that he was not. By the end of the 1980s Baudrillard's reputation was established as the 'high priest of postmodernism' and then became a fashionable target as the counter-movement to postmodernism gathered pace, as in A. Callinicos' *Against Postmodernism* (1989). Steven Connor's general discussion, *Postmodernist Culture* (1989) presents Baudrillard as one of the main architects of postmodern theory, but has some difficulty in so doing, as he notes (ibid:61), since there is not an obvious and direct connection between the two once the texts of Baudrillard are closely examined.

The irony is striking. During the period when Baudrillard was making important contributions to critical theory he was completely ignored. When the fashion for postmodernism began to take off his works were used as an emblem for the movement. It is clear from his writings that not only does the term not play any important role in his theory, unlike, say, a writer like Lyotard (1984), but that his position is one of great hostility to the whole phenomenon: 'I have nothing to do with postmodernism'.

THE MARXIST DEBATE

Douglas Kellner's rationale, for example, for presenting Baudrillard was expressly as warning and to provide an advanced critique which might deflect the enthusiasts on the political left. His critical attack was directed at Arthur Kroker's spectacular efforts to argue that Baudrillard had reinvigorated the Marxist tradition (in 'Baudrillard's Marx' in Kroker and Cook (1988:170–88)).

Kroker's 'panic' reading identified Baudrillard squarely as 'the post-modern scene itself', in its modality and its mood. Like the postmodern object itself:

> Baudrillard's writings are a geometry of signs of absence and lack which threaten to unravel in a fantastic eruption of creative energy as they trace the implosion of postmodern experience signified by the signs

everywhere today of dead labour, dead power, and dead truth . . . to read Baudrillard's most recent works . . . is to enter a terroristic universe, whose staged communications and abstract codings undergo a massive and feverish redoublement.

(Kroker and Cook, 1988:170–1)

Baudrillard speaks from the dark side of postmodernity (ibid: 171).

Kroker insists that the impact of the influence of Nietzsche is decisive: 'Baudrillard writes under the sign of Nietzsche: each of his texts are works of art which seek to arraign the world before poetic consciousness' (Kroker and Cook, 1988:171). Fundamentally it is Nietzsche's influence on Marx, mediated here by Baudrillard, which produces a 'tragic vision of abstract labour as the essence of postmodernity'. Kroker discusses four basic theses associated with this project: first the thesis of the death of the social body, second the deconstruction of the historical subject,[3] third the 'eclipse' of the commodity form, and finally the rupture with the purely accumulative theory of power. These together mark out the key postmodern assumptions.

Let us examine the last of these. Kroker suggests that Baudrillard has 'done the impossible. In a lightning reversal of effects, he has managed to radicalise *Capital* and make Marx dangerous once more' (Kroker and Cook, 1988:181). This radicalisation was possible only on the condition that Baudrillard fused Nietzsche's notion of the will to power with the theory of the alienated commodity. And now 'After Baudrillard, it is impossible not to confront the political and theoretical conclusion that *Capital* is the reverse, but parallel, image of the will to power.' His hard lesson for us is that *Capital* has to be read 'as a brilliant recitative of perfect nihilism' (ibid). In postmodernising Marx, Baudrillard made a detour via the work of McLuhan but only to reassert the principle that machinery was the message of industrialism for it is in this principle understood as the accumulation of dead labour power, that Marx's fundamental radicalism is to be read.

Nietzsche and Baudrillard have recognised that there is a third and decisive term: the will to will, or cynical power. The problem with Marx is that he compromised his theory, or as Kroker calls his brilliant 'vivisection', by turning to a naturalistic theory of labour (Kroker and Cook, 1988:188). In doing this Marx became himself an unwitting victim of capital's logic. It is Baudrillard who has become the essential analyst of capital in its final downward spiral. Baudrillard's 'silent majority' is simply Nietzsche's 'last men'. Going beyond Marx, Baudrillard has seen that the commodity form is in essence a form of the sign, and articulating this sign, the 'structural law of value' is the crucial mechanism of reproduction below which is the 'will to will'.

Kroker turns this around and claims that it is necessary to see that 'the interpretation of advanced capitalist society under the sign of nihilism is the basic condition for human emancipation as well as for the recovery of the tragic sense of critical theory' (Kroker and Cook, 1988:187). In this way the melancholy science is turned into a strategy for returning to questions of 'myth and enlightenment' (ibid: 188). Nihilism is not simply a pessimism, it should be read, as Nietzsche once said, as 'a projection of the conditions of (our) preservation into the predicates of existence' (cited in Kroker and Cook, 1988: 183). The point, says Kroker, attempting to read Baudrillard's practice, is to start with 'unrelieved pessimism', to think 'without illusions' and 'develop a realism of concepts on the basis of understanding cynical power' (ibid: 187) In this way a new realistic strategy of exploring postmodern experience becomes a possibility.

Kroker's reading, then, is idiosyncratic and has no hesitation in reaching the conclusion that Baudrillard is the postmodern theorist, even the postmodern scene, since this is a kind of nihilistic simulation of the object itself in an attempt to reach its fundamental structures (here conceived as dead labour), its dark side, where it is necessary to situate theory if it is to have any truth effect. The clear implication of Kroker's position is that it radicalises Marx by producing itself as an event in the excremental culture, it parades its truth in the form of catastrophic 'participation' in its object: 'we seek to create a theoretical manoeuvre in which hypermodernism implodes into the detritus of its own panic scenes' (Kroker and Cook, 1988: vii). The problem of this fatal strategy is that it continually falls into parody.

Douglas Kellner was, as I noted, appalled at these interpretations and suggestions, for his reading recognises that Baudrillard is the sworn enemy of radical Marxism. Kellner first identified the problem in two articles (1987, 1988) and then in a full-blown book-length attack (1989a). Kellner presents Baudrillard's ideas as postmodern social theory and then tries to subject the project to damning and puritanical criticism because 'the whole Baudrillard affair is rapidly mutating into a new idolatry of a new master thinker, and is in danger of giving rise to a new orthodoxy' (Kellner, 1987:126). Kellner's work, then, has a three-phased evolution.

1 His first reading suggests that Baudrillard's work is to be situated in a philosophy which rejects 'meaning and reality', as it is to be located in the French post-structuralist tradition and trapped in the the deconstruction of the subject. In horror Kellner recounts Kroker's view that capital has brought the end of the old gods and their enchanted world only to inaugurate the possibility of the superman. The launching base for this possibility is the new postmodern culture dominated by the hyperreal and simulations, and where all political opposition disappears: 'Baudrillard's story is as frightening and perhaps instructive as any of the great dystopias of the modern age' (Kellner, 1987:128). Marx was different since, says Kellner, 'Marx's story suggested the possibility of a happy ending for humanity.'

There is profound misunderstanding here Kellner remarks, for the difference between Marx and Baudrillard is irreconcilable: Baudrillard has moved out of the problematic of production altogether. In the new world, work is simply a sign, 'thenceforth capital and political economy disappear from Baudrillard's writing' (Kellner, 1987:129).

It is the dark side, of death, which now begins to assert itself in Baudrillard's thought, not social transcendence. Death becomes the ultimate signifier, and leads to the perspective which only sees the death of the social and the death of the revolution. Actually, says Kellner, Nietzsche himself stresses life as against death; it is with Baudrillard that the sign of death becomes dominant. Thus: 'Baudrillard's posture . . . indicates a move into the beyond, free from the ghosts and limitations of all the master thinkers of times past' (Kellner, 1987:130).

Baudrillard's work can be useful as a provocation to Marxism but in no sense should be combined or confused with it. Baudrillard's new theoretical space is at the borderline, and it is here, 'between the modern and the postmodern, that a critical interrogation of his thought should begin. Almost every article on Baudrillard in English seems to presuppose that he is right, that we are in something like a postmodern condition' (Kellner, 1987:131).

But, Kellner argues, this is naive and wishful thinking, for there is far too much weight given in Baudrillard to the mass media and its effects. He recognises this is a new version of Marcuse's one-dimensionalism, but at least Marcuse 'attempted to counter one dimensionality by desire, authentic art, libidinal reason, dialectical thinking, resistance and rebellion (the Great Refusal), and oppositional politics' (Kellner, 1987:138). This is curious comment from an author of a work on Marcuse who knows that 'one-dimensional man' draws back from these forms of opposition or produces them only as a remote chance. The space that Marcuse opened in that work is the space in which Baudrillard has sought to explore in a new way.

Yet even this is not as simple as it first appears and Kellner seems confused himself here for he also presents Baudrillard's advocacy of a modern cultural revolution on the basis of a culture of symbolic exchange and gift. Although Kellner criticises this as 'nostalgic' it is, as he is forced to admit a 'total refusal, total negativity, and the Utopia of radical otherness' (ibid. 140). It is for Kellner too extreme. It jumps directly from an ultra-primitive culture to an ultra-modern injunction that one should fight the system with a higher logic than the system itself: a catastrophic strategy which is 'not the least dialectical . . . (where) the system's own logic turns into the best weapon against it. The only strategy, of opposition to a hyperrealist system is pataphysical' (Baudrillard cited in Kellner, 1987:141).

For Kellner this new position has no radical charge; Jarry's pata-physics is simple caricature, not derision, as Baudrillard maintains. It is an imaginary cul-de-sac. What hope is there in this system which enshrines the principle of the denial of politics and alternatives? But Baudrillard's next step is even more 'bizarre' he says, for it proposes the triumph of the object over the subject. Here, even the very possibility of 'social theory' is denied – an interesting proposition in the light of Kellner's suggestion that this is postmodern theory. Out of this is only born he says, again contradicting his own presentation of Baudrillard's 'total refusal', 'a bleak picture, (for) Baudrillard no longer affirms any alternative, resistance, struggle or refusal' (Kellner, 1987: 143).

Kellner concludes this first presentation by saying that Baudrillard is of no help at all in understanding the 'contemporary era which is speeding towards the future and unable to overcome the past', a curious formula which comes close to one-dimensionalism.

2   In the following year (1988) Kellner, as if not content with these remarks, again reviewed Baudrillard's work, this time more confidently describing Baudrillard as 'the' postmodern theorist. Baudrillard 'describes a postmodern society in which radical semiurgy produces simulations and simulacra that in turn create new forms of society, culture experience and subjectivity' (Kellner, 1988:240). Indeed Baudrillard 'was perhaps the first to organise . . . a postmodern social theory' (ibid: 242).

At this point Kellner expressed Baudrillard's later theory as a move from explosive modernity, dominated by processes of production, to implosive postmodernity, defined as:

> the site of an implosion of all boundaries, regions and distinctions between high and low culture, appearance and reality, and just about every other binary opposition maintained by traditional philosophy and social theory . . . this signifies the end of all the positivities, grand referents and finalities of previous social theory: the Real, Meaning, History, Power, Revolution, and even the social itself.
>
> (Kellner, 1988:242)

But, says Kellner, now becoming altogether disillusioned with Baudrillard, 'it is not until the postmodern craze of the 1980s that Baudrillard takes up the term "postmodern" in relation to his own work'.

This is a crucial turn for Kellner, for he now wishes to find a point in Baudrillard where his thesis, that Baudrillard is postmodernism in theory, can be grounded. He cites Baudrillard to the effect as saying, 'I state, I accept, I assume, I analyse the second revolution, that of the 20th century, that of post-modernity which is the immense process of the destruction of meaning, equal to the earlier destruction of appearances' (from Baudrillard, 1981a:231–2). This becomes of capital importance in Kellner's argument, and he comments, 'Baudrillard's postmodern mind-set exhibits a contradictory amalgam of emotions and responses ranging from despair to melancholy, to vertigo and giddiness, and nostalgia and laughter' (Kellner, 1988: 247). Presumably Kellner himself has emotions which derive only from a commitment to revolution:

ardour, singlemindedness. If there is no room for laughter or melancholy there is for tedium and distress as will be apparent.

Kellner supports his interpretation with a reference to an interview with Baudrillard ('Interview: Game with Vestiges') from 1984, which seems to suggest that Baudrillard practises and embraces postmodernism (the quality of the translation here is crucial; I have been unable to check it):

> Post-modernity is neither optimistic nor pessimistic. It is a game with the vestiges of what has been destroyed. This is why we are 'post' – history has stopped, one is in a kind of post-history which is without meaning. One would not be able to find any meaning in it. So, we must move in it, as if it were a kind of circular gravity. We can no longer be said to progress. So it is a 'moving' situation. But it is not at all unfortunate. I have the impression with post-modernism that there is an attempt to rediscover a certain pleasure in the irony of things. Right now one can tumble into total hopelessness – all the definitions, everything, it's all been done. What can one do? What can one become?

And postmodernity is the attempt – perhaps its desperate, I don't know – to reach a point where one can live with what is left. It is more a survival among the remnants than anything else. [Laughter!]

(Baudrillard, 1984)

Again, postmodernism, says Kellner, quoting Baudrillard:

> is described as a response to emptiness and anguish which is oriented toward 'the restoration of a past culture' that tries 'to bring back all past cultures, to bring back everything that one has destroyed in joy and which one is reconstructing in sadness in order to try to live, to survive. . . . All that remains to be done is to play with the pieces. Playing with the pieces – that is post-modern.'

(from Baudrillard, cited Kellner, 1988:247–8)

What happens at this point is that Kellner reads this as describing Baudrillard's own intellectual position: Baudrillard 'reproduces certain trends of the present age which he projects into a simulation model of postmodernism as the catastrophe of modernity' (Kellner, 1988: 248). This interpretation is therefore a complex construction. Out of one article and one interview Baudrillard is said to provide a theory and practice of postmodernism.

3   Not content to leave matters there, Kellner published a full book-length study in 1989: *Jean Baudrillard: From Marxism to Postmodernism and Beyond* (1989a). Although being himself the main culprit he notes: 'During the 1980s Jean Baudrillard has been promoted in certain circles as the most advanced theorist of the media and society in the so-called post-modern era' (Kellner, 1989a:60).

Now Kellner's mood changes, he finds the whole project tedious, it becomes a:

postmodern carnival . . . (which) soon becomes repetitive and boring, and its novel attractions wear thin. . . . Still for a time it provides some novel amusements, as well as some rather frightening horror shows. So let us leave behind the concerns of traditional (does he mean modern? MG) social theory and explore the post modern carnival.

(Kellner 1989a:94)

He rehearses the theses outlined by Baudrillard, but again is tempted to attribute the attitudes and practices analysed by Baudrillard to Baudrillard himself. A key example can be found in the discussion of modern art (Kellner, 1989a:112). In an early essay (1972) Baudrillard discussed pop art as collusive with the modern world and not as many suggest critical of it. Kellner in a highly complacent misreading says this is a 'preview of Baudrillard's later surrender to the world of things' (Kellner, 1989a:112)

However, a lecture by Baudrillard at Columbia in 1987, clearly presented a quite hostile attitude to modern art, and this awakens a certain theoretical disquiet in Kellner. Yet he reproduces again the material from the interview of 1984 ('Game with Vestiges'). As Kellner gives more flesh to the interview it is apparent that Baudrillard may be mocking a position that is not his own. Kellner does not question the translation, but clearly a lot can hinge on just how liberal the translator has been with personal pronouns.

Things become more complicated now as Kellner begins to realise that Baudrillard refers to these contemporary cultural process up to 1980 as problems of modernism, after 1981 very occasionally as postmodernism (Baudrillard's 'cul-de-sac'). But now the perspective changes and Kellner admits that

for the most part throughout the 1980s Baudrillard does not offer an explicit theory of postmodernity beyond a few comments which I have cited. (To date the essay 'On nihilism' is the only one of his major texts in which he actually presents his own theory as delineating a new postmodernity.)

(Kellner, 1989a:120)

This marks a complete and unacknowledged volte face of Kellner's position. Gone is the insistence that Baudrillard thinks of his own theory in terms of postmodernism, and gone is the idea even that Baudrillard has a theory of postmodernism. Indeed:

in his 1980s texts . . . Baudrillard continues to use the term 'modernity' as the global framework for analysis, and the few times that he mentions a 'postmodern' phenomenon, he tends to be a bit churlish and critical, and so far has resisted spelling out a theory of postmodernity.

(ibid:121)

This suggests that Kellner's original analysis was wide of the mark, both as regards the object (postmodernism) and the style of Baudrillard's work. Logically this brings huge problems for Keller's notion that Baudrillard is the postmodern carnival.

It also suggests that it might be appropriate to re-examine the essay 'On nihilism', the only essay, according to Kellner to identify Baudrillard as postmodernist. Even in this particular essay (in Baudrillard 1981a: 229–36), there is only one reference to postmodernism (p. 231). A section of the essay has already been quoted. It is necessary now to put that quote into context: for, contrary to Kellner's reading Baudrillard does not 'scorn' modernity and embrace postmodernity at all. Baudrillard says:

> I state, I accept, I assume the immense process of destruction of appearances (and of the seduction of appearances!) to the profit of meaning (representation, history, criticism, etc.) which is the capital fact of the 19th century. The true revolution of the 19th century, of modernity, is the radical destruction of appearances, the disenchantment of the world and its abandonment to the violence of interpretation and history.

> I state, I accept, I assume, I analyse the second revolution, that of the 20th century, that of postmodernity, which is the immense process of the destruction of meaning, equal to the earlier destruction of appearances. Whoever lives by meaning dies by meaning.
>
> (ibid:231–2)

This longer quotation reveals that Kellner has misunderstood the position presented: Baudrillard does not 'scorn' the first to adopt the second. The incantation is expressly monotonous and takes equal distance from modernism and postmodernism. And if this is the 'only one' of his major essays to support the idea that Baudrillard thinks of himself as postmodern, there is precious little in the claim. Indeed, in what follows of Kellner's book (a further some one hundred pages of discussion) there is no direct reference to postmodernism. But then, suddenly (Kellner, 1989a:212), Baudrillard is again criticised for inhabiting a world that is an 'aleatory, vertiginous, indeterminate postmodern world of simulations, codes, hyperreality' (ibid:212). And all these, announces Kellner, are essentially conservative, even 'distressing' because it is:

> now, more than ever (that) a critical, reconstructive intervention into the field of radical social theory and politics is needed . . . I for one, am not ready to throw in the towel . . . () . . . it seems too early to surrender belief in the socialist project.
>
> (ibid:214–15)

POSTMODERNISM

If Baudrillard's comments in some interviews seem ambiguous, and comments in essays present a picture of distance from postmodernism (and modernism), a conference paper presented in New York in 1986, develops a coherent rejection of postmodernism. He notes that most of the culturally creative energies of the century were expended in the activities of the 1920s and 1930s. After this period the movements and currents split up, and reappear in the:

> ultimate configuration, that of 'postmodernism', undoubtedly characterises the most degenerated, most artificial, and most eclectic phase – a fetishism of picking out and adopting all the significant little bits and pieces, all the idols and the purest signs that preceded this fetishism.
> (Baudrillard, 1989a:41)

The characterisation of postmodernism is one of unrelenting and biting mediocrity, absence of passion, of challenge. All the old ideas that were swept away in 1968 are now restored 'in total eclecticism'. It is dominated by 'exhaustive representation' that is, he insists on their very state of 'exhaustion'.

Centuries of critical thought and action are brought to a sudden end: political and sexual revolution are finished. What follows is a new religiosity, a re-emergence of love. The dominant ideologies are soft and gentle. They belong to a new generation, 'that is discovering love, selflessness, togetherness, international compassion, and the individual tremolo.' The new ideologies concern:

> human rights, dissidence, antiracism, the anti-nuclear movement, and the environment. They are easy. . . . (This) generation has already succeeded in everything, already has everything, practices solidarity with the greatest of ease, bears neither the stigma of class misfortune nor the stigma of being cursed by capital. The members of this generation go about their business casually. They are European yuppies.
> (Baudrillard 1989a:43)

At the level of ideology, then, the new generation is the bearer of soft revivals, even of socialism. Its mediocre melange of insipid remakes leads to a general 'discouragement of everything regarded as adventurous' (ibid: 45). And this occurs in the void as 'postmodernism functions . . . by means of lack of events' (ibid: 41).

This discussion is salutary since it throws considerable light on the meaning of Baudrillard's interview (1984) and on other comments. Far from embracing postmodernism, Baudrillard's whole effort is to combat it. But Baudrillard's own conception of postmodernism is much wider than previously presented. It obviously includes what he calls soft feminism, liberal Marxism, green politics. These are not related to class politics as in some Marxist fundamentalism, for Baudrillard sees them as enfeebled ideologies available to the yuppies themselves. Ironically, it seems fairly clear that both Kroker and Kellner would now probably be subsumed by Baudrillard into this category. It thus becomes interesting to examine instances of discussion of Baudrillard's attempt to stay outside of the postmodern eclecticism.

There are, in the light of this, further ironies from writers like Callinicos who write against postmodernism and who identify Baudrillard as post-modernist: 'Unless we work towards the kind of revolutionary change which would allow the realisation of . . . (human) potential in a transformed world, there is little left for us to do, except like . . . Baudrillard, to fiddle while Rome burns' (Callinicos, 1989:174). But there is some contact here between Baudrillard and Callinicos: as both agree that Rome is burning, and Callinicos is right to see Baudrillard as working in a perspective of the apocalypse. The difference here is that for Baudrillard all notions of a praxis of creation of a new society, of a 'transformation' of society in the Marxist tradition, are now completely unrealistic. Callinicos can, therefore, only read in Baudrillard an essay in futility, and as such cannot allow any radicality in Baudrillard's development. He suggests that Baudrillard thinks:

> The only appropriate form of resistance in these circumstances is the refusal of any political action, which could only succeed in restoring in a perhaps more repressive form the imploding social, but the inert, apathetic absorption of the 'silent majority' in the images showered on them by the mass media . . . it is difficult to see his attack on any form of collective action . . . as anything more than a facile attempt to trump the Foucauldian concept of resistance.
>
> (Callinicos, 1989:86–7)

The problem is that Callinicos has not read very much of Baudrillard (and certainly not the key text, *Symbolic Exchange and Death* (Baudrillard, 1976) which is the basis of Baudrillard's comments on Foucault). But Callinicos is content to pick up what he sees as elementary logical problems in Baudrillard: it is impossible, he says outlining Baudrillard's notion, to 'talk of world independent of our representations of it, to distinguish between true and false, real and imaginary' (Callinicos, 1989:145).

The culture is dominated, he continues summarising Baudrillard, by the 'hyperreal' and the impossibility of critique, and in consequence the deradicalisation of all socialist practice. If this is so, the only thing left is belles-lettres, a kind of 'intellectual dandyism'. It is also logically flawed for 'how can Baudrillard – or anyone else trapped within simulation . . . describe its nature, and outline the transition from the real to the hyperreal? Baudrillard is caught on the horns of one of the characteristic dilemmas of Nietzschean thought' (Callinicos, 1989: 147–8).

But is Baudrillard actually caught in this way? Perhaps more to the point the naive critique of Baudrillard is in greater danger. In reducing Baudrillard to intellectual dandyism, Callinicos has risked falling into this himself: why read Baudrillard's poetry or general theory at all if everything is so predictably neat and transparently futile? He is willing to accuse Baudrillard of 'posturing' (Callinicos, 1989:87) yet what else has Callinicos done but to engage in what really amounts to anti-intellectualist posturing?

His lack of familiarity with Baudrillard is further in evidence in his discussion of the postmodern 'person'. He cites Lipovetsky against Baudrillard's supposed position (in which 'postmodern "seduction" (reduces) agents to alienation and passivity' (Callinicos, 1989:153)): 'Consumption compels the individual to take charge of himself, it makes him responsible, it is a system of ineluctable participation' (Lipovetsky, cited in Callinicos, 1989:153).

But had Callinicos either read Baudrillard or even Lipovetsky, who acknowledges that these ideas come from Baudrillard (Lipovetsky, 1983:70) he would have been aware that here we arrive increasingly at a series of remarkable transpositions: Baudrillard becomes fantasy and Callinicos gradually becomes Baudrillard. The idea of the new narcissistic individualism which interests Callinicos has Baudrillard among its initial theorists. Callinicos even goes on to argue that postmodernism is best understood as a product of the generation of 1968 as they come to terms with its failure. Baudrillard's reading is also generational but, as I have shown, identifies the yuppie generation as its true support. What is also remarkable is the way in which Callinicos is attracted (via the work of Mike Davis) to the concept of the pathology of the affluent capitalist society, which is the basic terrain of Baudrillard's social analysis.

Ironically however, instead of making these connections, Baudrillard is condemned himself as exemplifying the position of the yuppie (Kellner also makes this mistake), and it is in this sense that Callinicos asserts: 'the success enjoyed by . . . Baudrillard, quite out of proportion with any slight intellectual merit (his) work might have, thus becomes comprehensible' (Callinicos, 1989:170). Against what he imagines in Baudrillard, he simply asserts the possibility of revolution as the present forms of 'pathological prosperity' suggest the world is still fragile, and the Marxist project 'awaits realisation' (ibid:171).

BAUDRILLARD AND FEMINISM

Although some feminists have sought to identify Baudrillard's anti-feminism as a significant trend in postmodernism, for example, Suzanne Moore's notion of Baudrillard as a 'pimp of postmodernism' (in Chapman and Rutherford, 1988:165), others have seen this position as antagonistic to it and out of tune with a postmodern mood decisively inflected by the feminist movement. Kellner sees Baudrillard's provocation or affront to feminism as part of the postmodern carnival in which Baudrillard's 'loathsome' attitude is to 'let it all hang out'.

Baudrillard's attitudes to this question go back to his earliest writings on consumer society in the late 1960s when he developed the view that the sexual revolution was a cultural and sexual disaster leading to great oppression for women, an oppression of repressive emancipation. As women became liberated they were immediately trapped into a sexual order dominated by phallic values and the breakdown of symbolic exchange and ritual controls on sexual practice. The outcome was that woman's body became effectively a phallic object in an affluent society in which commercialism exploited and generalised the newly available resource. As the controls of the symbolic order were relaxed, a generalised pornographic culture emerged. At the moment of the sexual liberation, masculinity lost out and became fragile. Later, with the ending of the period of sexual permissiveness (the orgy), the position of women also became more vulnerable.

Against this scenario Baudrillard sought to develop an alternative to feminism. Against the new forms of obscenity which he identified as accompanying the sexual revolution, he attempted to protect and develop the principle of seduction. This suited a number of purposes. On the one hand, it stressed a basic shift in epistemology (from the subject to the object) which could be used in an attack on Marxism and on psychoanalysis. On the other, it seemed to offer a chance of finding, within contemporary culture itself, a resource very similar to symbolic exchange processes (as he had discussed in *Symbolic Exchange and Death* (1976)). What was dominant here was not the principle of love and happiness, but that of the (deadly) game of seduction and counter-seduction, at the level of pure appearance. The value of this could clearly be seen in a culture itself now without depth: women were then privileged players in this game, which, he argued had for time immemorial, been triumphantly waged by women against men. The feminist movement simply wanted to abandon this for a now obsolete masculine profundity.

Suzanne Moore cites Baudrillard and Jane Gallop:

> *Baudrillard*: it's the feminine as appearance that defeats the profundity of the masculine. Women instead of rising up against this 'insulting' formula would do well to let themselves be seduced by this truth.
> *Gallop*: A line if ever I heard one.
>
> (in Chapman and Rutherford, 1988:182)

And again Baudrillard and Moore:

> *Baudrillard*: Imagine a woman who faints: nothing is more beautiful, since it is always at one and the same time to be overwhelmed by pleasure and to escape pleasure, to seduce and to escape seduction.
> Please follow me.
> *Moore*: No thank you.
>
> (in Chapman and Rutherford, 1988:183)[4]

But some women critics have taken the debate further, and have not been content to accept a simple conflation of Baudrillard's anti-feminism and postmodernism. These tend to be writers who are interested in the postmodern project and who recognise Baudrillard's basic strategy is to stand outside. In so doing, they claim, he offers a valuable admission of basic anti-feminist values rather than, as others have done, dressing them up in philosophical disguises.

Louise Burchill analyses Baudrillard's essay on seduction (Baudrillard, 1979) and examines the argument for the reversibility of positions in the mythic play of seduction suggested by Baudrillard, especially in his discussion of Kierkegaard's 'Diary of a seducer'. She quotes Baudrillard's comment:

Seduction then changes its meaning from an immoral and libertine enterprise exercised at the expense of virtue, from a cynical dupery for sexual ends (which is without great interest), it becomes mythical and takes on the dimensions of a sacrifice. Which is why it achieves so easily the assent of the 'victim', who obeys, as it were, through her surrender to the orders of a divinity which wills all force to be reversible and sacrificed, whether it be that of power or the natural force of seduction.

(In Frankovits, 1984:30)

Burchill points out that Baudrillard's notion that the seduction has two poles, the masculine and strategic, and the feminine and animal (feline) are placed by Kierkegaard in dialectical relation but in Baudrillard in opposition. In fact, in order to make the process intelligible, there are positions and differences in modes of seduction. In the final analysis, it appears in Baudrillard's presentation that reversibility 'accrues to a position (women's metamorphosis engendering no "becoming man")' (Frankovits, 1984:40 and see Baudrillard's response in 1987c:95) and if this is the case the seduction ritual cannot entail the possibility that all forces are reversible. Baudrillard's system depends on an already constituted set of subjects which subvert the possibility of mutual metamorphosis. What happens as Baudrillard suggests himself: '(women) aren't devoured by curiosity for the other sex, rather they swoon away into their own. . . . By all the care that she takes of herself, she metamophosises into herself continually' (cited in Frankovits, 1984:40).

Another discussion, that of Meaghan Morris (1988b; summarising from Baudrillard 1987c: 94–5; and Baudrillard's discussion at length in 1983b: 176–83), picks up Baudrillard's notion of fatal strategy and the example:

set in some vague courtly context with the ambiance of a mid-eighteenth century French epistolary novel, (where) a man is trying to seduce a woman. She asks 'which part of me do you find most seductive?' He replies, 'your eyes'. Next day, he receives an envelope. Inside, instead of the letter, he finds a bloody eye. Analysing his own fable, Baudrillard points out that in the obviousness, the literalness of her gesture, the woman has purloined the place of her seducer.
The man is the banal seducer, She, the fatal seducer, sets him a trap . . . a banal theory assumes, like the platitudinous seducer, that the subject is more powerful than the object. A fatal theory knows, like the woman, that the object is always worse than the subject.

(Morris, 1988:19)

Morris notes the problem: that this only works if the position of the woman is deliteralised, and in this Baudrillard gains control from the woman and 'returns it to figuration'. Nevertheless, Morris wants to recognise a decisive quality in Baudrillard: 'a scenario that is so grim, obsessive, and in its enunciative strategies, maniacally over-coherent, a woman must tear out her eye to be heard', (Morris, 1988b: 19).

Compare that with:

the vox pop style of cultural studies (which) is on the contrary offering us the sanitized world of a deodorant commercial where there's always a way to redemption. There's something sad about that, because cultural studies emerged from a real attempt to give voice to much grittier experiences of class, race and gender.

(Morris, 1988b:23)

This kind of discussion seems to lead to a recognition that Baudrillard's strategy is to find a way out of the conformity of postmodernism leads him directly into reactionary positions. The paradox of this strategy is that it may appear to confirm the relaxation of political consciousness, leading to a passivity and quietism, or, on the other hand, to arbitrary and gratuitous provocations. One such example was raised in a recent interview (Baudrillard 1989c:54; interviewer Suzanne Moore):

Interviewer: you suggest 'One should always bring something to sacrifice into the desert and offer it as a victim. A woman. . . . What is the point of such a gratuitously provocative statement? Is the corollary to sacrifice a postmodern philosopher in the centre of the city? (It's clear the interviewer thought Baudrillard claimed to be such, and missed the humour in the reply (M.G.)).

Baudrillard: It would be a very good idea to sacrifice a postmodern philosopher.

Naturally there is a certain amount of provocation in the image of sacrificing a woman, but I don't necessarily regard the term sacrifice negatively. I see it as a positive thing. There is a certain amount of reciprocal sacrifice in seduction for example. Something has to die but I don't see it has having to remove someone – perhaps desire or love must die. Sacrificing a woman in the desert is a logical operation because in the desert one loses one's identity. It's a sublime act and part of the drama of the desert. Making a woman the object of the sacrifice is perhaps the greatest compliment I could pay her.

(ibid:54)

But there are moments when the discussion becomes literal. This is illustrated in Baudrillard's account of a moment of confrontation at a seminar on his seduction thesis. At this particular seminar there is both a feminist and a disabled man. On every occasion Baudrillard mentions disability or the disabled his tone becomes aggressive, and if he can provide a joke at their expense he will. In this instance as well he makes it clear that his antagonism to the disabled student is intense. The account is given in *Cool Memories* (1987b:104–5), and discussed by Douglas Kellner (1989a:182–4). Baudrillard describes how the woman:

> sat down next to the handicapped man and throughout her (aggressive) argument leaned tenderly toward him, slipping a lit cigarette in and out of his mouth to enable him to smoke. . . . Beautiful, provocative girl doling out her little revenge through a poor, impotent polio case. And him glowing painfully with the pleasure of this unexpected rape . . . she was soliciting me as she practically masturbated him before my eyes, she was saying to me . . . 'I am raping you through him and there's nothing you can do about it'.
>
> (Baudrillard, 1987b)

Baudrillard admits this was a 'stroke of genius'. Douglas Kellner is outraged by this account: 'Baudrillard lets it all hang out – shamelessly, unrepentently, good Nietzschean aristocrat to the core. No compassion for the suffering or willingness to engage in dialogue with feminism' (Kellner, 1989a). The English versions of this story to date omit a further paragraph which simply notes that Baudrillard admires the cruel settling of scores: 'I love that woman who shamelessly exploited a disabled man to promote her shitty feminism (*feminisme merdique*) as I love that other woman who offered her eye to her lover as a response to a compliment' (Baudrillard, 1987b:106). Whether or not Baudrillard won the argument on seduction at this seminar we do not know. What he does tell us (though Kellner misses this) is that the feminist brilliantly inverted the situation as she placed Baudrillard in the position he least wanted. However, in so presenting the scene as a defeat for himself, of course, Baudrillard also wishes to subvert the apparent victory of the feminist into a defeat: she practised the art which he preached, thus providing the proof he needed for the deadly game of seduction and the triumph of the object.

Baudrillard then evidently seeks to provoke the humanist consensus. Observers like Meaghan Morris point to the problem of metaphor here, and its apparent asymmetrical uses between the genders. Baudrillard, however, is perhaps even more extreme here than might be credited. In one section of his journal (1983c) he reports a case from 1981 of 'sentimental cannibalism'. One Issei Sagawa invites a young Dutch girl to a meal and then to read poetry. As she reads he shoots her, and then eats her. After a two-day 'repast', 'professing undying love, Issei Sagawa lay down on a bench and fell asleep' (1983c:43). In *Cool Memories*, Baudrillard remarks:

> the silence of metaphor accompanies the cruel act, thus the Japanese cannibal passed directly from the metaphor of love to the devouring of that marvellous young Dutch girl. Or that woman who made a gift of

her eye to the man who told her how much he appreciated her look. The effacement of metaphor is characteristic of the object and its cruelty. The words have only a material, literal tenor. They are not any more signs of a language. It is the silence of pure objectality.

(Baudrillard 1987b:189; 1990c:151)

With Baudrillard, then, we are not in the presence of a romantic; quite the contrary. Here we are faced with a theorist who seeks to find a provocative, cruel face of hyperrealism. Invariably it is the woman, none the less, who is blinded or who dies in the silence of the effacement of metaphor. What kind of exchange is this? Let us return to the infamous provocation that as the American desert was so magnificent it might be appropriate to sacrifice a woman to it. His words (1988a:66) were: 'Death Valley is as big and mysterious as ever. Fire, heat, light: all the elements of sacrifice are here. . . . If something has to disappear, something matching the desert for beauty, why not a woman?' His response to the question: 'What is the point of such a gratuitously provocative statement?' was to acknowledge the value of sacrifice: 'there is a certain amount of reciprocal sacrifice in seduction for instance. Something has to die but I don't see it as having to remove someone – perhaps desire or love must die' (Baudrillard, 1989c:54). This response diverts directly into the metaphorical, yet he continues his answer by saying 'sacrificing a woman in the desert is a logical operation because in the desert one loses one's identity'. This begins to equate male identity with a woman, as if to give a woman would be to regain the identity of the giver as man. But then his response continues in the provocative mode: 'making a woman the object of the sacrifice is perhaps the greatest compliment I could pay her'. This answer, then, is made up of a number of very disparate sections which tend to contradict one another. There is a continual movement from the literal to myth, there is a movement from the subject to the object, and a movement along the chain of the gift, from the subject to the object to the recipient (Death Valley), and back to the subject and then to the object (woman) who is paid the 'compliment'.

All these examples, which Baudrillard himself tends to accumulate and to compare and to group together, are certainly very different in structure. When Baudrillard talks of the fatal strategy which emanates from the side of the object as opposed to the banal strategy of the subject, and that cruelty is a characteristic of the object, some strange slips of analysis seem to be involved. There is a kind of cruel logic to the woman as object who donates her eye, in so far as this subverts the position of the man. For Morris this works, but only on condition that the woman's action is deliteralised, i.e. it works as metaphor. But Baudrillard wants to insist that it is only a cruel fact in the effacement of the metaphor, and that it is as such cruel to the subject (i.e. the man). On the other hand, Baudrillard wants also to include sentimental cannibalism and sacrifice also as instances of the cruelty of the object. It is extremely difficult to understand how this can be so: they appear, transparently, as the banal and cruel strategy of the subject, which is transfigured into significant metaphor only through the action of signs and language. It is quite the reverse of the process claimed by Baudrillard. In the case of the sacrifice in the desert, Baudrillard expresses its value in terms of the loss to the subject (the loss of his identity). It is tortuous indeed to see this as the action of the cruel desert since the desert is described simply as 'big and mysterious' and 'beautiful'. In the case of the other victim, the Dutch girl, no evidence whatsoever is given even of this possibility, since she is mysteriously consumed as an amorous act, unless being a beautiful young Dutch girl is in itself an offence.[5] When Baudrillard describes the action of the Japanese cannibal as passing directly from metaphor to its effacement, it is only the realisation of the pure silence of the object because the object is, in fact, dead. Here again that this is pure silence is not strictly true, since Baudrillard reports the sound of the gun shot and the fall of the body is recorded on tape. Although the process of the murder seems to have something of an air of ritual and sacrifice (presumably Baudrillard would argue that the Dutch girl is paid a compliment) in fact this is, like his other sacrificial images, purely artificial. They possess some of the characteristics of fateful events, as rituals do, but not the essential characteristics of rituals themselves.[6]

Baudrillard's arguments are also designed to offend democratic sentiments as well as humanist ones. But here, too, many of his examples run into difficulties. In the interview, for example, he says 'seduction is not just a sexual strategy and it's not one-sided. Both sides are deeply involved and the stakes are high', and he stresses: 'It's a very physical game and one of equality'. Now this is consistent with his emphasis on the nature of seduction as a play of challenge and response, and of reversibility of position, of metamorphosis of role, even of being. But even though this means an equality in the game in one sense, since initiatives can be reversed, he also says, that 'it's almost an ideology played out to the detriment of democracy' (Baudrillard, 1989c:54). This implies that somewhere or other there is a formal inequality, that the action is perhaps non-rational. Baudrillard flirts with different images. One is that the male and the female are like two different species: the 'model of amorous seduction, which also pursues the strangeness of the other sex, and the possibility of being initiated into it as into a different animal or vegetable species' (Baudrillard 1988c:45). But elsewhere Baudrillard spells out his idea that it is man who wants to be initiated and metamorphosed into woman, but woman only wants to be metamorphosed into herself: 'apparently they don't dream of being men. . . . They aren't devoured by curiosity for the other sex, rather they swoon away into their own.' This is expressed in the most forceful manner: women in their very narcissism express towards themselves an affection and scrupulous attention to detail so that they become a pure event, and they metamorphose into themselves continually. What is left for men, he queries, but to search through women this power of metamorphosis? (Baudrillard 1983b:185–6).

Women critics have been quick to point out that here is the basis for Baudrillard's apparent equivocation on sexual difference. Of course at one level, a game in which initiatives can pass is one in which there is chance and a degree of 'equality'; but now Baudrillard has revealed that in this game the positions of players have a basic structural differentiation which is essentially unequal. As he expresses it in this game the women are superior, but their superiority is not that of domination. It is related to the fact that their form of metamorphosis is inward (or shall we say that for Baudrillard this is their best option and what indeed defines woman). On the other hand, man wishes to cross from one species to the other, indeed to be initiated into the other species, and presumably can make the return journey. The drama, then, is on the side of the masculine. The charm, however, is on the side of the feminine. Even though Baudrillard constructs notions of reversibility on both sides, obviously the reversibility of the feminine is trapped in the feminine.

He thus asserts the strategic equality of the sexes in seduction while insisting on a structural or positional asymmetry. And when feminists attempt to attack the inequality of positions, his response is to say:

> I am not in agreement with hardline feminist ideology which says that a woman as seducer is a degrading role. In my view the strategy of seduction is a happy, liberating power for women. . . . Unfortunately in feminism everything that happens to be female is defended, *l'ecriture feminine*, poetry, any kind of artistic creation, and this makes it a kind of mirror of masculine simulation. This is a negative simulation, an unfortunate simulation.
>
> (Baudrillard, 1989c:54)

In the examples he provides here it does seem as if he believes woman are just not made for artistic creativity of any kind. Modern feminism induces a new bad simulation, just as Marxism provides, in his theory, a bad simulation of capitalism, a mirror of production. Where can his argument lead except to nostalgia? Against his expressions that his position is not nostalgic or reactionary, it is certainly backward looking; 'Men and women shouldn't oppose each other. I believe one can regain feminine seductiveness as a positive virtue. . . . But of course I risk being misunderstood' (ibid:54). But he will persist, moving even, in the last resort, to the highest provocation:

> Revolution – including the revolution of desire – is even less kind to those who think it has already happened than those who oppose it. Thus it is not the Revolution which will turn me into a woman. That will come about by my espousing here and now – passionately – the position of femininity itself. Now for feminists this is unpardonable. For this position

is more feminine, with all the supreme femininity it implies, than that of women will ever be.

(Baudrillard 1990c:7)

TOWARDS A FATAL STRATEGY

Baudrillard's writing in *Seduction* (1990a) is certainly intended as a challenge to the disaster of the sexual revolution and the 'phallic exchange standard'. It is really no surprise, then, that it is the latter idea, and 'panic sex' which is taken up and parodied by Arthur and Marilouise Kroker in *Body Invaders: Sexuality and the Postmodern Condition* (1988). The theme of seduction is perhaps an embarrassment. But it reveals the extent to which Baudrillard is prepared to go to attempt to avoid celebrating or being pulled into the eclectic but kaleidoscopic cocoon of postmodernism. In opposition, therefore, to the, as he sees it, cosy world of dialogue and human communication, with its aim of removing barriers to rational understanding, which he might call banal rhetorical strategies (exemplified by Habermas), Baudrillard develops a number of analyses of modernism and postmodernism under the thesis that the world has entered the phase of catastrophic cultural implosion. Only fatal strategies have any chance now of subverting the logic of this implosion: by hastening it or by perverting its own collapse.

Much of this again recalls the tone of the final passages of Marcuse's *One Dimensional Man* (1968).[7] There traditional forms of protest had themselves become 'dangerous' as they would tend to 'preserve the illusion of popular sovereignty'. Adopting an appropriately incantatory tone Marcuse announced that: 'in this period, the historical extremes may meet again: the most advanced consciousness of humanity, and the most exploited force. It is nothing but a chance' (ibid:201).

Clearly this chance had nothing to do with praxis; this was entirely a fatal possibility. Elsewhere in that text Marcuse insisted: 'the legendary revolutionary hero still exists who can defy even television and the press – his world is that of the "underdeveloped" countries' (ibid:68). This may well be Baudrillard's own position, but it is certainly his practice to adopt the tone of apocalypse for now:

> the present system of dissuasion and simulation . . . forcefully controls all the procedures for the production of meaning. It does not control the seduction of appearances. No interpretation can explain it, no system can abolish it. It is our last chance.

(Baudrillard, 1988c:74)

Having said that, however, Baudrillard does not make chance, the fortuitous, into a principle. In theory 'the term "fatal" has nothing fatalistic or apocalyptic about it' (ibid:87). Epistemologically, the fatal is situated in between the determined and the aleatory.

But in moving into the logic of the fatal, Baudrillard has altered his practice of writing both into the personal (he begins to fuse essay and journal), and into the poetic (into fiction–theory). Another issue has begun to emerge here out of these processes: the characterisation of different cultures as individual objects. His studies of France, Italy, America, Japan, Mexico, Australia indicate very different ways in which modernism is lived. In this respect again, postmodernism is a little-used term, and it tends to be reserved for the new complex of liberal eclectic culture. What is of interest is the brilliant surface of radical modernism and what he calls the strong cultures (Japan, Mexico), as well as the euphoric forms (Italy). In this perspective it is French modernism and postmodernism which is melancholy. His strategy avoids a banal apocalpyticism by simply anticipating it: it has already happened, as the world passed from an explosive to an implosive phase. But this is more complex than a simple reversal. The image of the mass as the black hole which draws to it all energy, is offset by a counter-image of an explosion in the cultural experience of time.

The rhetorical strategy is to refuse all intellectual and political blackmail, and to find, not soft cultural formations, but cruel imagery: Baudrillard's way is the theatre of imaginary cruelty, and to embrace a superlative language. In this way powerful enigmas can be thrown against the hyperreal as a kind of intellectual terrorism. The danger is to be caught in banal strategies (which accept the primacy of the subject) which will be pulled into the postmodern. Fatal strategies can only be launched from the side of the object, since the object is more ironic than the subject (a materialist thesis). But these strategies are not postmodern, banal playing with the vestiges, they are in deadly opposition both to radical modernity and postmodernism, they are developed in *La Transparence du Mal* (1990b) as strategies of the fourth order of simulation, that of fractal culture (which promises to be his theorisation of the postmodern), now conceived as strategies which rest on the basic thesis of the radical alterity of his position from western culture, or from the homogenised postmodern eclecticism, which can only establish exchanges within this field of manipulated differences.

In the light of these considerations it is interesting to examine the debate around the work of Fredric Jameson whose influential essay (1984a) 'Postmodernism, or the cultural logic of capitalism' marked an important step in the popularisation of the concept of 'postmodernism' as part of a reformulation of the theory of capitalism. The essay drew on a large range of intellectual resources in an attempt to evolve a synthetic perspective. One of the main influences, later acknowledged, was Baudrillard, as Jameson included in his essay a critique of the experience of the Bonaventure Hotel (built in 1977 in Los Angeles) in the mode of Baudrillard's critique (1977a) of the Pompidou Centre in Paris. Jameson used much of the same vocabulary and adopted something of the same tone with the exception that these buildings were identified as 'postmodern', and the basic object of the cultural critique was 'postmodern culture'. A comparison of these two essays is instructive (over and above the many critics who have pointed out that these buildings are, in architectural terms not at all postmodernist). Baudrillard's essay is an intense and bitter attempt to portray the Pompidou Centre as a work of anti-culture, of cultural dissuasion and deterrence, a conclusion he reaches as a result of an appeal to the nature of genuine culture (symbolic exchange, secret, initiation, ritual, reversibility). The masses, he suggests, should enter and make it collapse under their own weight (obviously a prototypical fatal strategy). Jameson's essay, in contrast to the taut, dense, agony of the 'Beaubourg Effect', is relaxed: it conjures a 'hypercrowd' (1984a:81), as a building it is simply in 'dissociation' with its city environment, yet there is 'excitment' – in the escalators and elevators which represent a 'dialectical intensification' of movement (they become signs of movement, and real human movement is abolished). Employing a Baudrillardian mode, he continues: 'I am more at a loss when it comes to conveying the thing itself . . . you are in this hyperspace up to your eyes' (ibid:82–3). And the crowd becomes 'a milling confusion, something like the vengeance this space takes on those who still seek to walk through it' (ibid: 83). Jameson ends his remarks by saying that this leaves us with a new problem, that of 'postmodern hyperspace' which has 'finally succeeded in transcending the capacities of the individual human body to locate itself . . . (bringing an) alarming disjunction between the body and its built environment' (ibid: 83–4). While, he argues with reference to Marcuse, late capitalism seems to abolish the 'semi-autonomy' of the cultural sphere, this is conceived as a process whereby the whole of society becomes 'cultural'. In this new social form all critical distance is abolished, even further, 'all distance in general . . . has very precisely been abolished in the new space of postmodernism' (ibid: 87).

Jameson, however, steps back, and appeals to the principle of the 'dialectic' which 'requires us to hold equally to a positive or "progressive" evaluation' (Jameson, 1984a: 88) which leads to reinvocation of the acting subject, a new project of 'cognitive mapping', a 'new political art in which we may again begin to grasp our positioning as individual and collective subjects and regain a capacity to act and struggle which is at present neutralised by our spatial as well as our social confusion (ibid: 92). Clearly the duty imposed by the 'dialectic' has enormous consequences: it appears dogmatically as a principle of salvation and in utter contradiction with the state of the world as portrayed by Jameson.

In an interview (of 1988) Jameson revealed that he had further embraced Baudrillard's position, marking perhaps a convergence with Arthur Kroker. Now, he stressed again, the culture had become one dimensional it had become evident that the task was: 'to undo postmodernism homeopathically by the methods of postmodernism: to work at dissolving the pastiche by using all the instruments of pastiche itself, to reconquer some genuine historical sense' (Jameson, in Kellner (ed.) 1989c:59). He then develops a positive notion of the 'beyond' of postmodernism in a way which implies opposition and transcendence:

> an attempt somehow to master these things by choosing them and pushing them to their limits. There is a whole range of so-called oppositional arts, whether it's punk writing or ethnic writing, which really try to use postmodern techniques . . . to go through and beyond. . . . The only way out of crisis of space is to create new space.
>
> (ibid:60)

Douglas Kellner was quick to seize on this flirtation with Baudrillard's fatal strategy, which Jameson simply calls 'postmodern strategy', but, says Kellner, Jameson has yet to:

> work out a radical cultural politics and such a project is the next logical step. It is to be hoped that an increased level of struggle by new social movements . . . will make such projects an increasingly important part of the Left's theoretical and political agenda.
>
> (ibid: 37)

Thus we reach another stage in the attraction and repulsion of Baudrillard's work: Jameson who has adumbrated a 'fatal' postmodern strategy as a response to a one-dimensional culture must now be encouraged to convert this into a radical oppositional cultural politics. Jameson, however, is insistent himself that texts themselves have become 'flat, one-dimensional and resistent to interpretation' (in Kellner (ed.) 1989c:29) and that is why postmodern strategies are needed. But there is a problem here. The 'new space' opened by the practice of pastiche is interpreted as a way out. How is this possible if, as Jameson also insists: 'pastiche is . . . a neutral practice, without any of parody's ulterior motives, amputated of the satiric impulse, devoid of laughter and of any conviction. . . . Pastiche is thus blank parody, a statue with blind eyeballs' (Jameson, 1984a:65)? For Jameson's (and Kroker's) pastiche is full of ulterior motives. Their attempts must fall either into self-contradictory parody, or into Baudrillard's hell (the infinite repetition of the same).

TOWARDS THE RIGHT QUESTIONS

The basic problem, certainly, is to ask if it is now possible to ask the right questions of Baudrillard? First of all, for example, just how is the gender issue related to fatal strategies? It appears that the seduction principle is feminine, yet the elaboration of fatal ironic strategies is a process of man becoming woman. This is elaborated in order that we do not fall into a perverse soft culture. This appears to be Baudrillard's most desperate attempt to find a principle of challenge which can be made into an attack on the permissive society. Here he is in line with some feminists (of the 'third wave') but his mode of deployment of these ideas is so tinged with problems of uncritical male chauvinism (apparent also in his *Cool Memories* (1987b)), that his argument is compromised.

Second, there is a fundamental epistemological problem. How do we really tell the difference between banal and fatal strategy, since to move to the side of the object involves deliteralisation, a move into myth: is it not catastrophic for Baudrillard to move out of myth at any time? His concept of mass worked as a decisive fiction. His concept of the yuppies can only play the role of a catastrophic breach of the whole edifice into the real and thereby provoke a loss of prophetic power. It is now clear that his concept of the 'masses' was developed specifically as a poetic, and as he says, a lumpen concept. It made possible the discovery of poetic affinities. The concept of the yuppie seems to be a suitable case for the same kind of treatment, but until it has received this transformation it sets off grave internal problems in the mode of writing and conceptualisation adopted: Baudrillard will indeed, in spite of himself, end up as a sociologist of late capitalism.

Finally, it is probably through the understanding of Baudrillard's literary background that some of the key parts of his project become clear. His epigraph for his study on *The Consumer Society* (1970) is taken from Dostoyevsky's *Notes from the Underground*: 'Give him such economic prosperity that he will have nothing left to do but to sleep . . . shower him with all earthly blessings, plunge him so deep into happiness that nothing is visible but the bubbles rising to the surface' (Dostoyevsky, 1972:37–8).

It is clear that Dostoyevsky is a crucial reference point, for Dostoyevsky's theme is precisely the naiveté of progressive humanism which believes that it can eventually master nature and produce a perfect society, indeed, the voice from the underground says:

> these laws of nature have only to be discovered, and man will no longer be responsible for his actions, and it will become extremely easy for him to live his life. . . .
> 'Then' (this is all of you speaking), 'a new political economy will come into existence, all complete, and also calculated with mathematical accuracy, so that all problems will vanish in the twinkling of an eye, simply because all possible answers to them will have been supplied. Then the Palace of Crystal will arise.' Well, in short, the golden age will come again.

(ibid: 33)

If this edifice is feared, in Dostoyevsky, it is because it is impossible, it overlooks something. This 'something' is: 'distinguished precisely by upsetting all our classifications and always destroying the systems established by lovers of humanity for the happiness of mankind' (ibid: 31). This something is akin to Baudrillard's principle of evil, for Dostoyevsky, on the other hand, it is: 'the greatest good, which is never taken into consideration because it will not fit into any classification, and the omission of which always sends all systems and theories to the devil' (Dostoyevsky, 1972: 34). By upgrading the 'devil's share' into a principle of evil Baudrillard has sought to place before critical theory a challenge that is both too simple and too subtle, too immoral and too moral, too passive and too active. Reponses to this challenge reveal, surely, the action of the principle itself. *Le cristal se venge*. The revenge of the crystal: Baudrillard is absorbed into the postmodern, as critical theory descends into eclectism and self-contradiction – becomes postmodernist? As Baudrillard says himself: 'for every thought one must expect a strange tomorrow. Theory is at any rate, destined to be diverted, deviated and manipulated' (Baudrillard, 1987a:99–100).

Part II

In the first great age of the substitution of machine for human toil Carlyle and the Pre-Raphaelites promulgated the doctrine of Work as a mystical social communion . . . Marx was an impressionable recipient of these doctrines.

(McLuhan, 1967: 60)

4   Baudrillard's attempt to develop Marxism

There is no autonomous problematic of objects.
                        Baudrillard (1972; 1981b:68)

Baudrillard published a collection of essays in 1972 called *For a Critique of the Political Economy of the Sign* (1981b), comprising essays from 1969–72, which cover some of the same ground as his earlier work on consumer societies, but intensify the Marxist elements of analysis. But this intensification, however, seems to bring in its wake some initial doubts and self-criticisms with an effort to repair some of the problems, eventually a full-scale radical change of theoretical position dramatically unfolds. There is a formidable internal drama in this particular work, therefore, which makes its critical neglect all the more surprising, for to my knowledge there is no adequate consideration, discussion or assessment of this drama, or the major theses of the work itself. Perhaps this is in part due to the way in which the book has appeared in the English translation: an inelegant translation, a gravely misleading introduction and added footnotes – often directly contradicted by Baudrillard's own formulations.

But this in fact is only part, and a superficial part, of the problem. The major difficulty is its theoretical abstraction, for, unlike *Consumer Society* (1970), this work does not contain long analyses of objects or ambience. It can also appear extremely eclectic: drawing on a large range of theoretical material of very diverse nature. It is written in an uncompromising style, at times appearing dogmatic and ill-tempered. Unlike the earlier books this book has a theoretical intensity which often forces problems and positions to extremes. Yet, despite these characteristics, the work takes on political and ideological problems in a far more direct way than in previous works. In this chapter I intend to discuss only about half of this particular work, for it seems that the work falls into two distinct parts: the first attempts to develop a Marxist conception of the analysis of objects and works its way to a general theory and a programme for further work. But there are already indications that all is not well by this point, and the second half of the book (which I shall examine in the next chapter) is really an effort to save Baudrillard's version of the Marxist problematic in the face of emerging doubts.

As I have said, I know of no adequate discussion of this work.[1] It seems particularly important to discuss some of the major arguments which seem widely misinterpreted and misunderstood. These essays in fact throw considerable light on the underlying theses of the two earlier books, they involve decisive theoretical clarification and are essential to their interpretation. But I shall do so really in the light of the existence of Baudrillard's own developing crisis in his approach to cultural analysis. As I shall argue, what is most interesting in this process is the way in which there is a genuine and profound displacement within Baudrillard's own theoretical position, that is, a change in the position from which his analysis is undertaken. Or, more accurately, if his analyses were always on two feet, in this period he shifts the weight from one to the other. It is quite clear that he believed that the direction of this change was to radicalise his perspectives fundamentally. In this chapter discussion will examine particularly his theses on social class, symbolic exchange and the conceptualisation of the sign.

CLASSES AND POWER

The initial essays in the book seek to go beyond an empirical description to what is conceived as a class logic, a 'strategic analysis of objects', as was presented in the book *Consumer Society* (Baudrillard, 1970), but here the theoretical detail is more precise and its political significance made apparent. What is important here is the way Baudrillard provides a general framework for all the analyses of the object and consumerism undertaken at this period. Very specifically he contrasts the preliminary phase of analysis as one which can see in objects an index of class membership with one which becomes class-strategic (that is, one which analyses the practices of groups and classes, in a structure of domination, an analysis which can account for social distribution of objects and their social meaning). Rather than finding an object which can be correlated with an already existing form of social categorisation, this analysis tackles the dynamic tactics of groups. It is not a question of the expression of group membership but of a practice of consumption as: 'a living element of . . . aspirations, which in a larger structure may coincide with other aspects . . . (professional trajectory, education of children, place of residence, network of relations, etc.), but which may also be partly contradictory to them' (Baudrillard, 1981b:36). This implies that objects have to be examined exotically, in terms other than themselves, very specifically on the 'terrain' of a field of practices in which signs predominate.

Here Baudrillard develops a clarification of the framework for the analysis of objects. It is quite wrong to assume, he reflects, that there can be any homogeneous field of objects, or any complete ambient totality which could express the experiential totality of a particular group. Such a phenomenon is internally complex, as is revealed not by an analysis at the level of the structural code, but by a 'strategic' analysis of the actions of groups in relation to the code. A naive correlation analysis, a simple sociology of objects, assumes that social groups directly express themselves in their objects. It is clear that any more adequate analysis will show that such groups are not the captive of social conventions in a pure sense, they tend to break rules and conventions in their tactical struggles against each other. In this sense it is necessary to begin to learn to read the existence of such struggles in the phenomena themselves, for in relation to the newly emerged ambience:

> this discourse must be read in its class grammar, in its class inflections, in the contradiction with its own social situation which the individual or group directs through its discourse with objects. A correct sociological analysis must be exercised of the concrete syntax of object ensembles . . . and in the lapses, incoherences and contradictions of this discourse . . . this discourse always expresses in this very syntax a neurosis of mobility, of inertia or of social regression.
>
> (Baudrillard, 1981b:37–8)

In this sense a 'phenomenology' of objects is only a very minor part of the preliminary phase of analysis, as is a mere 'formal reconstitution of the code of objects', for the aim of a Marxist analysis is of quite a different order, the understanding of the: 'ultimately disparate or contradictory relationship of this discourse of objects to other social practices (professional, economic, cultural)' (Baudrillard, 1981b:38, trans. mod.). The proximity of this formulation with those of the Althusserian school at this time are striking.

It is thus crucial here to understand precisely what this means for Baudrillard's approach to the study of ambience. At an important point in the argument Baudrillard provides a brief illustration in relation to the introduction of the television into different kinds of domestic milieux. The illustration appears rather slight and mechanical, and it is one of the very few discussions of any concrete case in the collection, indicating Baudrillard's basic avoidance of concrete enquiry.[2] Here, three scenarios are discussed. The first, the television as a physical object is simply introduced and placed on a table, shelf or pedestal, and the effect of the introduction dramatically polarises the lived space of the room in a way that the introduction of the radio did not. The room is reorganised into a viewing field. The second scenario is one in which the television is placed at armchair level on its own low table or console. It does not have such a polarising effect, the arrangement of furniture is not centred around it, for in this order the furnishing and lighting form an ambience. Finally, for the third scenario, the television disappears either into the wall or into a piece of furniture; it is completely disguised or hidden.

Actually what Baudrillard has done here despite his observations to the contrary, is a form of 'class analysis' very much still grounded at the level of correlations. But it is none the less, an important clarification, for it clearly implies the presentation of a social structure dominated by a threefold class division. The first (lower) scenario seems to indicate working and perhaps 'peasant' households, the second, middle-class households and the third, higher-bourgeois households. The analysis of objects is given wider social dimensions, and the new ambient culture is specifically identified as that of the new middle classes. But he remains formally dissatisfied with such a static conception, and moves forward to a form of analysis which will look beyond this system of inclusions, to one which will examine cultural distinction and tactical exclusion. This, he says, can only be one which is a genuine theoretical analysis of the ways in which an 'antagonistic social strategy is established'. Again reflecting an Althusserian theme, the way in which a 'social class logic' is evolved does not imply the existence of classes in any pure sense, for social groups are always interlocked in a complex fashion. Nevertheless, a 'cultural class strategy' exists on another level again, one on which it is possible to distinguish pure cases, a: 'social logic (subject to a theoretical analysis of the cultural system) makes two opposed terms appear, not the two 'poles' of an evolution, but the two exclusive terms of an opposition' (Baudrillard, 1981b:57), and he adds: 'these are not the two distinct terms of a formal opposition, but the two distinctive–exclusive terms of a social opposition' (ibid).[3]

Baudrillard's objective, as it emerges in these pages, is to rethink the problematic of objects in the light of a theory of 'cultural class logic', in an analysis of cultural strategies, but this largely remains a hollow ambition in this discussion which only develops on the basis of preliminary identification of classes, and specifically here the new middle strata, or what he sometimes calls the new petit bourgeoisie. Here the focus is:

> on the configuration . . . of rising, mobile, or 'advanceable' classes that have a critical and uncertain status, in the so-called middle classes, the floating hinge of a stratified society, classes on the way to integration or acculturation, that is to say, which escape the destiny of social exclusion of the industrial proletariat or that of rural isolation, without however enjoying the advantages of inheriting an already acquired social situation.
>
> (Baudrillard, 1981b:38)

The analysis which he develops concentrates on the way in which this new strata embody some of the key tensions, dilemmas and contradictions of society as a whole. These new groups reflect and are encouraged to develop aspirations of growth, progress and advancement characteristic of a society where higher standards of living are made possible. But in this process unrealistic and unrealisable ambitions and aspirations are aroused in the face of genuine constraints of the social order itself. Real inequalities continue, and are reinforced, even in the period of high capitalist affluence.

As well as advancement, social 'regression' is characteristic of modernity. Democratic ideology plays a role of 'overdetermining' certain basic social processes of structural inertia, for, in the face of these constraints, any excess of ambition has to be dealt with ideologically (there has to be a real compromise, and this is always first expressed in the object system itself).

Thus the analysis of objects is a primary sociological task, successful on condition that it now moves to a recognition of the object as a condensation of the strategies in these new social tensions. Baudrillard suggests the thesis that, in fact, the new ambient culture is a culture of social compromise, it is an attempt by the lower, upwardly mobile, social classes to follow the world of the bourgeoisie as it sees it (ironically only a reflection of previous periods of high style). In this light, the new strata realise that their world is also one that can be assessed and judged, and that a verdict will be placed on it from the outside. Baudrillard suggests that in relation to these new strata the: 'verdict is never a positive one: (and) their progress on the social scale is always relative and often ludicrous' (Baudrillard, 1981b:40). There is, for Baudrillard, a certain pathos here, for in the drive to accumulate the objects of the new ambient culture, there is only a gradual realisation that these objects are fundamentally inauthentic, and their acquisition is correctly seen as a 'rhetoric of despair' (Bourdieu, 1984), since the effort at social emancipation of these groups only results in formidable cultural defeat.

This defeat is lived and expressed in a number of ways, but they all have something in common: 'a logic and aesthetic of simulation, a simulation of the bourgeois models of domestic organisation' (Baudrillard, 1981b:41). The 'model' aspired to here is not that of the contemporary upper groups, but the styles of the bourgeoisie of an earlier period (themselves developed in the process of attempting to emulate aristocratic styles). In the new culture it is possible to identify two basic modes of the 'rhetoric of despair'. The first is an attempt to realise a 'saturation-redundance' pattern of consumption, the other is realised in terms of symmetry and hierarchy. The domestic household is thus the site of a complex class strategy of acquisition aimed at establishing its (class) distinctiveness: the cultural order is maintained through a new regime of moral fanaticism of cleaning and polishing, everything is seen to be in its right place. All the features of material possession are multiply overdetermined by the system of signs of a petit bourgeois class strategy which, on the one hand, seeks to exclude lower groups by producing its new forms of symmetry (it treats its objects as if they were children in need of discipline and civilisation) but one which has to compromise its aspiration to a place in society on the same terms as the bourgeoisie itself.[4]

Two elements of this process catch Baudrillard's attention. On the one hand the petit bourgeoisie introduce into the new ambient culture a regime which can only be described as a conspicuous morality of effort, perhaps a sacrificial effort to establish a form of new self-recognition and self-legitimation, but also along with it, the introduction of imitations of bourgeois forms which only render the attempt at self-identification into one ultimately stigmatised as derived and inferior. A system of cultural prestige and distinction created by these new groups themselves out of these elements is also a dead end, a trap. On the other hand, there is an internal differentiation or bifurcation which takes place, as this new strata itself divides into an avant-garde section and a petit bourgeois social mass which follows behind. In *this* instance the mass does not follow since: 'only a few elect will be able to accede to this stage of the aesthetic combinatory . . . (where) Mondrian-like, geometricism coexists peacefully with the psychedelic version of art nouveau' (Baudrillard, 1981b:48). This new social and cultural elite enters the world of high ambience, where all styles mingle, all textures begin to merge into a new sign system. The majority will remain in the more mundane – but fanatically disciplined – order (and, may not even become conscious of these new aesthetic tastes and objects).

In this light, he suggests, the concept of fashion has to be reconsidered. Looked at from the point of view of the structural situation of the new groups, it could be argued that the apparently emancipatory element of fashion, with its sense of dynamic progression, is in fact part of the trap laid by the social order for the newly enriched groups. It is, he concludes, an impasse, the results of a successfully diverted desire for real advancement. Looked at from this point of view consumption ideologies represent a blockage, a mask, not of change but of the inhibition of change, just as democratic ideology can be read as a compensatory order for the continued existence of real inequalities. So, in opposition to the dominant myths, consumerism plays its function in the process of social integration as hierarchy, it restores actual inequality against the modern egalitarian social fantasy. Indeed, it is possible to see consumerist ideas as a strategic compromise, but in the form of a game of changes, in which the old and the new become intermingled: modernity itself can be defined as the fusion of the two terms.

But if this is the case and the modern consumer is in a profound sense 'irresponsible', it matters little in the new ambience which values are retained as important elements, as long as the structure functions, in Nietzschean terms, as a 'slave morality'. It is a kind of class compensation, at the base of the social order, in the form of a cultural privilege and practice so articulated as not to challenge the system of power. At this point, then, Baudrillard had a surprise in store (for readers of the *Object System* (Baudrillard, 1968)) who thought the argument had concluded that cultural differentiation was to be regarded as a central force for social differentiation. What becomes clear in these essays is that it is not technical progress or the sign system which is ultimately important. The real forces are on quite another level altogether, and to grasp this it is necessary to read social relations in a strategic way, because:

upper class superiority . . . is precisely not established in signs of prestige and abundance, but elsewhere, in the real spheres of decision, direction and political and economic power, and in the manipulation of signs . . . and this relegates the Others, the lower and middle classes, to phantasies of the promised land.

(Baudrillard, 1981b:62)

Passages such as this are evidently of crucial importance in the understanding of Baudrillard's critical social theory, as they are relatively rare, and are often ignored, to the cost of any careless interpretation. For here emerges not only Baudrillard's commitment to Marxism, to a basic materialist position, but also to a specific version of the conception of society in (Althusserian) terms of a complex totality in which real economic and political class struggle are determinant, but contradictory, forces in the social process.

This particular set of formulations very obviously puts Baudrillard's principal critical ideas into a structural Marxist framework, and it draws semiological analysis into a dynamic relation to practices conceived as tactical and strategic. It clearly suggests that the fundamental issues here are those arising out of the production and reproduction processes of capitalist society. The analysis re-presents a view of the new ambient culture not only as the culture of the new middle class, but begins to suggest that it must be understood as a strategic cultural humiliation, as a culture of simulation and compromise produced as a failure of its excessive aspirations. In this light, the retrospective judgement on the writing on his earlier book the *Object System* (1968), is not only that it was a form of phenomenology, but also that it was a passive empirical analysis.

In working towards the level of strategic analysis proper, what we see emerging is an analysis which looks at the position of social strata in the larger system of social contradictions and in the way that these contradictions are reflected back into these strata. This theme was present in the analyses of *Consumer Society* (1970). Here, what is made clear is the attempt to create the various forms of social handling and defusing of social antagonism.[5] A number of these are identified in Baudrillard's work, underpinning them is the continued existence of immense inequalities within the reproduced class structure which run counter to the dominant myth of democratic equality, but second and most significantly the dominant pattern of egalitarian legitimation for the system is not the dominant mode of legitimation as such: the various patterns of inegalitarian legitimation which cluster around the object system and consumption are far more powerful. The formal description of the phenomenology of the object here gives way to another level of analysis: the ambient culture as a rhetoric of unavoidable social self-humiliation, a subaltern morality in which only simulation is possible. Yet, at base, even this structure of cultural struggle and legitimation, is not decisive, its logic is to be explained only by reference to the existence of production and power processes elsewhere and never analysed by Baudrillard.

But there is something else in Baudrillard's analysis which deserves attention. When at a crucial juncture in the analysis he suggests that an empirical correlation between cultural practice and class is not enough and that what is also required is a strategic analysis: this is specified as lying in the domain of cultural analysis, of cultural theory, of 'cultural class strategy'. (This is never called a political class analysis.) It is an analysis which brings into focus the construction of: 'cultural class privilege . . . [for] there are those for whom the television is an object, there are those for whom it is a cultural exercise' (Baudrillard, 1981b:57, trans. mod.). The opposition between the two is further discussed as a cultural opposition, and struggle between 'antagonistic cultural classes'. These cultural strategies exist in the pure state. It is necessary to examine in more detail what he proposes here, for he resorts to two quite different metaphors in order to complete the analysis.

First, he suggests, in another very clumsy attempt at concrete analysis, it is fundamental to see that the television is appropriated as an object–commodity, and its possession has a series of consequences. Whereas the upper classes may use the television as a cultural means, the subaltern classes tend to see it as an investment object, it has a fetish value at the level of commodity, and intend to get good return from it. Watching it becomes a necessary form of receiving this return on investment, but, he argues in an anti-McLuhanite spirit, this can, in such a passive mode never give rise to an autonomous cultural practice. This emerges only from an altogether different syntax of values and activities. But second, the television is appropriated as a social symbol, a token of social membership whereby the individual is integrated magically into the society as a consumer. As the television works, there is a production of a magical substance like mana, part of a magical economy of symbolic prestations, its 'ritual' value as fetish–object in the level of signs operates at an even deeper level of social constraint than that of the television as commodity.[6] It is important to notice that both these forms of value – commodity and social ritual – are contrasted to a level where autonomous, superior, cultural values are created and come into play (Baudrillard, 1981b:55), for there is a realm where values come into existence that are not 'subservient to . . . the latent imperative of revenue production'. It is precisely because of this that the bearers of the ambient culture face and suffer a specific form of cultural inferiority. This is realised in a ritualised consumption of television in the passive mode: a typical protest – 'they always show the same things' (ibid). Hence, the new petit bourgeoisie demands a culture from which it can profit, yet, in return it can only treat this culture with the resigned resentment of disappointed religious worship.[7]

LATENT THEORETICAL TENSIONS

What is highly significant in Baudrillard's exposition, is the intercalation here of themes from Freud, Durkheim and Mauss at a key moment, precisely at the point in the argument when the analyses of the fetishism of, or need for, objects comes to the foreground. These elements gradually intensify, and as I shall discuss in the next chapter force Baudrillard into efforts to save the Marxist theory of fetishism. Here, however, the theory of symbolic exchange appears in one of Baudrillard's earliest attempts to formulate it. The doctrine is that: 'an accurate theory of objects will not be established upon a theory of needs and their satisfaction, but upon a theory of prestations and signification' (1981b:30). Baudrillard provides a brief account of the kula and potlatch, from which he draws the (Durkheimian) conclusion that these exchanges are unique symbolic orders imposing determinate social constraint. He argues that: 'the fundamental conceptual hypothesis for a sociological analysis of "consumption" is not use value, the relation to needs, but symbolic exchange value' (ibid). However, this idea can not be introduced immediately for the obvious reason that modern capitalist forms have reduced the gift economy to diminutive dimensions on the margins of economic life, or so it appears. He maintains this is an error, and he proposes that: 'behind all the superstructures of purchase, market, and private property, there is always the mechanism of social prestation . . . (which is present in) our choice, our accumulation and our consumption of objects'. Indeed, even more emphatically: 'this mechanism of discrimination and prestige is at the very basis of the system of values and of integration into the hierarchical order of society' (ibid). So, it appears, the whole structure of capitalism is in effect a superstructure.[8]

These essays, then, dedicated to drawing the object and the concept of ambience into strategic analysis do so in a dramatic theoretical fusion of Marxist and Durkheimian ideas. At one level the conceptions which predominate are those which cluster around the object as a commodity in a capitalist society in which there is a determinant productive system. This has produced a new middle class and a culture which expresses its new social position, a conception remote to Durkheim and perhaps to Mauss, because it is fundamentally undertaken from a class point of view. But, as he moves towards the analysis of consumption processes themselves, and specifically towards the analysis of the object, it is clear that what Baudrillard constructs is a cultural analysis against the background of an emerging anthropological theory of symbolic exchange. It is adopted as a basic universal, a kind of substructural necessity, and therefore as a position from which a new challenge can be made to contemporary society.

The question which concerns us here is how these two can appear beside each other, how these two formerly bitterly opposed problematics are articulated at this point, how they are integrated in a single analysis. In fact there are rhetorical mechanisms in Baudrillard's analysis which allow the terms to come together. Essentially, the conception of the theory of symbolic exchange is presented in isolation from other important elements of Marxist theory. It would appear that Baudrillard has developed two quite different theoretical objects: one of production (in which Marxist theory predominates) and one of consumption (in which Durkheimian theory predominates). They coexist at the level of exposition but are normally held apart and even form a duel in the more fundamental argumentation. But they do come into contact, for example, at the point where the television is analysed as fetish object. It is here that Baudrillard's arguments are forced to their limits: the idea that as capital investment the television set must be watched as an effort of return on investment is highly speculative. Even more forced is the idea that the television set is an object of fetishistic integration of the masses through the exercise of the power of a 'supplementary mana'. Indeed at this point Baudrillard throws into the analysis so many contradictory images (the television as an object of ritual, of worship, of prestation and counter-prestation, as fetish, as mana, etc.) that the effect is one of confusion and loss of focus. Yet, the very suggestion of such a fundamental integrative process, one which, if effective, would apply to all social groups, highlights the counter-tendency, the specific function of cultural exclusion. Clearly the logic of Baudrillard's position would take analysis in this direction, to argue that cultural reproduction determines ambiguously the form of involvement in television (thus inverting McLuhan, and to argue that acculturation in hierarchical reproduction is the message in this instance).

It is clear that the idea of symbolic exchange plays a decisive role in Baudrillard's thought. It is developed more carefully in the second essay in the collection, on needs. Here a very important clarification is made: what is significant in gift exchange is not a 'norm of reciprocity', but the production of fundamentally ambiguous relations. For although what is given in such exchanges is, in itself, relatively arbitrary, and cannot be codified in a theory of distinctive elements or signs, the effect produced a tension of 'distance and relation, of love and aggression'. It is a transitive action. Yet this transitivity was broken, and the gift was transformed, by reification, into a consumption of signs.[9] Here the object: 'becomes autonomous, intransitive, opaque . . . it is "of" and "from" the reified relation' (Baudrillard, 1981b:65).

Thus, at this point we enter the realm of appropriation proper: a field of sign manipulation and coded differences. And, crucially, it is only after this moment that it becomes possible to talk of the 'consumption' of objects, because they have broken away from the determinations of the transparency of prestation and relations in ambivalence. In other words the symbolic-exchange relation (in which the gift is never consumed, but always seeks to be returned), has in modern society been caught, frozen and ruptured. In its place we see, he says, the rise of the new metaphysic of the subject, the object, and the need of the one for the other as one of consumability.

A GENERAL THEORY

Finally, Baudrillard reaches an attempt at unification, a general theory presented as a series of formulas, first in the form of specific transitions (e.g. from a use value to exchange value), and then in a series of structural correspondences. Finally, the discussion leads to a 'general proposition', before moving on to a programme for further critical work. It is a general theory in so far as all the basic ideas are connected together into a system of terms. It has a logic and a basic theoretical proposition, which undoubtedly brings Baudrillard's first general theoretical system into sharp contradiction.[10]

Baudrillard lays out for inspection twelve transitions of the form: use value/exchange value, exchange value/use value. These particular ones, for example, are described as marking the beginning and end of the capitalist cycle of production and consumption. These particular transitions are called *transformations*, as are exchange values into exchange sign values, and the reverse: here there is the intervention of the economy of the sign in conspicuous production and consumption. But the transition between use value and symbolic value and the reverse is called a *transgression*: the production of the gift, and the gift into use value. There is a radical destruction here, he argues, in the action of the symbolic value of the gift itself, just as there is in transgression of the symbolic value into exchange value, or into sign exchange value. In these latter forms we have, he suggests, the specific 'inauguration of the economic' as such (Baudrillard, 1981b:125).

In the second phase of the argument, Baudrillard considers structural correspondences of relations of difference in the theory working in three movements. First a specific set of relations, then a set which is logical but, he claims, theoretically incoherent, to a bursting of the formula and a general restructuring. So – first, the formula which is absolutely fundamental to Baudrillard's whole project: 'sign value is to symbolic exchange what exchange value is to use value' (Baudrillard 1981b:126). The thesis proposes that the same processes are at work on both sides. It implies the specific work of sign manipulation and its understanding in semiology. And it implies the possibility of a critique of this order as a critique of the political economy of the sign. This formula he calls a structural homology, it is an advance but not decisive. A further move is to argue that 'sign value must be to exchange value what symbolic exchange is to use value.' The problem here is that no theoretical relation exists, or has been established between, the latter two terms. In fact, the order of transition is quite different even opposed, since between the latter two terms there is a rupture. Thus the homology is not extended and the formula ends in incoherence.

The next move, he suggests in the attempt at reaching a theoretical unification, is to deconstruct the sign into its component parts, signifier and signified, and to argue that, if the exchange value of a commodity is to the use value as signifer is to signified, a new coherence can be introduced and symbolic exchange 'expelled from the field of value' (Baudrillard, 1981b: 128). In the end the most radical reduction is not between exchange value and use value, but between the system of value and that of symbolic exchange. Here emerges the principle that the field of symbolic exchange is exterior to the field of value.[11] As he expresses it himself: 'all the logic of this entire system (of value) denies, represses and reduces symbolic exchange' (ibid:128). The critique of the political economy of the sign and the theory of symbolic exchange therefore are 'one and the same thing'.

From this Baudrillard draws up three main tasks: the elaboration of a theory of symbolic-exchange proper, a radical critique of use value 'in order to reduce the idealist anthropology' by which it is still dominated, and finally, a critical theory of the sign form in its relation to the commodity form. This is specifically spelt out as a programme of work, and I shall refer to it as the programme of 1972. It brings to an end the first part of the book (Baudrillard, 1981b), and before going on to look at the way that Baudrillard tries to answer these theoretical issues and problems it is appropriate here to make some observations on his 'general theory'.

The major difficulty comes in relation to Baudrillard's efforts, here as elsewhere, to deal with the relation of symbolic exchange to all the other transitions and transformations. This problem is raised acutely in the first half of this book by the temptation to talk, on the one hand, as if the processes of consumption in all systems are related to symbolic exchange and that in capitalist systems exchange value and sign value are 'built upon structures of more basic symbolic value' (Baudrillard, 1981b:30), and on the other as if symbolic exchange was external to the system. Second, Baudrillard has also suggested (ibid: 87) that use values do not exist within the advanced capitalist economy since everything is reproduced in the system, and yet use value remains a term in the general table.

One way out of Baudrillard's dilemma would be to make use value indeed something which was the product of internal ideological work of the system combined with other cultural processes, just as Marx himself had suggested (English workers 'need' beer, French workers 'need' wine), but then to follow this through the active processes of consumption: wine is both produced for the market and not for the market (the two processes are not completely independent), and wine is distributed both as sign and as exchange value, but also as gift and prestation. In the domestic milieu, for example, the consumption of wine is dominated by a complex interweaving of symbolic exchange and sign consumption. The problem in Baudrillard's exposition is that having at the level of initial definition stated that there is a radical and unbridgeable gulf between exchange value and symbolic exchange, he cannot do other than arrive at a conclusion which reproduces it. But this is a decisive moment in Baudrillard's intellectual career, for from this moment his theoretical position shifts to a critique of the political economy of the sign not from the position of the oppressed and exploited and alienated classes, but from the external position of the symbolic exchanger.

5 A change of position

we have to be more logical than Marx himself.
Baudrillard (1972; 1981b:131)

Baudrillard's attempt to set to work on the 1972 programme led first to a reconsideration of the Marxist concept of 'use value', and this was to lead on to critical reflection on other fundamental Marxist terms: ideology, superstructure, alienation and fetishism. These were not to be treated in isolation from Marxist semiology, or theories of the sign which had been imported into Marxism by writers like Barthes. The initial critical phase, which consisted of an attempt to rework, and to update Marxist theory in this way, produced the essays in the second half of *For a Critique* (Baudrillard, 1981b: Chapters 7–11). The impression made by these chapters is of a writer working under great pressure to remain within the orbit of Marxism while attempting to radicalise it systematically. Some, but perhaps not all, of the influences which lead Baudrillard in this orientation are apparent: politically his intensified opposition to capitalist consumerism, but also the impact of the Tel Quel group and especially the work of Derrida and Kristeva which now become of critical importance in Baudrillard's development. The essays of this phase do form a specific unity. Their attack continues and develops the critique already established of the network of notions which cluster around the terms need, use, subject, object, alienation, etc., previously subjected to systematic epistemological and theoretical examination and critique. It is clear, however, that at this moment although Baudrillard's project was an extension of what he regarded as Marx's great critical work on exchange value to other underdeveloped parts of Marxist theory, and, if his approach, in this regard is certainly consistent with that of Althusser's idea (involution) of working from one (advanced) part of theory to another (less developed) his break with the Althusserians with respect to the theoretical content of Marxism takes place during this phase (Baudrillard, 1981b:166).

It would, of course, be wrong to say that this critical period stands on its own, for as I have already noted, Baudrillard's work, from the start, is marked by a very radical attack on any theory, like Marcuse's, which postulates an identifiable set of essential, innocent, human needs which can be thrown as a challenge against the modern system. During this phase, the critical moment is carried through to other adjacent theoretical objects, and particularly, at first, to the concept of use. There can be little doubt that this is a key term by which Marx sought to reveal the specifically capitalist form of the emergence of exchange value (for the market) in articulation with the value of the product in its use. Baudrillard's critique here has no empirical element at all (though this perhaps might be reconstructed from suggestions). The analysis is conducted at a purely logical level (Baudrillard, 1981b:130–42), but its consequences are far reaching for the whole of Baudrillard's later work.

USE VALUES AND WORK

The argument begins with a presentation of the idea that for Marx things in their use are not 'comparable' to one another, and are quite unlike, and in principle exist in another register from, all things and values that are in commodity exchange. But, says Baudrillard, there is a problem here, because for exchange itself to take place, the basic fact of social usefulness as a feature of the world of objects has already to have been established: objects are not innocent in this respect; they are already deeply marked by the principle and fact of utility. This implies the thesis that there is more to the complexity of this level of social activity than a mere coincidence of certain, already given, use values and the emergence of exchange values in relation to them. Relations between the objects themselves have to be considered, and only on this basis is it possible to to begin to see that the connection of use and exchange is *already* predicated in the forms of equivalence that appear in commodity exchange – quite contrary to Marx's own expositions on this point. What occurs can be defined as an emerging form of abstraction at the level of the use value. This can be expressed as analogous to those used in the analysis of exchange: between use values there is already established in capitalist societies a 'rational–functional common denominator' (Baudrillard, 1981b:132).

But it is not only an extension of the principles adopted in the analysis of exchange value which permits this feature to come into view. It is also clear that, at this level, a decisive move is to contrast use values with the highly personal and unique nature of the gift exchange: gifts, he argues, can never be reduced to any such functional common denominator.[1] If this comparison is made, it is clear that the useful object has long entered into a very specific code of functionality which governs and subordinates it to its own logic, independently of any subjective meaning it may come to have for the individual user. Thus, if this level can be analysed by analogy with exchange, it does not mean that this level exists as an analogy with exchange; it is, quite the contrary, a level of reality in its own right and thus determines its own range of functional equivalences (Baudrillard,

1981b:132). If this is the case then the idea that there exists a fundamental and unchanging essential basis of human needs and useful objects which satisfy them, as an eternal substratum of human life, is an illusion. This level can be examined by analogy with Marx's analysis of exchange, where he shows that there is an abstract element in exchange (called abstract labour) which forms the basis of the possibility of a system of equivalences. (Baudrillard comments: just as Marx uses the terms *Arbeitskraft*, and *Arbeitsvermögen* (abstract labour power), one could say *Bedurfniskraft* and *Bedurfnisvermögen* (abstract use) (Baudrillard, 1981b:132)).

If this analysis is correct, Baudrillard suggests, it shows just how far it is necessary to go to rid Marxism of its Saint-Simonian heritage (as, for example, the phase 'from each according to his ability to each according to his needs' which requires not only a critique of needs but all its associated metaphysics, which seem to cluster around the idea of the individual, now separated from obligations of a collective kind which have hitherto played a role in defining social ties, the individual is liberated to find for himself, as autonomous being, his own destiny as consumer). This can only mean in fact that the object has a destination already written into it, it is already a rational, functional and objective phenomenon. This is an altogether different problematic from that of the gift in its specific play of ambivalence. Clearly use value requires demystification of a kind which will follow through all its ideological ramifications. Very specifically, for example, these seem to be tied to the way in which bourgeois economic theory appears to give sovereignty to the individual producer and consumer, whereas in fact: 'far from the individual expressing his needs in the economic system, it is the economic system that induces the individual function and the parallel functionality of objects and needs' (Baudrillard, 1981b:133). There is a tautology here, insists Baudrillard, which bourgeois economics is powerless to overcome, for it rests on the most impenetrable elements of its ideology (supply and demand) as a moral theory of the individual faced with an absolute ethical order (hitherto always multiple and profoundly ambiguous).

The new principle is that of the infinite functionality of all things, or, in this system the fact that all things become objects governed by secret order of human utility. In this way Baudrillard himself begins to elaborate, very simply at first, a revised model of Marxist theory which induces a new radical complexity at the site of Marx's own theory of use value. Two elements are noticeable at this stage. First, in opposition to use value Baudrillard has an alternative order of values marked out as the terrain of symbolic exchange value. But second he has inserted another level of abstraction into the theory of use value in order to break up the term into the product (in use, like the commodity in exchange), and its actual utility (as it takes its place in a system of rationality and functionality). Because this order becomes more complex, it is important to realise just how significant Baudrillard's choice of terminology is, especially in relation to concepts of the 'product', the 'object' and the 'commodity', on the one hand, and equivalence and non-equivalence on the other. Unfortunately:

> by maintaining use value as the category of incomparability, Marxist analysis has contributed to the mythology (a veritable rationalist mystique) that allows the relation of the individual to objects conceived as use values to pass for a concrete and objective – in sum 'natural' – relation between man's needs and the function proper to the object.
>
> (Baudrillard, 1981b:134)

Theoretical critique is essential in order to wrest Marxism out of this matrix of western metaphysics.

Perhaps one of the reasons why Marx found himself in this false position, Baudrillard suggests, was that he accepted as valid the distinction between the private sphere (of the concrete application of use in which resistence to the capitalist order could be sustained), against the public, reified and alienated structures of market exchange. If so, Marx missed a crucial point, noted even by some classical economists, that, even in consumption, what was consumed was not only the commodity but also its utility. But what was not noticed by classical economists was that this does not apply in the case of the gift or of the objects of symbolic exchange. For the classical economist, this is a world of irrational processes (the object does not have a use or utility which can be consumed in its social cycle, it is consumed in a process of pure loss). In failing to make this distinction, clearly Marx did not get to the root of the capitalist process, and thus his analysis is compromised – not at the level where he, rightly, criticised all ideological notions of the eternal private individual as acquisitive, but at the level of the conception where the individual can define himself in the use of objects for the realisation of his own being. Today this has to be pushed further, for it is clear there is no sphere which any more escapes the process of capitalist alienation, all needs including personal ones are deeply influenced by society's 'consummative mobilisation'.[2] Today everything which may appear to result from individual desire and initiative is: 'dissociated and catalysed in terms of needs, more or less specified in advance by objects . . . and all ambivalence is reduced by equivalence' (Baudrillard, 1981b:135). So the mode of appearance of the sovereignty of the individual to the classical economists is an effect of this prestructured field which paradoxically turns the individual subject into one of the 'most beautiful of these functional and servile objects' (ibid: 136), and then, *a fortiori*: 'this utilitarian imperative even structures the relation of the individual to himself'(ibid).

For Baudrillard, then, there is a certain fatal ambiguity in Marx's own theory of the individual as producer and consumer, for his ideas are never developed to the point of an irrevocable break with utilitarian myth. It seems that even Marx required some reference to the individual beyond the alienated structures of the exchange relationship in order to guarantee the roots of his analysis. But if Marx wanted this guarantee in the individual, he was in fact only to be caught up himself in its very ideological system, for it is not here that phenomena escape the effects of capitalist reproduction; indeed it is here, for Baudrillard, that some of the mysteries of the system are found in their most intense form. Fundamentally, then, here we come across a level of ideology (or fetishism) which functions not only in the same way in both classical political economy and in its most famous critique, but also as something which acts as a common support of the most basic assumptions of each corpus: this level reveals a harmony between all its elements (subject, need, scarcity, producer, utility, object and consumption) which is also the most basic set of terms of all the social ideologies of the period: relations between individual and society, individual and nature, between the individual and the body, and the individual self and others. In this light, the most radical critique of this harmony, has now become the touchstone of revolutionary theory itself.

It is important to stress that in these formulations Baudrillard is at pains to point out that it is Marxism which has made the critique possible, and it is Marxism itself which has to be the basis of a 'reinterrogation' of the 'repressive . . . metaphysic of utility' (Baudrillard, 1981b:139). For Baudrillard, in the pages where Marx seeks to ridicule the individualist illusions of political economy (in its Robinsonades), Marx falls into the trap of the naturalist ideology of transparent individual needs himself: but 'if Crusoe's relations to his labour and his wealth are so "clear" as Marx insists, what on earth has Friday got to do with it anyway?' (ibid:141).

SIGN VALUES AND IDEOLOGY

From this point Baudrillard returns in the subsequent essays to the dominant questions of the critique of the sign (particularly, Baudrillard, 1981b:142–63), which is now accomplished more and more directly by taking up a position 'beyond the sign' (in the problematic of symbolic exchange itself).[3] Radicalising the field in this way makes it possible to arrive a the conclusion: 'Only total revolution, theoretical and practical, can restore the symbolic in the demise of the sign and value. Even signs must burn' (ibid:163). This repositioning, this declaration in support of the restoration of the symbolic, is joined from now on in these analyses with an increasing appeal, itself an important repositioning, to the deconstruction of the (Saussurean and Barthean) notion of the sign, as well as the (Althusserian) notion of base and superstructure. Here the work of Derrida becomes an important lever.

But this is not done in a single move. There is a further radicalisation of the critique of humanist theoretical assumptions in the theory of alienation. Here Baudrillard's analyses even extend Althusserian theoretical anti-humanism. Indeed, the line of critical argument in the process of establishing the network of essentialist notions around individual use values seems heavily indebted to Althusser, but, developed here curiously into an attack on the formalism of the Althusserian notion of overdetermined totality (economic base and ideological superstructure), as a magical system of connections into which a basic set of already separated elements are put together by intellectual 'bricolage', by means of which the (genuine) Marxist dialectic is destroyed (the 'dialectic lies in ashes because it offered itself as a system of interpreting the separated contents of material production' (Baudrillard, 1981b:146, 166)). Instead of radicalising the Marxist critique of capitalist forms, the Althusserians, he maintains, have only succeeded in creating subtle but acrobatic incantations.[4] Against the Althusserian approach to the concept of ideology which tried to contrast it critically with scientific knowledge, Baudrillard tries another tack, to contrast it specifically with the reign of the symbolic order itself (ibid: 146). The ideological realm is now conceived as a specific means by which capitalism begins to 'traverse all the fields of production' and which Marx again uncritically accepts (alas, says Baudrillard). This view of ideology defines it as a system of representations grasped independently of, in transcendence of, its content: its internal elements circulate round it as though they were commodities on the market.[5] This 'ideological' order has to be contrasted with a symbolic order which maintains an ambivalence of content. If this is understood, the specific forms of destruction and reduction of the symbolic by ideology come into view. The ideological process is a devastating shift to the formation of rational, discrete, positive elements in thought, the formation of specific structured codes.

It is clear, he argues, that 'Marxist research' must now:

> come to terms with the fact that nothing produced or exchanged today (objects, services, bodies, sex, culture, knowledge, etc.) can be decoded exclusively as a sign, not solely measured as a commodity; that everything appears in the context of a general political economy in which the determining instance is neither the commodity nor culture . . . no longer properly either commodity or sign, but indissolubly both, and both only in the sense that they are abolished as specific determinations, but not as form . . . this object is perhaps quite simply the object, the object form, on which use value, exchange value and sign value converge in a complex mode that describes the most general form of political economy.
>
> (Baudrillard, 1981b:148)

This passage reveals something of the internal problems of Baudrillard's thought in this period. On the one hand, his position is drawn towards a rejection of the idea of a determinant instance in the Althusserian sense and, specifically, the idea of separated levels of practice. Yet his own position seems only capable finding the unity he desperately requires in the form of the object, as if the crucial issue concerned the conceptualisation of the connection between the elements in the various productive forces themselves.

It emerges that the form of the object now has to be approached in a radically new way, for the next critical exercise involves a rejection of the Saussurean idea of the sign (a critique of Benveniste's defence of the referent), and a rejection of the distinction between connotation and denotation that he had hitherto used himself (a critique of Barthes). Both are stigmatised as ideological, to be understood as attempts to escape the rigours of the code itself. Instead of finding this leads to a defeat for analysis, it must lead, as he remarks, in a consideration of the strategies launched from within the system, (a critique of Enzenberger and Eco), to a rejection of ideas of playing with,[6] or 'breaking up' the code itself in favour of more effective ones: 'What is strategic in this sense (revolutionary strategy) is only what radically checkmates the dominant form' (Baudrillard, 1981b:184). The only principle which can do this is one which counters the nature of 'ideology' itself: this, he identifies, is the very force of the symbolic order, which makes it possible to go beyond the sign.

It can be seen, then, that Baudrillard's way of tackling the critique of the sign, is to pose the most subversive of questions: what if the structural theory of the sign, with its tripartite distinction of signifier, signified and referent reproduced the same metaphysic as the theory of use value? In effect he believes that this is precisely what Derrida and the Tel Quel group have argued, as opposed to the positions of Benveniste and Barthes. These latter writers remain within the apparatus of a system which accepts the possibility of the existence of a transparent real world which language appropriates (here as the referent). This mistaken view can only lead, he suggests, to a hidden moral agenda. The world becomes a transparent determinant of the sign, is a 'long sermon' caught within the confines of western methaphysics (a favourite phrase of Derrida's, see Gane, 1989:55–77).

In a crucial gesture, at this point, Baudrillard opens a daring attack on the sign itself from the point of view of the symbolic order, for in the last resort it is the principle of ambivalence in the symbol that is the mortal enemy of the sign (which functions to transform everything into positive terms). It is not with respect to the existence of the real world, with its apparent ability to intervene as last resort, that the circle is to be broken, since the real world is not available, (and is never available except as the myth of semiology itself). Only the symbolic, in its radical negation of the positive term, can act effectively as a counter to the 'formal correlation of the signifier and signified.' Baudrillard does not evade the obvious problem here. There is a difficulty, 'for the symbolic, whose virtuality of meaning is so subversive of the sign, cannot, for this very reason, be named except by allusion, by infraction' (Baudrillard, 1981b:161). This is demonstrated, he notes, by Derrida's attack on the positivity of the sign, and ironically, Lacan's demonstration of the repressive nature of the sign. The necessity for revolutionaries to burst this particular theory as a form of positivity, of repression, of rationality, is evident. It is only possible through the assertion of a different modality, of ambivalence, of that which is beyond the sign itself and threatens to explode it. The logic of this argument has profound implications for Baudrillard's work, which radicalises it in a tendency to the symbolic, to literature and to poetry.

Up to 1972, then, it is possible to situate Baudrillard's position as one which attempted to reconstruct Marxism so as to make it an effective base for the critique of modern capitalism. His theory depended on the notion of a monopoly stage of capitalism (Baudrillard, 1970:168, 272), and the emergence of a new middle stratum which acted as social support for the compromise culture of ambient modernity. But his revision of Marx, his attempt to update Marxism, brought him into confrontation with crucial weaknesses in the theory of use value, base and superstructure, and the notion of ideology. In his next phase, this critique turns to an attempt to locate and isolate all the consequences of productivism in Marxist theory.

6   Baudrillard: theoretical critic

He is truly a revolutionary who speaks of the world as non-separated.
Baudrillard (1975a:166)

It is clear as the collection *For a Critique* (1972) comes to an end, and with it the critique of the sign, that Baudrillard's critical reflections on Marxism, psychoanalysis, structuralism and critical theory had really only just begun. Here I shall examine his critique of structural Marxism, psychoanalysis and his critique of Foucault (as in some senses a representative of modern social science).

EMERGENCE OF THE CRITIQUE OF MARXISM

Baudrillard's critical rejection of Marxism was published in 1973. It was the first work of Baudrillard to find its way into English (in 1975), and is certainly not one which draws back into a comfortable middle-class revisionism; rather it drives forward in the other direction towards deepening radicalism. Whereas in 1972 his position was still evolving on the terrain of Marxism, either as a Marxist or as an internal critic of Marxism, the work of 1973 reversed previous judgements and concluded that Marxism was irretrievably caught within the framework of capitalist relations itself. Marxism was not the revolutionary breakthrough that had been hoped for, but catastrophically, it was a particular elaboration of capitalism's own principles: it was the mirror of the principle of (capitalist) production itself.

In a sense this line of criticism was a latent possibility in Baudrillard's work from a very early period, for his own way of working as a Marxist was to approach the question of consumption as independent from production. It was, of course, never claimed that this domain (production) was the the site of the all-determining processes in the system as a whole. However, very little ever appeared as a direct reference to the productive labour process, or indeed to the political power processes of class struggle.[1] When his critique eventually took shape, it could be seen simply as the complete elimination of this site from his theoretical vision. When Baudrillard's critique arrived it followed others who had already moved in this direction

(Glucksmann 1972, orig. 1967) criticised the formalist implications in the Althusserian reading of practice as the key term in Marxism, but Althusser himself had already taken the decisive step of moving from the perspective of production to that of reproduction – certainly a radicalising step, and one to be followed in a curious way by Baudrillard).

One way of appreciating the nature of Baudrillard's thought is to recall that at this period in France there were two quite different ways of relating to Marxism. One derived from the humanist reading, which developed an understanding of the world principally in terms of the reification and alienation effects of capitalism, and contrasted this with a revolutionary perspective of the recovery of human society in the future communist society. The alternative to this was a structural Marxism inspired by Leninism polarised towards the view that Marxist theory was to be developed as a science and fused with proletarian social forces in a vanguard party. It is clear that Baudrillard, if he was ever deeply influenced by the former, had certainly moved away from any simple existentialism or theory of the alienation of essential human properties in capitalism.[2] From the moment his writing appeared his position was decisively orientated to a structural Marxism. His position even reached a degree of scientism that could match other structuralists[3] for he was never satisfied with a theory of simple immanent transition to socialism. His theory is characterised by a powerful search for the principle of transcendence, a principle of alterity, just as it is for a sense of the points of dramatic closure within the system.[4]

It is clear, however, that in the formation of his sociology as a whole, no one paradigm ruled exclusively. Not only did Freudian and Lacanian ideas from psychoanalysis play a decisive role, but other sociological traditions intervened at crucial points. Some commentators have pointed to the role of Frankfurt Marxism, others to the influence of theory from Veblen to McLuhan. But as his theory evolved it became clear that the most important centre of gravity outside Marxism was curious Nietzschean Durkheimianism. In a strange sense it could be claimed that instead of a theory of the essence of man derived from phenomenological or existential theory, his conception of alienation was constructed out of a fusion of Freudian, Nietzschean and Durkheimian elements. In other words, Baudrillard elaborates an anti- or non-humanist theory of alienation.

It is noteworthy that his final pages of *The Mirror of Production* (1975a) are devoted to a critique of the naiveté of alienation theories. At each period, he insists, human society is complete: the meaning of a felt lack, is always *in* the present and its meaning always remains in the present.

Many commentators have noticed, however, the apparent nostalgic element in his work, as if there was a basic nostalgia for a golden age of human society which had been lost: his orientation to the present, especially after the fading of the revolutionary period of 1968, is unremittingly hostile. And during the intensification of his critical about-turn all his previous theoretical allies came in for critical rejection: semiology, psychoanalysis and Marxism. All of them rejected for a perceived complicity with the workings of the repressive social order itself.

In a significant sense, therefore, his criticisms are self-criticisms, but unlike Althusser, there is not the slightest hint, in Baudrillard's critique of Marx, that he had ever made any errors himself. This did not tell against him, however, for it was the unorthodox Althusserian mode which found least popular favour.[5] In his own critique his main enemies are the structural Marxists (humanists having become innocuous). Thus there are long refutations of Godelier, Kristeva, Althusser and others, among whom is Marcuse. One notable source of support is found in Walter Benjamin, but he also notes other sociologists like Weber, and also, of course, Bataille.

Strangely, perhaps, there is no real change of basic terminology at this point. What occurs is to be understood far more as a displacement of position, as a change of attitude, a re-evaluation and a retargeting of critical objects. It is not as if, for example, the deconstructional analysis of the subject (common to both Althusser and Derrida) is abandoned. On the contrary, Baudrillard tries to assess the extent that the application of the idea was kept within a narrow framework which should now be broken. On the other hand, it seems very unlikely that Baudrillard could escape completely, in one move, the whole of his previous formation. For example, even in the important judgement: 'to the extent that it is not radical, Marxist critique is led despite itself to reproduce the roots of the system of political economy' (Baudrillard, 1975a:67). Evidently here he is on the verge of saying that, in so far as Marxism does not 'produce' something different from political economy it 'reproduces' it.

But this raises and leads to an important point. For it is clear that for Marx, it is not use value, but the proletariat, a class logic, which is seen as the force for the negation of the existing order. Baudrillard now rarely discusses this, preferring to remain on the ground of the object form. Perhaps this is a feint, and these elements are all intimately connected. This is only revealed by implication, yet it is perhaps the most important underlying thesis of the work of Baudrillard, a point to which I shall return at a later moment. Suffice it here to note that since Marx, he suggests, only the analysis by Lukacs of the principle of reification constitutes a critical line of consideration of the object form (Baudrillard, 1975a:121); but this has to be placed in a context of the acknowledged displacement of capitalism towards a monopoly stage (Lenin), in which: 'It is the control of demand (Galbraith) that becomes the strategic articulation' (ibid:125). This comment is significant in the sense that it reveals the fact that Baudrillard still adheres to something of the Marxist programme, and retains the significance of Marx's critique (or 'deciphering') of aspects of capitalism.

The essay, *The Mirror of Production*, is made up of five sections, which attack the Marxist conception of labour, nature, primitive society, slavery and feudalism, and its general epistemology as developed by structuralist interpretations.

THE WORK ETHIC

The idea of *labour* is identified as a key term in Marx, as can be seen in Marx's decision to select the notion of production as essential to the definition of humanity itself. He quotes Marx (from *The German Ideology*): 'The first act is thus the production of the means to satisfy these needs, the production of material life itself' (in Baudrillard, 1975a:21). Marx fatally mistakes the liberation of the productive forces with general social liberation, and identified productivity as characteristic of culture: Marx again says: 'men begin to distinguish themselves from animals as soon as they begin to produce their means of subsistence' (in ibid:22). And this critical observation is linked to the analysis already accomplished of the notion of use value, now turned into an analysis of Althusserian interpretation which specifically pointed to Marx's last words on the interpretation of his theory (cited in Althusser's works), stressing the significance of the concept of use value. Baudrillard's point is that Marx draws back from radicalising his analysis here, refusing the idea that 'use value is produced by the play of exchange value' (ibid:25). (Baudrillard is perhaps half-aware of the irony of his own formulation here with its appeal to production. But he does not see the quotation he uses from Marx which says against Baudrillard: use value is a crucial term but is not dealt with abstractly only as it arises from the analysis of a given economic form, not from reasoning this way and that about the concepts' (Marx, cited in Althusser and Balibar, 1970:79).)

What is necessary, Baudrillard reiterates, is to see that a generic definition of man as 'productive man', *homo faber*, is actually caught within the effects of rationality of capital itself; any adequate critique has to 'shatter' the conception in order to reach a grasp of the full workings of the mechanism. Baudrillard follows Marx's analysis of the formation of abstract labour in eighteenth-century artisan forms, and tries to show that Marx misses the fact that concrete, differentiated, incommensurable labour appears in opposition to, and yet is used to designate, all other activity. That is: 'it signifies the comparability of all human practice in terms of production and labour' (Baudrillard, 1975a:27). Ironically, he claims, it is Marx's concept of abstract labour which brings concrete labour into existence as such, and yet misconceives it in the same moment.

In an important aside, Baudrillard claims that there is a parallel outcome in Marx's discussion of the division between the technical and social division of labour. This split is used he suggests, to provide basic elements in the social theory of both the contradiction between forces and relations of production, and the distinction of alienated and non-alienated relations of production. Yet these are 'fictions' which are used to carry and propagate the universal principle of production, loaded this time with the inevitable weight of technical rationality. Baudrillard cites Marx's own remarks to the effect that production creates needs: 'the extent to which historic needs . . . which are themselves the offspring of social production and intercourse, are posited as necessary, the higher the level to which real wealth has developed' (in Baudrillard, 1975a:28). In this, says Baudrillard, Marx can no longer see beyond the principles of the social order of capital since social wealth is now *only* ever visible in relation to labour and production. (But, again, close reading of Marx here does not altogether support Baudrillard's contention, Marx continues:

> Necessary needs are those of the individual himself reduced to a natural subject. The development of industry suspends this natural necessity as well as this former luxury – in bourgeois society, it is true, it does so only in antithetical form, in that it itself only posits another specific social standard as necessary, opposite luxury.
>
> (Marx, 1973:528)

In other words, Marx points specifically to the 'suspension' of the natural subject in bourgeois society, in favour of one that is relative to new levels of wealth.)[6]

In principle, Baudrillard maintains, this idea of labour as essential to the analysis of all societies is 'arbitrary and strange', and judges that: 'the analysis of all primitive or archaic organisations contradicts it, as does the feudal symbolic order and even that of our societies' (Baudrillard, 1975a:29). (Yet again, Baudrillard avoids Marx's famous argument that the analysis of higher forms (of man) can be used in the analysis of lower (apes), and that the whole of Marx's strategy is based not on arbitrary principles those established in biology.)

The analysis, in Althusser, of theory as a productive process, means that the notion of ideology becomes modelled on capitalist processes, and, as a system of thought, only reduplicates its object as separated and alienated: theory and revolutionary practice are neutralised by this failure. Yet Baudrillard adopts, ironically, a version of Althusserianism to express his own thought:

> man is not only quantitatively exploited as a productive force by the system of capitalist political economy, but is also metaphysically overdetermined as a producer by the code of political economy. In the last instance, the system rationalises its power here.

By suggesting it is in the sale of their labour power that workers are alienated, Marx only prevents a far more radical idea to emerge: that workers are alienated through the very 'inalienable' powers to labour ascribed to them (Baudrillard, 1975a:31).

In this sense, he argues, Marx never gets to the position where he can challenge the thesis that the human is characterised by the capacity to produce, to transform his various environments in relation to his purposes. (Obviously Baudrillard is not able to attack Marx on the division between mental and manual labour in the same way, since for Marx such problems become resolvable through the theory of production.) But for Baudrillard it is the fact that production comes to play such a key role as integrator of ideas of science, technique, progress, history and indeed praxis, that: 'it circumscribes the entire history of man in a gigantic simulation model' (Baudrillard, 1975a:33).[7] If one is to get out of this trap, he suggests, it is essential to begin to limit the idea of mode of production itself. Far from making it a universal, it must be strictly limited to the capitalist process of producing. The universal reproduction of the separated structures of this particular society has to be prevented at the level of theory, for this society is exceptional (a Durkheimian style of analysis). Thus what remains of Marxism as a critique is a strictly logical analysis of exchange processes.

It is not only French Marxism which comes in for criticism. Marcuse is also cited as having adopted central elements of a theory too uncritical of its assumptions: 'In the last analysis, the burdensome character of labour expresses nothing other than a negativity rooted in the very essence of human existence: man can achieve his own self only by passing through "externalisation" and "alienation"' (Marcuse, in Baudrillard, 1975a:36). Baudrillard remarks, this shows: 'how the Marxist dialectic can lead to the purest Christian ethic . . . this aberrant sanctification of work has been the secret vice of Marxist political and economic strategy from the beginning' (Baudrillard, 1975a:36). He contrasts Marcuse with Walter Benjamin's observation to the effect that within the German workers' movement there was a clear transition from a Protestant work ethic to a similar socialist celebration of the liberating powers of work: 'Nothing was more corrupting' (Benjamin). (Yet, again, the note on Marx's comments on the German position as indicated in the 'Critique of the Gotha Programme' (1968), do not quite endorse this position, since Marx is at pains to point out that it is the bourgeois reading which ascribes a 'supernatural power' to labour, that in modern conditions – where a part of society have become owners of the material conditions of labour processes it is precisely ownership of labour power which is the hinge of the system of exploitation. Marx seems to be completely aware of the ambiguity of the formulation that 'work is the source of all wealth and culture'.) Baudrillard nevertheless forces his argument and concludes: 'Confronted by the absolute idealism of labour, dialectical materialism is perhaps only a dialectical idealism of productive forces' (Baudrillard, 1975a:37).

CONCEPTIONS OF NON-WORK PROCESSES

The tendency in Marxism to treat the means of production as an absolute principle is itself part of a wider strategy to disengage and break up elements of the social whole into autonomous processes, even introducing such separations into the conception of the dialectic itself. (All this has its consequences in social democratic revisionism on the one hand and Stalinism on the other.) There are yet further consequences in the implications for the conception of the relation of work to non-work processes, and this makes Marxism 'defenceless' agains the subtleties of bourgeois aesthetics. Thus in Marcuse, a particularly clear case of this tendency, the problem is always posed in terms of aethetic play, transcendence, disalienation on the basis of an ethic of productivity, a 'dialectical culmination of man's activity of incessant objectification of nature and control of exchanges with it' (Baudrillard, 1975a:40). All the main concepts applicable to non-work processes are profoundly affected by the interruption of ideas of use and labour. Even if this sphere is posed in the most radical way, avoiding the obvious pitfalls of a simple notion of the extension of leisure in the new society, the conception of the sphere of play, now without a defined content, is always formally dependent on the contrastive term, 'work', which it mirrors. The critique always misses its target at this level, since the pure form is always determinant.

Baudrillard's next target is an attempt by Julia Kristeva to find within Marx's own writing a more sophisticated position which might deflect Baudrillard's attack. Kristeva, in many aspects working within the same literary problematic as Baudrillard, here searches to answer the same problem as Baudrillard in connection to the critique of the sign, to find a basis for this critique in Marx. She says, as Baudrillard cites:

> Marx clearly outlined another possibility; work could be apprehended outside value, on the side of the commodity produced and circulating in the chain of communication. Here labour no longer represents any value, meaning or signification. It is a question only of a body and a discharge.
>
> (in Baudrillard, 1975a:42)

Baudrillard's reply correctly points out that no such conception can be found in Marx, that Kristeva has introduced into Marx a purely extraneous conception (from Bataille) which runs counter to the whole of Marx's ideas on human activity: 'if there was one thing that Marx did not think about, it was discharge, waste, sacrifice, prodigality, play, and symbolism' (ibid:42). For Marx social activity is conceived in terms of the production of values, and of material phenomena. It is quite the contrary in Bataille who argues that the sacrificial economy is exclusive of political economy, it is a different analytic field which will not tolerate the concept of labour: a 'choice has to be made between value and non-value'. The concept of production itself is trapped within an analytic field which has to be understood as a whole – only possible on the basis of an altogether alternative conception, one which does not carry at any point the implication of use or *utility*. Kristeva's reading, he claims, is a futile effort which only leads to a misunderstanding of Marx's text. Her conception of a 'body and its discharge' is caught within a framework of productive non-reciprocating entities.

Baudrillard appeals to the analysis by Jean-Joseph Goux against Kristeva, which suggests that all conceptions of a 'realm beyond value is confounded with the sphere of use value' which means, if it is correct, that in Marxism 'all transcendence is locked into this single alternative within the field of value'. As this is evidently conceived in Marx as a rational relation of means to purpose, the ideas which are found in this field always conform, even with regard to sexuality, to a principle of work. Marx did not grasp the nature of the fundamental contradiction here. This is to be found not in the relation of a concrete to abstract labour, but between work and non-work (pure expenditure or symbolic exchange). He missed the fact that political economy 'overdetermines' production in the simple sense with a deeper level of rationalisation of productivity, and this can only have been arrived at by a decisive *break* with all notions of the symbolic exchange order: the symbolic is ambivalent, the rational capitalist order demands that this is reduced to unambiguous efficiency, a 'positive', destined to accumulation: 'the mirror of production, in which all Western metaphysics is reflected, must be broken' (Baudrillard, 1975a:47).

Baudrillard ends the discussion of this first topic with remarks on epistemology, which suggest that Marxism wanted to produce an analysis which was both scientific and critical, but having taken production as a key term it fails to establish itself as other to the system, it simply becomes a double of it beginning from one of its (insufficiently criticised) repressive elements. In this respect, and to this extent, Marxism is a 'repressive simulation' of capital (Baudrillard, 1975a:48). In opposition to this analysis it is necessary to say, he argues, that in other societies there is no mode of production, no unconscious, no dialectic in the sense developed by Marx and elaborated by structural Marxists.[8] Against this body of thought which has become obsessed with the analysis of barriers to revolution, it is strategically necessary to bring the questioning of primitive societies to bear against Marxism (and psychoanalysis and linguistics) itself (ibid: 49).

TOWARDS A CRITIQUE BASED ON SYMBOLIC EXCHANGE

First of all it is necessary to rid anthropology of structuralist notions imported illegitimately from outside. Baudrillard turns to a critique of Godelier, but before entering into the details of this he provides a brief analysis of the evolution of the conception of nature since the sixteenth century and its implications for the way in which hidden assumptions have entered modern social theory by this route. This is, in fact, no minor digression, even though Baudrillard's discussion only raises the general lines of an analysis, which might therefore appear overly schematic.[9] His argument suggests that the modifications to the ethic of capitalism in the nineteenth century are the late results of a long history born out of the

Judao-Christian tradition: a separation of body and soul (the latter in the image of god, the former for use). The later crucial phases of this development involved an other worldly ethic of renunciation, followed by the puritan ethic of work. Nineteenth-century political economy was only a continuation of this tradition, and could not escape its assumptions.

Thus, in the seventeenth century, there still existed a rough equilibrium of society and nature: Spinoza's notion of god as nature was already predicated on a positioned relation of subject and the world, but nature could be conceived as the totality of laws which guarantee the working of things. A century later nature is discovered as more than a law, it is now a set of powers. On this is based a definitive split between nature and society. The former is conceived as 'reality', as referent. This occurs at the same time as the idea of production rises as the dominant principle of mastery over nature: production aims to subordinate nature. Marx was mistaken to think that the labourer still worked on nature as if on a fertile mother. This mythology is obliterated in the historical degradation of nature. But there is still an ambiguity in the attempt to understand nature. On the one hand, science reproduces nature as a separated essence, yet it does this in the name of nature's own purpose. Ironically, even nature becomes a 'metaphor of freedom and totality' (Baudrillard 1975a:55).

Whereas Marx went some way to think through the problem of the break-up of the traditional community and the appearance of class stratification, he did not fully attack the myth of nature and its accompanying set of anthropological assumptions, especially those around the idea of needs, the purposeful nature of products and the underlying idea of the usefulness of nature as a function of productive work. The new (bourgeois) ideology again splits into a good nature (dominated and rationalised) and a bad nature (polluted and hostile). Marxism simply aligns itself on the optimistic model, and continues the idea of a virgin nature waiting to be dominated. It maintains the idea of necessity, and the effects of necessity enter into the entire system of explanation through the economic, which expand the realm of necessity as society advances. Marx proceeds on the illusion that previous societies have known this system of natural needs and physical realities, whereas this only becomes effective under capitalist formations. The problem of scarcity is a modern invention. The consequences of this theoretical misrecognition are serious, for Marxism burdens itself with an 'idealist over-determination by political economy' (Baudrillard 1975a:59). Thus in Marx, Saint-Simonian principles are not questioned: 'scarcity' is to be overcome in a society of abundance, where each will receive according to natural 'needs'. The development of the productive forces will make this possible according to Marx (who therefore has fundamental 'need' for these needs). Marxists like Marcuse in modern times believe this is imminent. But the problem is this, Baudrillard argues: the technological spiral is never complete and cannot be completed in this system. The myth of productivity and its inherent revolutionary potential is the key blockage to genuine revolutionary theory, and it is intimately connected to the myth of nature as revealed in the concept and mythology of scarcity (fundamental to political economy and uncritically accepted into Marxism).[10]

In societies where symbolic exchanges are predominant this idea does not apply. (Indeed the problem goes further for neither law nor necessity, repression nor the unconscious in the Freudian sense, really apply. The way that the theory of the oedipal complex is applied to these societies has to be completely rethought.) Even when the Christian tradition became established and displaced genuine symbolic orders, there were repeated appeals for a rehabilitation of nature in the Cathar, pantheistic, mystical, libertarian and millenarian heretical doctrines. Extreme calls for the end of the world were made, and for 'paradise now'. The response of the church was to reassert the break with nature, and to align itself with doctrines of work, just as Marxism has done.[11]

Baudrillard's vigorous critique suggests that Marxist anthropologists such as Lévi-Strauss and Godelier only set up primitive societies as a distinctive Other to modern capitalism through a feint; the oppositions of primitive and modern thought are, in the end, defused. Baudrillard, himself, from this moment, takes on the role of a kind of *ultra* of primitive societies. He devotes himself to countering the philosophical, sociological and ideological incorporation of these cultures (via a generalising theory dominated by ideas which project the advanced but separated and stratified structures of modern, western society). Primitive culture becomes the subversive principle of critical analysis, which structuralist concepts have sought to displace and cancel (structural concepts become unwitting carriers of the western cultural 'virus' to primitive peoples).

The problem is the way that historical materialism has been constructed on the model of the capitalist mode of production which 'reproduces' (Baudrillard, 1975a:69) the categories of nature and history from with the capitalist code itself: they are its 'referential simulation'. The dialectic is installed behind these conceptions as a law, either of history or of nature itself. But the way that this is developed is quite different from any critique which has as its aim the deconstruction of imaginary worlds (as is Nietzsche's). The aim of the work of a Marxist anthropologist like Godelier is to dismember these societies in the mode of a 'bad' butcher.[12] For Godelier it is apparent that primitive societies do not have a separated structure of economic production. He insists that these societies do nevertheless have a basis in kinship and a superstructure in myth. This, says Baudrillard, is only to preserve Marxism in the face of the extreme *heresy* presented by primitive orders. The problem arises in an acute way for a Marxist like Godelier since he acknowledges that these societies do not have a convenient institutionalisation of 'relations of production'. If this is the case they really can have no mode of production. Godelier persists in applying the concept even if there is no corresponding formation. The dialectic is saved as a formal procedure, or rather, says

Baudrillard, as a *formal simulation of capitalism* projected onto these societies.

For Godelier the task is specified very clearly as the analysis of the 'role of the economy in the last instance' in these societies, and in relation to this the action of the dominant social structures 'which at the same time fix non-economic functions'. This follows Marx's own formulation that 'the middles ages could not live on catholicism, nor the ancient world on politics' so that explanation cannot follow these ideational structures as if they were determinant. Rather, Marx argues, it is through the analysis of the ways in which these societies produced their livelihood that is the key to explanation. This was a key reference in the Althusserian interpretation of Marx, which tried to identify two concepts here: the dominant layer in the social formation and the determinant structure (the economic) which 'explains why here politics, and there Catholicism, played the chief part' (Marx). Maurice Godelier tries to develop this idea in relation to primitive societies but links it directly to historical progression: 'As soon as humanity exists, the functions of economics, kinship and ideology exist with a determinate form. This content and this form are transformed with history and by it' (cited in Baudrillard, 1975a:73). So, says Baudrillard, Godelier begins in the present, from the separations established in bourgeois society and in bourgeois political economy, and makes these the eternal grid for the interpretation of all social forms. The separations become differentiated abstract functions held in place by a new 'dialectic' legitimised as scientific. Under the impact of this productivism, historicism and scientism, Marxist anthropology creates an object in its own image, one that is internally dislocated so that it can be manipulated theoretically.

This is a problem, Baudrillard suggests, because it appears that the Copernican revolution in anthropology has not yet occurred; Marxism and western anthropology simply fill the gap by projecting its own ethnocentric matrix onto this *unknown* object.[13] But this is a mistake: 'The very least requirement would be to reexamine the whole matter starting from this non-separation', (Baudrillard, 1975a:74). Without this, analysis immediately runs into problems of a most elementary kind: in these societies there is no production, no producers, no needs and no satisfactions in the sense attached to them by bourgeois or Marxist theory. Yet Godelier simply suggests that 'in a primitive society the producers own their means of production and their own labour' without having attempted the very least critical transformation of these terms, ensuring they carry no trace of a suggestion of productivism. It is extremely easy to fall into error here as the 'exchanges' occurring in these societies can be understood simply on the model of exchange in capitalist society. But to do so misses the main point about the nature of the gift and gift exchange.

Consider the question of economic or societal surplus. Western analysis confuses this because it can only start from the basis that the production of an economic surplus is natural, and so it proceeds to examine why one is not produced in these societies, or why there are blockages to its production. Consequently it is relatively straightforward to define these societies as subsistence societies, functioning directly in relation to natural 'needs' (which always seem to be minimal). There is here an intervention of a number of conceptions which function simply to impede a close analysis of these societies and their key articulations, for if these societies do have an order, and a principle, it is not that of separation and overdetermination. Such a principle is in its way simply another form of vulgar utilitarianism. For example, if these societies are organised around a principle of symbolic exchange all ideas of subsistence and function, even of survival, must be subordinated to it. These societies may even defend themselves against the intrusion of such elements, for example:

> symbolic exchange . . . excludes any surplus: anything that cannot be exchanged or symbolically shared would break the reciprocity and institute power . . . () . . . this exchange excludes all 'production'. The exchanged goods are apportioned and limited, often imported from far away according to strict rules. Why? Because, given over to individual or group production, they would risk being proliferated and thereby break the fragile mechanism of reciprocity.
>
> (Baudrillard, 1975a:79)

And if this is the case there are a number of important consequences, for exchange of this kind could be said, he suggests, to be a kind of 'non-production' and an unlimited reciprocity between persons, based on a strictly limited exchange of goods. This disappears from view as soon as the imported term 'production', and mode of production is introduced.

It must be noted that Baudrillard's formulations here do appear divided between a dogmatic adherence to the importance and difference of symbolic exchange, and a certain hesitation in relation to the question of whether symbolic exchange, thus understood, is a barrier to production and surplus (they are 'negated and volatised by reciprocal exchange which consumes itself'), as if primitive cultures do in fact have some sort of presentiment of the existence of these problems and indeed seek to exorcise them. The difference between Baudrillard and other writers is thus in part not simply a question of theoretical content but also of position (of *partisanship*). Baudrillard's work appears at times as immanent criticism, as epistemological deconstruction, but at others as the formulation of a contrast: for example, Godelier has simply got it wrong through a mania for structuralist procedures. At this point Baudrillard presents a specific doctrine of the nature of primitive societies (based on Mauss and Bataille) against the ones proposed and developed by structural anthropology. The implication at this point is that Marxism must give up its attempt to generate a theory of social evolution based on an understanding of the capitalist mode of production as a higher form.

Take, for example, the analysis Godelier makes of the role of magic.[14] Godelier's position inevitably leads to a misunderstanding of the means–end relation in these societies since his own approach still rests on uncriticised assumptions of action and reason. Godelier suggests that the primitive labourer seems to know that he must labour to produce a product but then realises that his technique is insufficient by itself and is in need of a bit of magic to make it entirely effective: 'By his magical practices, man thinks he can insert himself in the natural order's chain of necessary causalities' (cited in Baudrillard, 1975a:81). The many false assumptions here are exposed: a crude western social psychology of a pragmatic type is inserted into a notion of the primitive as governed by superstition, coupled by an imposed western notion of causality and nature.[15] Against this view Baudrillard cites other analyses – especially that of J.-P. Vernant – of ancient Greek society, which argue that it is quite foreign and inappropriate to think of labour in these societies as a 'factor of production' and that there is some direct calculation of the expenditure of effort which is primarily 'economic', or that the 'fruits of harvest' are related to a calculated moment of 'input'. If these societies are those in which there is a symbolic exchange through the gods, there is no place for 'scarcity' as such, which is shown to be a specific conception linked to linear progression, not to a cyclical motion of gift and counter-gift. The modern notion of magic is always posed against its opposite – reason. Thus, to introduce it into the analysis of the 'labour process' in these societies adds a misconception onto a misconception in order to 'seal a disjunction' felt by the analyst.

Marx's own thought in this respect is entirely rationalist. For Marx, mythology is an attempt to 'master and dominate' nature. It will, then, logically disappear with the increasing control of nature produced with technological progress. Two problems arise here, says Baudrillard. The first is that Marx's position 'completely masks the entire problematic' of symbolic exchange beneath layers of rationalism, scientism and functionalism. But second, the implication for contemporary societies is also false, for technical progression does not lead to the disappearance of mythology or the imaginary in society. In fact it: 'generates a fundamental contradiction connected with, its abstractness and its very rationality, which primitive symbolic exchange, which is more concrete in this respect, does not have' (Baudrillard, 1975a:84).

AN ALTERNATIVE ANALYSIS OF CLASSES

Baudrillard's analysis of ancient slave society and artisan modes of production does not so much insist on the false intrusion of the principle of production as an obstacle, rather it bases its argument on the failure in Marxism to pick up the radical critique of modern capitalist forms that can be made from the position of these earlier forms. Such a critique is again blocked, he suggests, by the western illusion that the passage to wage labour is a 'progression' or indeed 'liberation', a view supported by: 'western humanist rationality incarnated in the thread of history by the abstract political state, which, when instituted, attributes all earlier forms of domination to the irrational' (Baudrillard, 1975a: 96). But no effort of forming a concept through a recombination of elements, from the position of the worker who sells his labour power, to that of the slave or the artisan, will ever be adequate to their specific features. In contrast to Althusser's own critique of the essentialism of certain Hegelian forms of concept formation, Baudrillard attacks the notion of concept formation by deduction from a later to earlier state. It is a kind of retrospective essentialism which fails to reveal the specific characteristics of the earlier fusion of elements because the premisses of the later forms are never relinquished.

In relation to slavery specifically, what the imposition of Marxist categories fails to notice is the unique forms of reciprocity developed.[16] Baudrillard's discussion here is brief and is obviously open to criticism if read as a general theory of slavery. If read critically, however, with all necessary precautions, Baudrillard's effort, paradoxically, is to strengthen Marx's own argument concerning wage labour as an alienated formation. For what is missed in the simple construction of a comparative table of forms of exploitation, or labour systems, is the possibility of learning something from slavery about the nature of power. In slavery the worker is not separated as a free employee, and the slave owner is not separated as a free employer. There is inevitably a form of reciprocity established, yet not one that is dominated by individualist concerns of altruism and egoism dominant in modern, western societies. The symbolic order is still active in these societies and this is always passed over when the question is posed in Marxist terms.

It is hardly necessary, says Baudrillard, to go into the forms of reciprocity in any detail to see that, in fact, counter to many well-entrenched assumptions, Marx himself, perhaps, did not pay enough attention to the forms and depth of alienation of the modern worker (humanist assumptions again preventing analysis here). Where Marx sees the process of alienation as located in the sale of labour power, this is only made possible on the basis of the control the labourer has of himself (for he is 'free' to sell his labour power on the labour market). This gives to the labourer, says Baudrillard, an extraordinary and 'exorbitant' privilege, one which even escaped the slave owner. And this throws considerable light on an important problem in Marxism itself, especially its conception of liberation which is based on the: 'interiorisation of the separation, . . . of a subjective, abstract essence (in this case labour power) over which the identity of the subject comes to fix itself' (Baudrillard, 1975a: 95). Thus there is a remarkable difference with slavery in which there is a fundamental *connection* at this point. The form of domination is personal: the slave is not an object in the sense that labour power becomes an object in the market. Domination does not require or establish, necessarily, a transcendental form of authority: this only arises in a system of separations of the capitalist type, which, paradoxically, Marxists view wrongly as a progression *from* a more extreme, even a maximal form of exploitation.[17]

Baudrillard's discussion of the artisan, focuses on the Marxist conception of the craft mode of production as predicated on the fact that the artisan is an independent worker who owns his means of production, and his own product. Alongside this structure is the organisation of exchange and consumption through guilds and communal networks (kin, village, neighbourhood). This latter fact is decisive, he argues, since it is:

> a mode of social relations in which not only is the process of production controlled by the producer but . . . the collective process remains internal to the group, and in which producers and consumers are the same people, above all defined through the reciprocity of the group.
>
> (Baudrillard, 1975a: 97)

The situation is directly parallel to the exchanges established in a language community, everyone is both producer and consumer, or rather these terms are inappropriate, he says, since in fact there is neither separated production nor consumption, for what occurs is based on reciprocities and on equivalences. But the parallel between gift exchange and artisan exchange is not perfect, since the latter introduce conceptions of use and value. Nevertheless, because personal connections still remain, the strict separation of producer and consumer is not fully established. The distinction between the labourer and his own means of production could not be recognised as such, without a false element entering into the analysis.

The important element which is always missed in Marxist analysis here is the continuing presence of symbolic exchange structures. These make it quite wrong to speak of pure economic investment in the work process. What occurs is much closer to a form of reciprocity, of gift, expenditure and resolution. Craft art is still a world away from simple utility and usefulness. The work of art bears: 'the inscription of the loss of the finality of the subject and object, the radical incompatibility of life and death, the play of an ambivalence' (Baudrillard, 1975a:99). The work of art in symbolic exchange is thus irreducible to formal economic exchange. The implication of Marxist conceptions is to reduce all these systems to, or relate them all to, economic rationality of a capitalist type. This has the further implication that conceptions of liberation derived from them are also caught within the network of a system which is profoundly repressive. Again, pressing this argument to an extreme instead of seeing that the evolution of 'free labour' is repressive, Marxism seems to link autonomy and mastery as an unqualified progression. The logic is implacable in leading to the glorification of work and labour as the source of value, and is unable to see that in this process the 'slave has become his own master'. Instead of subjecting this to a critique, Marxism simply adopts the position of political economy and reproduces its nostalgic celebration of the 'instinct of workmanship' (Baudrillard, 1975a: 105).

This notion exercises fascination across a number of perspectives, he argues, and for understandable reasons. It is the basis not only of ideas of improving the quality of working life, of job enrichment, with all its overtones of re-establishing a golden age of the craftsman, but it is also behind much of the inspiration for flexible working, or polyvalent working (as defined by Proudhon), which, in their own way, attempt to establish a new mastery. It is in the end always also bound up with the individualist principle of labour as sublimation. In this sense it is parallel to the new notion of the body and sexuality, where the individual is the free autonomous agent in control of his or her own instrument of the production of pleasure: a parallel goal of liberation as repressive desublimation. It is, says Baudrillard, more a fantasy of self-management, on the model of the artisan, and as a doctrine of liberation, completely caught up in a system of the reproduction of alienated separations, unable to transcend them.

In a final discussion, Baudrillard turns to discuss more directly his real target, the Althusserian conception of the dialectic and historical materialism. For this conception, the contradiction between the forces and relations of production becomes the single positive space for historical progression. In fact, the earlier periods, earlier modes of production are not analysed as definitive, they only make sense in this framework as forming part of a historical series, historical accumulation. In the earlier periods, the social forces were blind; only later in the capitalist period does social opposition become for the first time rational and scientific. Thus the idea of the revolutionary overthrow of capitalism is based on a qualitatively different kind of experience which enables the antagonists in the process to bring the process of oppression to an end. But, says Baudrillard, 'this is a little too neat'. It is a little too neat that just as the mode of production appears in history, the theory of scientific history based on it also makes its appearance. This is only to give current history and current formations an exceptional privilege. It is to say that these forms are closest to the universal (scientific), which is the claim Hegel made in his day of his society, a claim which Marx had previously ridiculed.

Althusser's analysis of the irreversible 'epistemological break' in the work of Marx, therefore, has as its real function only one of legitimation: it permits Marxism to believe itself a superior form of social analysis. The epistemological problem can be seen directly in Marx's own argument (taken up by Althusser): 'It requires a fully developed production of commodities before, from experience alone, the scientific truth springs up' (in Baudrillard, 1975a: 116). There is an intimate connection between commodity production and the Marxist conception of science. As Althusser says, 'the present form of capitalist production has produced scientific truth itself in its invisible reality'. Baudrillard immediately denounces this, first as a vicious circularity (the science is intimately bound up with the social order it is supposed to transcend), and second, as Marx was bound to a particular phase of capitalism which has since become history completely new forms of scientificity would render Marxism obsolete.

These two points sum up Baudrillard's own predicament at the end of this critique of Marxist theory. On the one hand, his position has moved decisively towards that of symbolic exchange which has now become a firm basis for launching a critique of bourgeois and Marxist theory. On the other hand: 'one preserves the fundamental form of the Marxist critique of political economy but forces its content to break out beyond that of material production alone' (Baudrillard, 1975a:118).

WHAT IS LEFT OF MARX

Thus, Baudrillard still wants an option on the possibility of developing Marxist theory into a new period. Indeed this is one important way to read Baudrillard's theoretical development and has been one of the ways in which his work has been adopted and used by other writers. At this point in his work he argues that if a development of Marxist theory is possible, it would point to a new phase of capitalism and its features would involve a perspective in which the sphere of productive forces is so expanded that the distinction between the base and superstructure, between the economic and the cultural has broken down completely. Traditional Marxist theory cannot respond to this without itself undergoing a complete transformation. The problem, he asks rhetorically, is whether Marxism remains Marxism if it is pushed to the limit in this way?

Baudrillard's point of departure in discussing these problems is a formulation of the evolution of capital in Marx (from *The Poverty of Philosophy* by Marx), presented by Baudrillard as a critical genealogy. Its first moment is the society in which important sectors remain outside of commodity exchange and only certain forms of surplus are exchanged, the second, is the society in which the whole of industrial product is exchanged (capitalist society), the third, is the society where previously protected areas also enter the sphere of exchange value (virtue, love, knowledge, etc. fall into this sphere in an era of 'general corruption' and 'universal venality'). Baudrillard says, 'it is necessary to give this genealogy all of its analytical force' (1975a:119).

This is in part attempted by Lukacs in the theory of reification, and by the situationists in the theory of the 'spectacle'. But these are still securely fixated with Marx in a conception where infrastructure and a class struggle are sited in production. Very few critiques of modern capitalist cultures get further than reducing culture to the commodity form and criticising it as prostituted. But what if Marx's own genealogy is forced to the limit? In that case 'it is the form-spectacle that is determinant . . . this step, truly overturns perspectives regarding politics, revolution, the proletariat and social classes' (Baudrillard, 1975a: 121). The obvious objection to this idea, that commodity forms still dominate, is in fact to confuse generality with domination, a mistake he insists Marx himself never made.[18] The point is that despite generality, the commodity form has given way to the sign form. This means the code of equivalence has become more significant than the exchange of commodities. This conception is to be distinguished from any simple notion of the prostitution of culture or the reduction of culture to money (a view that can be found in the *Communist Manifesto*). Value, henceforth, is dominated by exchange sign value, which is deeper and involves a form of oppression more profound than that of simple exploitation: more extensive, open to manipulation and is yet even more illegible. Instead of acting on relations of work and exploitation, these structures like those of reification, act on the definition of reality. The principal site of social conflict does not any more concern ownership of the means of production, it is now within the operation of the code; yet the new code, increasingly active throughout the society, is largely lived in the unconscious, a completely materialist proposition (if the term is still meaningful, he suggests (Baudrillard, 1975a:123)). The project here is to test the extent to which Marxism is still meaningful, and whether its logic can be developed to account for a new period:

> to rescue it from the limited dimensions of a Euclidean geometry of history in order to test its possibility of becoming what it perhaps is, a truly general theory. . . . It postulates a dialectical continuity between the political economy of the commodity and the political economy of the sign.
>
> (ibid)

Baudrillard returns to Marx again on the concept of monopoly (*The Poverty of Philosophy*) to show that at one point for Marx, labour and production may one day cease to be the decisive elements. This prediction may now be the case, and, if it is, the whole strategy in the system has moved to a different level, a level in which the dialectical progression may not operate.

This new strategic level is that of consumption and the control of demand. Here the new forces focus on needs, culture, information and sexuality, which are at the same time defused and manipulated. Previous contradictions are now neutralised or integrated into a new framework: one in which demand based on new ideology of needs arises on the basis of a new mode of simulation. New responses, new technical means, are induced into the the system in a new phase of indulgence: it can play with revolutionary signs and can annihilate them, through its control of the code. The new order is an immense game, where all values are equalised and can be exchanged in a cross-societal levelling. This spells the end of the sign as something which could produce status distinction in conspicuous consumption. The referent, 'reality', as a basis for the production of distinction is abolished: 'the signifier becomes its own referent'.

The implications of this are further elaborated as mutations within capitalism: with monopoly capitalism sign value becomes dominant, and as it does so it begins to eclipse the notion of use value as a basis of the world of commodities. Need as an ideological category has ceased to be autonomous; it is henceforth socially coded. Consumption itself is not anymore simply a field of enjoyment but is still under the constraint of production, which paradoxically, becomes meaningful only in relation to itself. As production for its own sake begins to assert itself it becomes abstract, and neutralises all opposition. This is the moment when finance capital becomes autonomous from industrial capital on an international scale. It must be read as the triumph of the code of general equivalence of all things, the increasing possibility of sign exchanges of all realities. The cost is the dialectic, which no longer finds a place in the social order; production is relegated to a particular instance of a wider process (which in turn dominates it). The 'capitalist mode of production' is one which corresponds to an early phase of the development of the system, in fact more broadly determined as the system of political economy. Now the 'centre of gravity' has been displaced monopoly capitalism should no longer be regarded as a mode of production: finance capital is the dominant form of capital, determined now by the structural law of the code.

The new phase also alters the complex pattern of the forces of opposition and dissent. Essentially, he argues, it was in the phase of early capitalism that the primary tactic of the system imposed the discipline of the proletariat in the process of production. If ever there was a possibility of dialectical struggle! In the new phase the tactic has changed and the meaning of work also. Instead of workers being the centre of revolt it is those excluded from work who are alienated. It is the 'reverse of capitalism's initial situation' (Baudrillard, 1975a: 132): for now all social groups appear to struggle to get into the process of production, and the alienated are those who are not included. New sectors, the 'irresponsible', are created, and it is these that carry on the revolt. The forces of opposition are themselves not located within the structure, they attack it from without. The system now finds it has to educate and socialise and to counter the possibility of disaffection and subversion which arises from sites outside the productive order.

These include students, blacks, women, youth and the non-integrated apathetic silent majority. As the system becomes established and concentrated, it begins to exclude deviant groups. In the past, it was the mad who were confined outside society. Today, he argues, the whole society has become a place of confinement. It is our culture which has produced the rigid distinction between male and female and between black and white. Now the women's revolt or gay liberation are not aimed simply at democratic equality but more profoundly, he argues: they threaten the code which condemns and excludes them. They threaten, that is, the imposition of the law of value in the domain of sexuality (the phallus, the masculine as general standard of value equivalence). Again, blacks do not simply attack discrimination on the grounds of its economic cause or consequence. The system cannot respond other than by renewing the code in which the discrimination is produced. In the case of youth, again, the question is not intelligible in economic terms. Youth is expelled to a non-place, not to a social-class space, it cuts across other categories, it is marked by its formidable irresponsibility. It is thus paradoxical he argues that in the new situation with the oppression of youth, women, blacks, the aged, etc, Marxism itself becomes exploited as an ideology as soon as it begins to assert the primacy of the economic: 'the system now plays on the economic reference . . . as an alibi against the more serious subversion that threatens it in the symbolic order' (Baudrillard, 1975a: 139). And the new subversive elements cannot be made visible within the old framework of prolonged dialectical struggle. Today subversion has become transversal[19] (not connected necessarily with the economic base), and non-dialectical (since the repressed term does not necessarily imply negativity of a dialectical type).[20] More significant today is that which transgresses,[21] and deconstructs.[22] There is no longer a paradigmatic revolutionary class subject to which all can be related or reduced.

FOR A UTOPIAN PRACTICE

If there is no revolutionary subject, there is nevertheless both the open revolt of the dissidents on the one hand arising outside of the system, and especially the political system, and the 'immense, latent defection, the endemic, masked resistence of a silent majority' which is itself 'nostalgic for the spoken word and for violence' (Baudrillard, 1975a: 141). There is more than this; there is an inherent weakness at the heart of the present order, to be found at the level of production but not in the way predicted by Marx. The critical problem in modern capitalism is that it has a 'fatal incapacity to reproduce itself symbolically'. In all orders where the symbolic order is violated, production feeds directly into a system of power and exploitation. In fact it appears, to look at it the other way round that, he says, the symbolic exchange system is now the 'radical negation of capitalism'. Capitalism cannot escape this consequence (for 'liberation' is possible under capitalism only in the one form: production).

And consumption? After the slump of the 1930s it became paramount for capital to conquer the realm of consumption, to mobilise the consumer. This was achieved through the illusion of participation, of symbolic simulation. Yet it has never been able to recapture the festival as a form of symbolic exchange, since the fundamental connection in the capitalist order between consumption and production breaks it up. Consumption has to be accomplished in such a way as to reproduce production. Even leisure is caught in the system, and cannot be allowed to escape the connection with production: it cannot be wasted or idled or disconnected from value.[23]

The same problem is found at the level of power and the control over exchange of communication. Once the spoken word is monopolised there, a power differential is created. Given the control over exchange of words, the symbolic order is destroyed and integration rests on manipulation. The paradoxical consequence is that the system becomes sick from tolerance, permissiveness. The system appears to give way, yet this marks new hyper-repressive forms (Baudrillard, 1975a: 146). Against the apparent relaxation in fields like information and ecology, there is a real increase in management and controlled manipulation. The effect is to block even further the action of the symbolic order: it is a further universalising of the code:

> but against the triumphant abstraction, against irreversible monopolisation, the demand arises that nothing can be given without being returned, nothing is ever won without something being lost, nothing is ever produced without something being destroyed, nothing is ever spoken without being answered. In short, what haunts the system is the symbolic demand.
>
> (ibid:147)

This leads Baudrillard to conclude that the principal struggle today is not a political but a cultural revolution. Or rather, even more decisively, his formulation is that the cultural revolution 'must make itself against the economic–political revolution' (ibid: 151).

Baudrillard begins to connect the poetic and the utopian vision to this conception of culture. It is as if Marx was right, he says, in general, but in the form of a misunderstanding. Out of the radical utopias which existed at the time of the *Manifesto* (1848), Marx theorised a social revolt. But instead of this objective analysis, there is something else, the direct word of the poet – communist prophecy. For the poet the political analysis is a postponement. These utopian movements are the equivalent of those which fought the rupture of symbolic exchange itself. Poetry was never directly connected with this rational Marxism (for which the revolution will come in its time). For the poet, the important thing is the immediate realisation of utopia. 'Poetry and the utopian revolt have this radical presentness in common . . . the actualisation of desire no longer relegated to a future liberation, but demanded here, immediately' (Baudrillard, 1975a:165).[24]

Finally, in this critique, Baudrillard tries to define his new position: unashamedly utopian. In contrast to the Marxist conception of revolution as an outcome of alienation, of a conception of humankind as bound to a total project, utopia is not really connected to a conception of alienation at all. Time, in this conception (symbolic) is quite different. It is not linear, or historical. Utopia, in this conception is not to be regarded as something in the future, to be waited for. In Marxist theory the actual moment of revolt, is only an aspect of the revolution. For symbolic theory, every society is already a complete totality, always already present. Here there is no room for a theory of alienated essence which will be recovered at some future point. For each person is completely present at each moment. The communards were not concepts, they were the revolution, and their speech is not aimed at any recovery of an alienated essence: it is symbolic, and complete. Utopia is a violence that is non-cumulative; it is lost, annulled in the revolution. It does not transform itself into power. What the revolutionary demands is not the taking of power by the exploited at all (a completely false and dangerous demand), but rather the word against power (and its reality principle).

In the last section of this chapter, I will consider Baudrillard's critique of psychoanalysis, and then of the work of Michel Foucault.

PSYCHOANALYSIS, MIRROR OF DESIRE

Baudrillard's main critical writing against psychoanalysis is developed in the mid-1970s against the concept of the unconscious, in order to clarify some of the implications of his theory of symbolic exchange for Freudian theory.[25]

Baudrillard's argument is that modern psychoanalysis has to be placed in a larger context which will relativise some of its overly ambitious claims. In the first instance it is necessary to suggest that the claim for the universality of the individual unconscious may be completely false (this is argued in the main body of the text, where Baudrillard supports Ortiques' view that in primitive societies the oedipal relation is socially structured (Baudrillard, 1976: 208–15)). Second, the critical, and deconstructive work of Freud has now been turned around into a positive formal entity, and hence has become a problem of the same type as that of Marxism. Baudrillard's strategy throughout his discussion of Freud and psychoanalysis is to work on the difference between the topography of the psyche as assumed in Freud and, again, that of the social process of symbolic exchanges. Just as the symbolic is incompatible, in Baudrillard, with the sign and with modern linguistics based on the notion of the universality of the sign, so his position develops a consistent attack on the notion of the unconscious as involving the same kind of assumptions. Thus he poses in the most direct way the question: 'what is the status of desire and the unconscious in poetic discourse?' (Baudrillard, 1981c:60).[26]

His argument is posed in the form of a challenge: it is necessary to read psychoanalysis from the point of view of the symbolic (after all, he says, wryly, 'analysis must always be reciprocal' (Baudrillard, 1981c: 60)).[27] It is also clear in the light of Baudrillard's own intellectual biography with its very heavy dependence on Freud and Lacan that what is involved here is perhaps a recovery of a position lost in the period of this *rapprochement* with Althusser and Lacan. Essentially, he argues, the symbolic must not be identified or confused with the Freudian notion of primary process, and second it must not be confused with the unconscious. His argument is that in a key text like that of Freud's analysis of jokes, there is a theoretical failure to distinguish between the analysis of a symptom, and a work of art as such. The concept of 'sublimation' in psychoanalytic literature is poorly defined and open to all kinds of abuse. If there is something in the poetic work of art which makes it different from the slip, parapraxis or joke, there is a fundamental and fatal gap in psychoanalytic theory. In generalising an inappropriate – in the last instance, idealist – concept to the poetic, psychoanalysis becomes reductionist and vulgar. Freud's theory is intimately bound up with a notion of an economy of energy, and this is used to explain the displacements which erupt in the joke as a function of the pleasure principle. In the same way there is a vulgar form of analysis which tries to argue that the pleasure derived from the poetic is a form of accumulation of energy, a kind of 'pleasure profit' on the model of a capitalist enterprise (Baudrillard, 1981c:62).

Behind this term (energy) it is not difficult to find a notion which might be called the mode of production of the unconscious, a conception of pleasure as either a saving or a surplus (note, he insists, not an excess, not a process of destruction and annihilation of energy). The elaboration of Freudian theory gives rise to the idea of the individual mind as a 'gigantic laboratory' of processes, forms, displacements, available as a site for the release of repressed elements. The medium of the joke permits the relay of energy and material so that the signifier never produces its own effects. This occurs only through the route of desire. This is also evident in the theory of propping (*étayage*) where the body's own physiological processes are diverted so as to invest a new zone with libido. There is, also, an appeal to 'needs' of the psyche, a fundamental, theoretical misunderstanding, linked, via anaclisis, to an unquestioned notion of elemental desire (this parallels some of the assumptions in linguistics around the notion of the motivation of the sign). These are at best provisional links and are sustained only on the basis of theoretical assertion. (In fact, he concludes, they are wholly misguided and illegitimate connections.) The notion of an autonomous desire, for example, is entirely an effect of the way in which illegitimate models have been uncritically imported into analysis.

Yet psychoanalysis does itself bring about a shift in the relation between signifier and signified in the direction of the poetic: the representation of a loss. This negativity does not appear in linguistic theory, with its theory of the arbitrary nature of the sign. In psychoanalysis, on the other hand, the relationship to the lost or absent object is a necessary, not arbitrary relation. For example, Leclaire says:

> In psychoanalysis the concept of representation would be situated not at all between an objective reality on the one hand and its significant image on the other, but rather between an hallucinated reality, a memory image of a lost satisfying object, on one hand, and a substitute object on the other hand, whether that would be a formula-object, like the one that

constituted the fantasy, or an instrumental gadget, such as a fetish might be.

(cited in Baudrillard, 1981c:64–5)

Equivalence at the linguistic level is lost. And again in what Baudrillard calls a remarkable passage, Mannoni is quoted at length:

It is when the signifier is introduced that meaning is toppled over. And that is not because the signifier carried with it a collection of signifieds such as could be charted by a semantics of the traditional sort. It is because we interpret Saussure's ellipsis as if it kept the place of the signified empty, a place which can only be filled in the different discourses of which a unique signifier is then the common feature. If we, too, relieve the signifier of the weight of the signified, it is not in order to turn it over to the laws which linguistics discovers in all manifest discourse, but so that it can be said to obey the law of the primary process, by which it escapes, if only for a brief, faltering moment, from the constraints of the apparent discourse, which always tends towards the unequivocal even when exploiting an ambiguity.

(cited in Baudrillard, 1981c:64)

For Baudrillard, this represents a proposition in psychoanalysis which is entirely self-subverting: the possibility of submitting the linguistic categories to this manoeuvre may 'blow up' the bar between the signifier and the signified. (On the nature of these Saussurean categories see Gane, 1983a: 10–15.)

Again, a discussion by Benveniste of the problem of non-contradiction in language is cited by Baudrillard as establishing a fundamental problem:

The specific feature of language being to express only what it is possible to express. . . . To imagine a stage in the development of a language . . . in which a certain object would be denoted as being itself and at the same time any other, and in which the relationship expressed would be itself and other than itself, thus neither itself nor other, is to conceive a purely chimerical notion.

(cited in Baudrillard, 1981c: 65)

Baudrillard is scathing in his comment on this remark:

Benveniste knows what he is talking about, for the entire linguistic rationalisation exists specifically to prevent that. The ambivalence of the repressed does not risk surfacing in linguistic science, because that science is entirely part of the mechanism of repression.

(ibid)

The thrust of Baudrillard's argument here, then, is to question the absolute insistence of the linguistic relation of the signifier and signified, and its Saussurean implications defended by Benveniste, against the apparent contradictions in psychoanalytic theory. The very equation, says Baudrillard, 'must be broken' (1981c:65). Psychoanalysis seems caught in a dilemma and just makes the best use of the available tools: if the bar (between the signifier and the signified) has changed its meaning it still functions to produce linguistic value (through repression). It is caught, Baudrillard suggests, between equivalence (of sr/sd) and the complete dissolution of value as such. It is at this point that the poetic becomes a challenge and threat to the established assumptions, since the poetic is the route to the dissolution of value as symptom, fantasy or fetish. The fetishised object is saturated with values in its striking opacity. The system of values cannot be unlocked, there is, in contrast to the symbolic process, an obsession: the 'accomplishment of perverse desire . . . fills the empty form with meaning' (ibid: 66). In psychoanalysis, therefore, the assumption is that the object is displaced, not resolved, and finds its reality on 'a surface indexed on the heavy reality of the unconscious' (ibid).

The poetic must be thought outside this system as: diffraction, dispersion, irradiation, anagrammatic in its very nature. This cannot be grasped under the notion of a law of value, as there is no repressed content which can remain the subject of a systematic displacement. What exists here is lived without anxiety as dissemination, extinction of value: in total and non-perverse pleasure. In art there is, he insists, no repression, no residue and no return: there is a suspension of inhibition. It plays the hand of its own death, without reserve or restriction, to the dissolution of meaning. Meaning, on the other hand in psychoanalytic theory, is played at the cost of silencing a voice, and the return of the repressed continues to haunt it. The poetic does not silence anything, and nothing returns to haunt it. It does not, in fact, mean anything, since death, nothingness and absence are spoken and resolved. Indeed: 'death is manifest, at last it is symbolised, whereas it is symptomatic in all other formations of discourse' (Baudrillard, 1981c: 68). If this is so, it spells the end for psychoanalysis, for if death itself speaks, psychoanalysis, notes Baudrillard, has nothing more to say.[28]

Take the position of a poet like Rimbaud, Baudrillard suggests. He (Rimbaud) says of his poetry: *it is true in every sense*. There is nothing hidden, nothing is concealed. Linguistics and psychoanalysis take the opposite view. The difference between these two positions is fundamental and irresolvable. On the one hand, the symbolic order possesses no signified, there is no dream thought behind it, no latent process, no energy potential and no productive economy. For psychoanalysis there is separation, castration and repression: that which is said and that which is silenced. An economy productive of energy always finds a remainder, a surplus, a meaning.

To establish this difference more clearly Baudrillard returns to the example of jokes, and to the possibility of a completely different theory (from that of Freud). Instead of proposing a pleasure based on 'savings' it may be possible to propose that pleasure comes from: 'a point prior to the very discrimination of structures, and therefore prior to the differential movement of cathexes and therefore from a point prior to or outside the realm of psychoanalysis and its order of logic' (Baudrillard, 1981c: 70). This, at least, raises the possibility that pleasure may be derived from another source, a short circuit, a conflagration. Words may lose meaning in a direct *rapprochement*. Indeed, the poetic moment of the joke may be beyond desire or fantasy, and may lie in the annihilation of the repressive moment. This idea was already known to Kant, whom Freud quotes: 'The comic is an expectancy which is resolved into nothingness, which dissolves into nothing' (Kant, in Baudrillard, 1981c: 70).

Baudrillard gives the example of a joke by Lichtenberg: a knife has a new handle and a new blade: this knife is without 'its' handle and has lost 'its' blade. Baudrillard says a knife is the product of the separate naming of handle and blade: 'if the separation between the two is removed (and the blade and handle can only be joined in their respective disappearance . . .) there is no longer anything there at all – except pleasure' (Baudrillard, 1981c: 71). For Baudrillard this is a key form of poetic wit: there is a resolution, but into nothing, and there is nothing behind this nothing. It simply represents the end of separation, it is the end of the unconscious. And all the examples which Freud gives, says Baudrillard, can all be recognised as having this form.

Baudrillard takes another example, in the German: *Eifersucht ist eine Leidenschaft, die mit Eifer sucht, was Leiden schafft* (translated as 'jealousy is a passion which obstinately seeks that which causes suffering'). One interpretation obviously has implications of a 'capitalist' type: the technique is one of accumulation, of addition. The other is radical; what happens here is a cancellation, as Saussure has suggested, in the anagrammatic form. The effect is an excess of pleasure, 'not in the transversality of the signifier under the effect of the primary process, but in the total revolution of the signifier upon itself' (Baudrillard, 1981c:73). This analysis is very different from that of Freud's which insists on the importance of condensation effects as the explanatory category, and the lifting of inhibitions allowing a release of energy to the surface; in effect, a reinscription 'in terms of content, of an original "source" or "liberation"' (ibid: 74).

Finally, Baudrillard points to the social character of humour and jokes. If the effect of the joke is, as Freud claims, a release of energy in the individual, the joke would be largely an individual phemenon. In fact its social character evokes its shared nature. Stories and jokes are exchanged and consumed like all symbolic prestations, like gifts, even to 'a veritable potlatch of stories, produced in succession one after another, in which an entire group is mobilized' not as an effect of individual choice but as the necessary effect of the obligation of the group itself.

THE CRITIQUE OF FOUCAULT

As a postscript to this period of critiques it is possible also, perhaps, to add Baudrillard's discussion of the work of Foucault (although this appeared as a separate essay a little later, in 1977 (Baudrillard, 1977b)). Its main lines of criticism are similar to those already developed, where a conception of symbolic cultures are used as a basis for contesting Foucault's whole conceptualisation of power.[29] It is clear that, from Baudrillard's point of view, Foucault, too, has not been able to escape the entrapment of the modern code, for discourse is not simply about power, it is in itself of power:

> It flows, it invests and saturates, the entire space it opens. The smallest qualifiers find their way into the slightest interstices of meaning; clauses and chapters wind into spirals; a magisterial art of decentering allows the opening of new spaces (spaces of power and of discourse) which are immediately covered up by . . . meticulous outpouring. . . . In short Foucault's discourse is a mirror of the power it describes.
>
> (Baudrillard, 1987c: 9–10)

This is obviously an important comment, not just on Foucault but in its ramifications for the reading of Baudrillard's own work. From this point in his career Baudrillard was concerned to develop new forms of writing. Here is a brief indication that Baudrillard continued to enlarge and defend his view that there were in fact only two very basic and contrasting cultures and each had its own form of writing: one, based on the accumulation of meaning and effects (and power), the other which is based on symbolic exchanges, a form, which very precisely cancels and annuls the accumulation of power.

Baudrillard's own relation to Foucault is itself interesting. In some writings and interviews, it is Foucault above all who had come to carry the mantle of French intellectuals after Sartre. But later, in his autobiographical essays, Baudrillard had some severe comments on the way that Foucault allowed himself to be surrounded by uncritical admirers. In theoretical style, and in method, there really could not be greater contrast between Foucault and Baudrillard, and Baudrillard makes this plain immediately: power is dead and Foucault's discourse is only possible because power is dead. Indeed, Foucault is the 'last great dinosaur of the classical age'. In a sense, however, he says: Foucault was probably aware that his writing was not a simple empirical account of power. It is not in its ability to reveal truth that this writing is seductive, but that it mirrors power, and it probably 'has no illusions about the effect of truth it produces': it is mythic. The problem appears to be that the writing itself is too perfect. Indeed 'too perfect to be true'. This is indicative of the fact that perhaps the age of power is over, devoured in a new reality.

From the start something fundamental had escaped Foucault, Baudrillard argues: although the genealogy of power passes from the despotic, to the microcellular the underlying axiom is the presumed existence of power as both a truth and a reality. This is parallel to Foucault's own discussion of sexuality. It may well be, quite inconsistently with Foucault's own idea, that these are in the process of disappearance. When a stage of thinking is reached where it is suggested that 'everything' is sex, or power, this could well indicate the crisis of this phenomenon not its omnipresence. The problem in Foucault's own theory is that it is completely dependent on traditional definitions of the object, despite his radical reformulations.[30] His conception of sexuality says Baudrillard is fundamentally a semiological one, and incapable of following current spirals in which unprecendented doublings and redoublings occur. Barthes, on the other hand, has said, quite correctly, that 'sexuality is everywhere except in sex'. If this is true, Foucault is too late, just as is his theory of power: magisterial, but obsolete.

Foucault discusses and rejects any universal principle of repression in sexual relations, of, for example, given sexual drives, which might be diverted into production giving rise to some notion of sublimation. But in discussing this, says Baudrillard, Foucault passes too quickly over another possibility: that repression might originate from farther away and might be a repression through sex not of sex. This might work from discourse to discourse, governed by exactly the same 'ultimatum' as that found in production. Instead of reduplicating this mechanism, it has to be recognised that 'to produce is to force what belongs to another order (that of secrecy and seduction) to materialise' (Baudrillard, 1987c: 21). If this is the case, then modern culture is truly pornographic and dependent on a new notion of the real as related to separate social instances or layers, including sex itself. It is this which Foucault uncritically adopts.

The way this can be made visible is through an understanding of other cultures:

> which maintain long processes of seduction and sensuousness in which sexuality is one service among others, a long procedure of gifts and countergifts; love making is only the eventual outcome of this reciprocity measured to the rhythm of an ineluctable ritual.
>
> (Baudrillard, 1987c: 23)

This no longer makes much sense in our own society, where the conception of the sexual is that of a realisation of a specific desire. Here ritual is subordinated to the natural. The idea that the soul is to be saved is abandoned in favour of a principle of the use of the body. Just as capital drives towards use, so too is the body used, it must accumulate pleasure. Thus the body seems to have no other purpose than a functional one.

In fact, Foucault, in the end, arrives at this view, perhaps in spite of himself, says Baudrillard. It is not repression that is the key term, it is still production. Foucault has not grasped that they are, in fact, no different. The fact there is no repression in primitive or earlier societies is simply the result of the fact that only in our own society is there 'sexuality' as such. It is

made apparent in certain kinds of theory which appear at a specific moment
of history: this can mislead understanding completely. The crucial question
to ask of a theory such as Foucault's is what existed before sex. Foucault in
fact says it was 'the body and its pleasure' (*ars erotica*). Baudrillard notes,
in violent, bitter contrast, that sex put an end:

> to something more radical, a configuration where not only sex and desire
> but even the body and pleasure are not specified as such. . . . Foucault's
> 'pleasures' are still opposed to the 'exchange value of the sexual' only
> insofar as they constitute the use value of the body.
>
> (Baudrillard, 1987c: 32–3)

Thus it is certainly not innocent to begin to specify that which has been
denied.

In the case of power, for example, it is possible to ask if it is not the
case that the previous powers to create the real have not simply declined.
If power simply reproduces itself and in so doing arrives at the more real
than real, then it, too, is threatened: the end of the real will also be the end
of power and of sex. It is probably no accident, says Baudrillard, that the
theories of power of Foucault and of desire in Deleuze, are so remarkably
similar. Foucault, in fact, specifically avoids talking about desire, and for a
very good reason: should he do so the whole problematic of power would
convert into that of desire. If they are mirror images, there is only one
adequate way forward, says Baudrillard, 'forget them both' (Baudrillard,
1987c: 19).[31]

But this kind of crisis of power cannot even really be conceived in
Foucault's theory since power is a kind of eternal substance, power
does not have catastrophic vicissitudes. In its latest form it has simply
become microphysical. And here there is another complicity, this time
with modern genetics (Monod). It appears that this new cellular form of
power is radical, but it is important to see where this is leading. In fact it
does not contain any revolutionary principle at all, as can be seen clearly
in Deleuze and Guattari's analysis of Kafka where the transcendental law
is counterposed to that of the immanence of desire. In fact, desire is only
the 'molecular version of the law' (Baudrillard, 1987c: 35). There is no way
out here.

But the the type of analysis found in *Discipline and Punish*, the object
of Baudrillard's critique, is, he argues, quite different from that of his
earlier works. Foucault could have constructed a genealogy which would
have shown say in relation to sexuality that it would have gone through
a confinement stage (similar to that of madness), where it could ferment
and become the excluded term of a reasoned and repressive discourse.
Sexuality and madness would become close terms and interchanges would
be possible. But the way in which Foucault's analysis works out, the
universe is always full, sex and power are everywhere. Yet it remains
a mystery: the world maintains a unity but only the unity of a 'cracked

windscreen'. It is like Pere Ubu's polyhedra, like crabs which march off in all directions.[32] It comes as a 'divine surprise', says Baudrillard, that there is a 'resistance' to power. But this is only more power to which everything returns. And instead of being broken down at the microlevel, it still functions as a structural term. In this framework power cannot be surpassed, reversed or undermined. At any moment, one particular form of power dominates and is refracted in Foucault's analysis, and it is this which ultimately fabricates the reality of power, as a 'dictature without appeal'. It does not cancel itself, it is always the last word.

Foucault is simply quite wrong to conceptualise power in this way, power can always be reversed (Baudrillard, 1987c: 42). If power could be held as a substance in any case, it could not exist, it would be cancelled in one way or another. Foucault's notion is that power is distributional. But the same objection holds: either power would have crushed all resistance and would have collapsed under its own weight. Something, in the end, actually resists such expansion to the infinite. And this is true throughout the culture. There is always something which prevents ultimate accumulation (to death). This is decisive, and this is what is absent from Foucault's theory: power is something that is in fact exchanged, not in a crude capitalist sense, 'but in the sense that power is executed according to a reversible cycle of seduction challenge and ruse. . . . And if power cannot be exchanged in this sense, it purely and simply disappears' (Baudrillard 1987c: 43).

The implication Baudrillard maintains is that the terms dominator and dominated have to be reconstructed or abandoned, but: 'exploiters and exploited do in fact exist, they are on different sides because there is no reversibility in production, which is precisely the point: nothing essential in fact happens at that level' (Baudrillard, 1987c: 44). There are no fixed positions where something significant does happen, where in other words there is a genuine 'cycle of seduction'.

This is why, in the end, seduction is always stronger than production: it is always reversible. Power can seek a form that is irreversible, it seeks to become real, to become unilateral. But it can never escape the seduction which envelops it. In fact, production itself would never interest anyone if it were not for seduction elsewhere.

Now having completed his discussion of Foucault, Baudrillard is tempted to lay out a kind of positional statement, rather in the way that earlier at the end of *Mirror of Production*, he presented a vision of cultural revolution. It has, as its epigraph, a phrase of Kafka which marks a decisive change of mood in Baudrillard's work: 'The Messiah will only come when he will be no longer necessary. . . . He will not come on the day of the Last Judgement, but on the day after.' Baudrillard gives into this in theory in the most dramatic way possible: the revolution has either been accomplished or it will never occur, or, if it occurs, it will only be because it is no longer necessary (a sign that it has happened). An entire period has come to an end, yet few have realised it: 'And they will play the game of linear revolution, whereas it has already curved upon itself to produce its simulacrum, like stucco angels whose extremities join in a curved mirror' (Baudrillard, 1987c:50).

Theoretically this is a vital point for Baudrillard's later position: 'All things come to an end in their redoubled simulation – a sign that a cycle is completed.' All things, as they approach their death, he suggests, fall 'far behind the horizon of truth'. And this might well be the case with power itself. The immense proliferation of appearances of power are available only on condition that it is dead. Power was never a thing, it was always a play of theatre: when this is operationalised, it is a sign that it is in a state of collapse. Power is not even an instance, it is only a 'challenge'. All the contemporary forms of the appearance of power have as their function the concealment of the death of the social which is its complement. In these conditions it is the challenge which is escalated to the limit, and which: 'Dares those who hold power to exercise it to the limit' (Baudrillard, 1987c: 54). In the past, power was part of a symbolic order, and it could not transcend death. But even when power has sought to escape the order of the symbolic it is still haunted by death. It is always haunted by the challenge, and against this it has found defences in liberal democratic structures.[33] In fact, these have only further weakened it. Modern analyses completely fail to grasp that the challenge is not dialectical, not cumulative.

Take feminism, he suggests. The feminine always exerts a possible reversibility towards the masculine. Indeed the feminine challenge is to:

> reserve sex and to deny pleasure (women's), continuous refraction of sexual power into the void has always exerted an incalculable pressure, with no possibility of response . . . except headlong flight into phallocracy. Today phallocracy is crumbling under this very challenge, taking with it all forms of traditional sexuality – and not at all due to social pressure from any sort of feminine liberation.
>
> (Baudrillard, 1987c: 56–7)

Thus the perspective that develops here on historical struggles is quite different from that of Foucault's, or even that of Marx, whose writings on French history is specifically political. The French working class, however, in 1848 and 1871, and of the oppressed classes even in 1968, tried not to act on the real, but, says Baudrillard, to act out the 'death of the class itself – it chose to implode' and did not opt for hegemony at all. This is only explicable at the level of symbolic exchange.

Thus, for politicians power becomes a problem when it does not exist. This is the same for the church: its power is greatest when the clergy realises that God and His power do not exist, but the masses think He does. Only on this basis is the political force of parody explicable, far more deadly than direct confrontation:

Power is only truly sovereign when it grasps this secret and confronts itself with that very challenge. When it ceases to do so and pretends to find a truth, a substance, or a representation (in the will of the people etc.) then it loses its sovereignty.

(Baudrillard, 1987c: 59)

This is the meaning of Kafka's phrase. When talk of power is omnipresent, it is a sign that it is too late. It is only a form of nostalgia, fascinating because it is dead. It is obscene, its forms are like so many resurrections. Its forms of appearance even are exacerbated as in fascist forms which bring a kind of aesthetics of death. Indeed Foucault's fascination is of the same order of simulation as that of fascism.[34] But power cannot be saved, the cycle cannot be subverted. Its end can happen in an instant.

Part III

*We find the avant-garde in the cool
and the primitive*
                    (McLuhan, 1967: 36)

7 Cultural implosion

. . . the inversion of received scenarios.
Baudrillard (1983a: 11)

A series of short papers followed the period of critiques, considering, in a new unprecedented style, some remarkable theses: the death of the social, and the implosion of meaning in the media. (These papers were in *In the Shadow of the Silent Majorities* . . . 'Or, The death of the social' (1983a, 1–94), 'The implosion of meaning in the media' (1983a, 95–112) and 'The masses: the implosion of the social in the media' (1988b: 207–219): they date from 1978–85). These essays provoked a wide discussion (see for instance Zylberberg (ed.) 1986) and have been the object of a fierce criticism. Here the main objective is to present and assess their main ideas in the logic of Baudrillard's overall project.

NEW STYLES

These papers inaugurate a different and highly original continuation of his Marxist phase, and in some senses this is acknowledged. It is difficult to locate his position within any orthodox classification for as he says, it is neither optimistic nor pessimistic. This mood is elusive, it is rather a genre of inverted utopianism (if this can be grasped). Certainly the key concept is that of the mass. Yet it is never defined in a specific, or coherent way. There also appear to be some awkward reconceptualisations. Essentially he wants to develop a black imagery of the mass as the centre of gravity of the society, a version perhaps of the Marxist thesis that the masses make history but in the age when there is no history to be made; yet even this stands in some tension which his apparent concentration on the immanent logic cultural forms in his work more generally, in which social-class analysis is little in evidence: classes are absorbed (pataphysically) into the mass.

But these papers actually present a dramatic recasting of Baudrillard's social doctrine, and is, in a sense, a possible basis for a new, and perhaps half-resigned, ironic reconciliation with forces in the current system (not the system itself, of course). Previously, Baudrillard's main social analyses concerned the class logic of culture in modern society, in terms of cultural simulation: the bourgeoisie simulating the tastes of the aristocracy, the petit bourgeoisie the bourgeoisie, and so forth towards the ambient culture of compromise. Now Baudrillard replaces the term petit bourgeoisie with that of the mass, but viewed in a peculiar way, very remote from classical Marxism's identification of the heroic character of the oppressed classes. It might be called a new exercise in the analysis, not of class logic, but mass logic (though Baudrillard does not use the term). But first it is necessary to look at some of the principal ideas, before returning to the question of the definition of the mass.

The new approach to the examination of these phenomena was provocatively presented as the opposite of sociological reasoning:

> sociology can only depict the expansion of the social and its vicissitudes. It survives only on the positive and definitive hypothesis of the social. The reabsorption, the implosion of the social escapes it. The hypothesis of the death of the social is also that of its own death.
>
> (Baudrillard, 1983b: 4)

Nothing could be clearer: the terms of social analysis have to be totally reconstructed in the new conditions. In this respect Baudrillard attempts to develop a violent and regressive overturning of all the major propositions of modern sociology.

The mass, deprived of its internal structures, heavy with implications of brute reality, is retrieved as a suitable term for the analysis of new relations and processes in a society at the end of a historical cycle. The processes of cultural and social homogenisation (through the mechanisms he has already identified) have dissolved former segregations. Crucially, the basic temporal form of society, however, is no longer that of a progressive, expanding or historical society (itself no doubt partly mythical, with constant entanglement and amalgamation with earlier forms.) Evolution has now not just slowed down, it has entered a phase of contraction in which whole new series of laws apply: a society in a phase of inward implosion. It can now be seen how tempting it is to make Baudrillard's analyses support a thesis of postmodernity, since his writing points to a dramatic, or rather, *the* most dramatic turning point of all, where all the major parameters have to be reconstructed in order to understand what is happening. Baudrillard tries to mark this transformation through the elaboration of a new vocabulary, and new way of writing. He has also tried to find and indentify other analysts who have discovered the same processes at work: these are utopians who fuse powerful poetic imagery and fatal theory. If this change of style, or mode, of writing is fundamental, it also leads to new questions about how to read and assess this new writing.

This has to be understood against the background of Baudrillard's arguments that it is the poetic which is the most radical threat to the current and conventional understanding of language and expression. And it is towards the poetic that his styles are polarised. If this is true, then it is no good to assess these essays on the basis of a previous canon. In Baudrillard's own terms, critics have only been able to accept and grasp his trajectory up to the point at which this kind of writing is compatible and consistent with orthodox Marxism: from the moment that another framework or paradigm or in this case another 'mass position' instead of 'class position', begins to assert itself, critics simply consign it to the sphere of the 'funhouse' (Norris, normally reliable here misses some black humour, 1989) or the 'madhouse'. However, from the point of view of the problems of the new context this is to fall behind the present horizon not to go beyond it. It is clear that Baudrillard's aim is to attack the present order not only from the past, and from the continuing theme of the symbolic order, but from within its mass logic. And it may well be that here, paradoxically, Baudrillard is more consistent with Marx than his Marxist critics.

The discussion of Baudrillard, then, from now on, will follow a new mode of analysis which has explicitly renounced any attempt to go beyond appearances to the unearthing of a latent structure from which it might be possible to read the world. This is not at all to suggest that Baudrillard has made a headlong dash, after years of theory, into the fact, the empirical. Part of the attack on traditional social sciences is precisely, according to Baudrillard, that they are founded on a metaphysic of the real (not aware that this is produced only at a specific historical moment), and which even with its own culture is now no longer tenable. Social sciences from now on partake of that special nostalgia for things which are dead, or in the process of disappearing. Thus, too, it is no longer a question of producing a rational argument for a rational audience to consume by producing a replica of the 'real' as its truth, or of revealing it by tearing away its veils.

On the other hand, it is certainly a mistake to think this is a simple anti-intellectualism, or a form of writing where anything goes.[1] In fact the poetic exercises its own discipline on language. His reconstruction of the theory of primitive cultures as cultures of symbolic exchange, lead to the proposition that Mauss and Saussure converged to a theory of the discipline of these exchanges, which at the level of the poetic could be conceived as anagrammatic exchanges. His own poetic writing (*l'Ange de Stuc* (1978a)), follows this discipline. Paradoxically, instead of ranking alongside aleatoric postmodern poetry, Baudrillard's poetry seems more in line with the highly disciplined styles of earlier French poets (Mallarmé): in a formal sense, a nostalgic modernism rather than some kind of futuristic effervescent postmodernism. Baudrillard's ideology, if this term is appropriate, is certainly very different from that of someone like Durkheim who thought aesthetic experience inherently lacking discipline (a reaction against the ideology of the free, individual spirit creator and excessive egoism). On the contrary, what is evoked is the discipline of ritual obligation in the work of art itself. But if Baudrillard does not appear as avant-garde in poetry, the initiation of a style of (anti-)sociology as prose–poetry, fiction–theory became, immediately, avant-gardist, in a field increasingly dominated by technocratic modes of analysis.

In his earlier writings, Baudrillard approached the analysis of modern consumer societies through an in-depth examination (that is as a complex and overdetermined totality, determined in the last instance by economic structures). This model is now abandoned, it is now, he says, as if each sphere over determines itself (Baudrillard, 1987d: 30), the end of the social itself. The social has dissolved into the 'mass'. The mass is an important and particular image, he suggests,[2] but it is necessary to disassociate it from implications possibly derived from two earlier uses. One from Marxism, which suggests that it is the masses who make history (a term and a concept revived by Althusser). In Marxist theory the masses are the oppressed who form the exploited classes. There is, as Raymond Williams once pointed out in a notable discussion (1961), another connotation where the mass (now equivalent to the working classes) is confused with the 'mob', or the crowd as conceived in the work of Le Bon (see Berthelot in Zylberberg, 1986). These are both active and positive notions.

Baudrillard is not interested in either of these two conceptions. He is only interested in invoking the image of the mass in quite new conditions which will themselves again alter (see the response in his latest work, 1990b: 47). In the social imagination, the 'mass' is either passive (the silent majority) or is frenzied (the mob), but today the condition and meaning of the mass as a silent majority has completely changed: their alleged passivity itself has taken on a new significance. The mass can function now to absorb energy of the social: it, too, has neither history or future, yet it is strategic. It is in the present that the masses are both silent yet have the capacity to absorb and neutralise all that comes from without. The mass, he argues, in a phrase which indicates that he has not altogether lost touch with Marxist principles is 'always superior to any power' acting upon it.

In Baudrillard's imagery, therefore, the mass functions like an 'earth' in an electrical system. It does not irradiate energy, as in other systems, it is inert, neutral and it attracts only to neutralise. And when it absorbs energy in this way no traces are left behind. This mass is implosive, is 'characteristic of modernity' itself.[3] It is outside and functions to block the process of meaning, and contributes itself to the process of the collapse of meaning in society. In an intensification of images, just as is achieved in his essay on the Beaubourg building in Paris, Baudrillard then likens the mass to a 'black hole' collapsing under its own weight: it heralds the death of the social in society. Any sophisticated or subtle attempt to capture this phenomenon in precise empirical categories is to miss the point, he argues. The mass itself corresponds only to this lumpen analytical notion: 'it is by prowling around these soft, and acritical notions (like "mana" once was) that one can go further . . . to want to specify the term "mass" is a mistake' Baudrillard, (1983a: 4–5).[4]

Any attempt to proceed to give a content to a phrase such as 'a mass of workers' is misguided, since the term is the outcome of a statistical mode of constitution of a subject: in this case, he insists, the mass is not a subject or an object. Even if there is a theoretical side to such discourse the 'mass' here is simply an unintegrated endpoint of analysis (its 'refuse'). It has no 'sociological reality' and no reality at all outside this purely statistical construction. He insists that 'it has nothing to do with any real population, body or aggregate' (Baudrillard, 1983a: 5)

Since this mass acts in the neutral, it is not even a polarity. And as the mass is a black hole there is no internal circulation of meaning within it as such. Marx, himself, noted that peasant society was formed on the model of a sack of potatoes permitting no totalisation of meaning; Baudrillard sees the mass in an updated image (making him officially a high-tech theorist) as 'instantaneously dispersed, like atoms in a void' (ibid: 6). It is also without speech, yet is always accompanied by spokesmen who have nothing to say (it is thus certainly not fascist or totalitarian which implies energy and direction). The mass is, as an entity, that which remains 'when the social has been completely removed' (ibid: 6–7).

But Baudrillard's conception of the mass is not simply a force of neutralisation, for it neutralises in a specific way. For example, the idea of God does not reside in the mass, it is a belief of the religious elite. In the mass, this idea gives way to the enchantment of saints and martyrs, the last judgement and sorcery. Even worse, for the elite the mass has never been the subject of the 'anguish' of sin and salvation. Thus, it is not here a question of reading Baudrillard as simply musing on the foibles of a catholic population.

Baudrillard's mass as a social phenomenon today is like the peasants who appear in Carlo Levi's *Christ Stopped at Eboli* (that is outside of history and Christianity, distrustful of all political intentions).[5] In other words, it has remained primarily pagan all along, and has only superficially been touched by Christian or civilised values. Seen in this way the practices of the mass form a specific refusal of meaning but in a participatory manner (while Levi's peasants felt excluded and inferior). There is often the illusion of commitment, the visible sacrifice to a particular cause, but what is not accepted is the 'sublime' demand of religion: anticipation of transcendence: 'for the masses, the Kingdom of God has always been already here on earth, in the pagan immanence of images, in the spectacle' (Baudrillard, 1983a: 8).

Against all the pressures of the religious institutions, the masses have absorbed religion and neutralised its transcendent ambitions. And this is true of all such transcendental religions and ideologies: these have only ever been supported and borne along by a certain segment of the upper strata, whose ideas and values have found popularity only in vulgarisation and distortion. Even the idea of the 'social' does not find itself accepted into the mass, this idea is only 'shattered' in it.

MASSES AND POWER

It is wrong therefore to believe, as is popular amongst the elite he says, that the masses have become cultured or even that the masses want culture.[6] The idea of raising cultural standards and of producing a better-informed society is a hopeless task actually now attempted only by a tiny fragment of the elite. The mass do not want this, and whatever is attempted will always be subverted as if by a counter-strategy. This strategy seems, says Baudrillard, to be one which converts significant signs into idols, as if the crucial point is not meaning but spectacle. The notions of deep or transcendent meaning, of dialectical seem to be rejected as foreign to it. Arguments to the effect that the masses do not know what they want, or are profoundly alienated or mystified, are false. The masses do not gravitate to enlightenment or to reason. The masses by contrast profoundly distrust political reason:

> they scent the simplifying terror which is behind the ideal hegemony of meaning, and they react in their own way, by reducing all articulate discourse to a single irrational and baseless dimension, where signs lose their meaning and peter out in fascination: the spectacular.
>
> (Baudrillard, 1983a: 10–11)

Although this is not new, the annihilation of meaning, power, culture by the mass continues in deeply antagonistic new forms today. Instead of believing meaning is crucial and determinant, it is necessary to grasp the fact that meaning is always marginal and on the periphery: meaning is an 'ambiguous and inconsequential accident' (ibid: 11). Even as individuals we inevitably become part of the mass, and therefore live in 'panic or haphazardly' outside the sphere of meaning itself.

The staggering indifference of the mass which maintains itself after the immense impact of organised socialisation, education and social training, including political revolution, mass-media-information revolutions and so on, is a primary fact, something which should be recognised in its own right. When a significant political or cultural event clashes with, say a football match, it is always tempting to reach the conclusion, when the masses prefer the football match, that the masses are manipulated or mystified by sport (even theorised as a state apparatus). But this overlooks the fact that such an analysis precisely displaces onto the state a power it does not in fact possess; and it denies the masses a strategy which it always has. Baudrillard's argument is that it is precisely this indifference to political meaning that 'has to be analysed in its positive brutality'. The preference for spectacle, for example, the preference for the football match, which is claimed with enthusiasm by the masses over the political event, is a fact no theory has grasped.[7] Instead of talking of mystification, analysis should understand:

the much more dangerous fact that this indifference of the masses is their true, their only practice, that there is . . . nothing in this to deplore, but everything to analyse as the brute fact of a collective retaliation and of a refusal to participate in the recommended ideals, however enlightened.[8]

(Baudrillard, 1983a: 14)

A glance at the genealogy of the political sphere itself is pertinent here, he argues, in an attempt to link the general theory of simulation with that of political power. Late-medieval and Renaissance politics was a new structure dominated by the play of strategies and signs unconnected with any idea of the representation of truth as such (like the world of the Jesuits later it played on a specific absence – for the Jesuits it was the absence of God, and this was the secret of their power). In this sense, then, the political space of the Renaissance belonged to the same order of simulation as the 'mechanical theatre', or perspective in painting. It was thus in the order of the game, not an 'ideology' in depth but a strategic field. In this sense it is not surprising, says Baudrillard, that it gave rise to technical virtuosity. Generally speaking, therefore, Machiavelli is misunderstood when thought of as advocating a purely manipulative politics, cynical in a moral sense. In fact, political force is found principally in the game, in the rejection of moral ends and ultimate meanings.

Since the eighteenth century and particularly since the French Revolution, things have changed and the political order has become, in contrast, charged with meaning and significance. It is now considered the site of representations, and it has become invested with 'social' significance. The will of the people was incorporated into the new conception of politics as a fundamental signified. Signs were given depth, and the represented came to be considered as 'real', indeed the very reality of history and politics simply expressed it. A period passed when the political and the social were in rough balance (perhaps, he claims, a golden age of bourgeois representative systems). Liberal political thought still plays on a nostalgia for this golden age. Marxist thought and practice pushed, however, for the dissolution of the political into the social, towards an 'absolute hegemony' not of an ideology, but of the 'social'.

The 'social' itself has now, says Baudrillard, triumphed definitively and the political hardly exists as an independent realm, having been saturated with the (previous) structures of the social order. The effect of the disappearance of this difference between the social and political, parallels the disappearance of the social as an autonomous realm. Thus the social is not the source but the recipient of energies and its 'specificity is lost' as it becomes undifferentiated, anonymous. In a word, becomes a mass.[9]

It is this undifferentiated form, says Baudrillard, that has to be analysed. Given the decline and fading away of the class system as a system of meaningful referents, which could be made to appear as content at the political level (interpreted as a process of representation), a new situation has arisen. This needs to be grasped radically, the disappearance of any basic underlying 'reality' in the society as donator of meaning to the political process. There is in fact only one element left acting as the final referent: the 'silent majority' which is now, however, nebulous, floating and, in the final analysis, purely statistical. It makes its appearance, therefore, not in the form of a representation or as a source of meaning, as hitherto conceived, it cannot be represented or given a meaning, but rather in the form of a statistic. It can be regarded as 'a simulation of the horizon of the social, or rather on whose horizon the social has already disappeared' (Baudrillard, 1983a: 20).

Since the masses do not any longer express themselves, they are investigated, tested and polled. In this way a new order of simulation is created but staggered back onto an earlier one (a stage dominated by the idea of representation) as it is only in this way that it can become meaningful. The new simulation relates not to a meaningful subject or social agent, but only to a 'model' of such an agent constructed in relation to new statistical techniques. A new (theoretical) couplet is brought into existence: the unity of the silent majority and the statistical survey. Here, there is no system of polarities, no differentiation of terms, no flow of energy, no field or flow of currents. The mass is born short-circuited in 'total circularity'. What seems to occur he argues is a circulation around simulation models, and a collapse of the complex system into itself. In the end Baudrillard works towards the following image 'bombarded with stimuli, messages and tests, the masses are simply an opaque, blind stratum, like those clusters of stellar gas known only through analysis of their light spectrum' (Baudrillard, 1983a: 21). This is the only way to understand the silence of the mass, as it refuses to speak in the terms and sense of the previous system of representations. Understood positively this is not a new form of alienation effect, he suggests, it is, rather, a strategic one which has to be seen as a strategic weapon in its own right.

Indeed, reading it in this way, he argues, it can be seen that it is a fundamental mode of non-alienation in the mass. For no-one, no organisation, as has been the case previously can any longer speak with confidence 'for' the mass. The mass in ceasing to be a subject in the traditional sense can no longer pass through the stage of the formation of political identities (through a kind of 'mirror phase' as argued by Althusserians). The mass has 'withdrawn into silence' and can no longer be alienated as a subject (which implies at the same time the end of any appeal to it as the subject as a revolutionary force). The idea of the revolution by the oppressed groups always assumed the oppressed had an identity, were alienated and that they acted in a sacrificial struggle. This explosive mode of action is not that of the masses as they are established in the present period: now it is a question of the neutralisation by the mass of all such transcendental possibilities (liberation, history, etc.). This new mode can be conceived more as revenge, retaliation and defence: this spells the death of the political sphere as such. Previously, to be sure, Baudrillard comments, apathy was in part cultivated by the administrations and has been an essential basis of the powers of certain bureaucracies. But this is possible only up to a certain level beyond which modern systems and political organisations alter their strategies and seek to involve the mass and to encourage it to 'participate'. However, says Baudrillard, 'it is too late' (1983a:23) the contemporary mode is established once and for all.

The modern problem, he writes, only arises because, in this new situation, it is felt necessary on all sides to try to give this mass some 'structure', some coherence. Yet something even stranger happens he suggests. All this immense effort of producing meaning only produces more of the same non-meaning, only more 'mass' is created. Differentiation is never the outcome of attempts to create meaning in the mass, it is impossible to achieve a change of fundamental qualities in this way. What happens is the mass becomes something to be investigated, becomes a 'case'. It is investigated as to its state of health, its pulse is taken. It then becomes an object which has to be seduced and solicited. A new order of divination is created in an attempt to establish indirectly what the mass actually thinks. Unfortunately, this is based on the false assumption that increasing the quantity of information will lead to some form of communication. What happens is that a mechanical relation is imposed: the form of a mass to be informed confronts a mass of information, like an input–output machine (simulation chamber). But this fails, the energy is lost and the 'social' collapses in failure. It produces the inverse of its intended outcome: not the creation of a meaningful order in the 'social', but rather the extension of the mass (as it is further created in surveys). The mass is then atomised, nuclearised but not alienated. It is also, not a hot, frenzied mass, but on the contrary, a mass that is frozen.

The new problem for the system is to find a way to prevent itself from collapsing under its own weight. A vital new imperative: today it is a question of creating both the demand for goods (in the economy) and the creation of the demand for meaning (in the culture). In the past this was accomplished quite spontaneously. Today there is a gap: 'it is the production of this demand for meaning which has become crucial for the system' (Baudrillard, 1983a 27).

When it is impossible to achieve the creation of demand in this way the whole system is in danger of coming apart. The masses are constantly under interrogation in an attempt to find a meaning, to establish a sense, but it is a hopeless search and reveals nothing for the mass is profoundly 'without a conscience and without an unconscious'. An impossible situation is created for the political elite. But for the mass it is a strategic triumph, for the mass is not without cunning or strategy. It realises the 'paradox of being an object' and of simulating the social. It is its very 'hyperconformity' which has to be understood as an 'immanent form of humour'. All attempts to grasp the mass are doomed to failure since it is in its nature diffuse, decentred, its movement is Brownian: it vanishes just at the point at which it is about to be seized. Opinion polls prestructure responses in order to grasp it, but only end in producing tautologies.

The end result of such techniques is not an objective science but a science of imaginary objects, a pataphysics (Baudrillard, 1983a: 33)[10] which has as its object the created object of hypersimulation. The 'involuntary' humour of the masses would lead, in the pataphysical, to the unburdening of all metaphysical problems. All uncertainty is ruled out in statistical objectivity. And because the answers are undoubtedly objective the researcher cannot but believe in them. The masses, however, do not, as such, make an assessment, they do not choose. They are not critical. They are fascinated by the new media, and this is realised in the very neutralisation of any message that might be transmitted.

This leads Baudrillard to a new proposition: just as in jokes pleasure arrives from the neutralisation and cancellation of meaning (see the earlier discussion p.119), so here, too, it is possible to see that communication occurs 'outside the medium of meaning itself' (Baudrillard, 1983a:36). Take the political system. This only survives in the modern situation on the basis that the masses hold opinions (this is the presumption of all polls). But the system converges with entertainment, and the masses are its public audience. This creates a fundamental problem, the apathy of the mass is 'the effect of an implacable antagonism between the class (caste?) which bears the social, the political, culture – master of time and history, and the un(in)formed, residual, senseless, mass' (ibid:38).

It is also possible to see, he continues, in the 'apathy' and in this depoliticisation, not a crude political ignorance, but a strategy situated paradoxically and threateningly on the other side of the political altogether, beyond politics. The retreat into the private, the domestic, is a strategy of the annihilation of the political realm itself. This is not as a result of a dialectical struggle, and there is no dialectical subversion of the system, however much it is interpreted as a negation. It is nevertheless to be situated in a perspective of resistence, an aspect which is always neglected. All the so-called great advances of the social system (education, medicine, housing) have all been accompanied by this kind of resistence. The dominant culture is diverted by the mass in many different ways (the doctor is transformed into a magician), and everything is diverted into the spectacular and divested of meaning. It is often thought that it is the mass media which causes this to happen through its technical capacities (sociology is always searching for the ways in which the masses are manipulated by the media), but the fact is, says Baudrillard, that this is always at the cost of not seeing the more basic (indeed Marxist) fact that the mass is stronger than the media. The masses in fact envelop the media and it becomes one entity. All mass consumption quickly diverts meaning into spectacular forms, a baffling phenomenon for all rationalist social scientists. The masses seem to know that there is no liberation or transcendence apart from a hyperlogic of the system itself.

THE NEW PROBLEMATIC

Baudrillard situates his position in the following way: it is not, he says a naively optimistic vision, like some optimistic version of McLuhan's works suggest that in the global village there can be a new transparency of consciousness in information; and it is not either a view that a socialist progressive struggle can be launched in the media in the way that say Enzenberger has suggested. The key, central issue here, as for the whole of Baudrillard's work, is opposition to these. He remarks, 'I once believed in a possible subversion of the code of the media and the possibility of an alternate speech and a radical reciprocity of symbolic exchange', though not in a conception of high optimism like Enzenberger (Baudrillard, 1988b: 208).

What has happened in this gigantic change of position? Essentially I think it is a bizarre continuation of the early theses of cultural class logic. In the first period the analysis of cultural simulation (bourgeois and petit bourgeois were analysed as class strategies of a complex and ambivalent kind). After 1978 the analysis of cultural simulation is drained of all social-class content: the simulations are posed as a genealogy of forms, and formalism is their primary vice. Baudrillard inverts the problematic in order to investigate the other side of these strategies which depended on the positive action of class subjects. What interests him now, framed in the new social context, are rather obscurely and inconsistently defined object-mass strategies of resistance (thus of *ressentiment*, though he rarely uses the term).

I say this problematic emerges inconsistently because at this stage in its formation (1978) Baudrillard refers both to the 'strategy of the object' and to the fact that the mass is 'neither Subject nor Object'. He says the social disappears into the mass, yet can elaborate a clear picture of the social elite in relation to the mass. He can identify the mass as a purely statistical phenomenon, yet talk of the mass as following their own 'explicit and positive counter strategy – the task of absorbing and annihilating culture, knowledge, power, the social . . . a deep antagonism which forces the inversion of received scenarios' (Baudrillard, 1983a: 11). Thus there appears some crucial logical problems, which seem to arise because Baudrillard wants to achieve some contradictory purposes. The most notable of these is the desire to present the mass as an essentially ambivalent phenomenon.[11] Yet this is itself a problem and causes severe theoretical difficulties. He confronts them by saying a number of conflicting propositions: first the term mass should remain unspecified, and undefined. He proceeds to evoke an image of an 'opaque nebula whose growing density absorbs all the surrounding energy' (ibid: 3–4); but at the same time suggests that what is really happening is that the mass 'realises the paradox of being both the object of simulation and a subject of simulation' (Baudrillard, 1983a: 30).

It is important here to return to the question of Baudrillard's problematic – his epistemology and his theory. The term problematic has today lost much of its precision (as it attained in Bachelard, Althusser and Lecourt) and therefore much of its power of discrimination (it is now used to describe a theoretical framework). It is with Baudrillard's theoretical transition here that the terms again become essential, for Baudrillard's work reveals a complex combination of an (apparent) epistemological regression, coupled with a progressive opening up of a terrain of new forms of mass resistance to the social system. The specific terms, problematic and theory, have to be clearly distinguished here: problematic concerns the level of forms of explanation, verification, conceptualisation, theory defines the object and its field.[12] The notion of an epistemological break is thus a phenomenon at the level of the problematic (the way in which the problems are posed). What Baudrillard proposes, in effect, is a double problematic: one as an (apparently) regressive break with rationalism – towards a position which suggests concepts should not be defined or specified; the other is the integral development of theoretical substantive theses which depend on the action of rigorous concepts, and whose problematic remains structural.

Thus Baudrillard wants the poetic evocation of the mass to stand as a symbolic force of ambivalence, its 'representation is no longer possible' (Baudrillard, 1983a: 20), it neutralises semiological positivity; yet he also wants the positive definition of the mass, to grasp the position of the mass as ambivalent (just as he had tried to define the ambivalent position of the petit bourgeoisie and its ambient simulations). This explains why he defines the position of the mass as 'neither subject nor object', yet this is evidently in conflict with his discussion. In the end he resolves this dilemma through a definition of the situation of the mass as one of double bind. Baudrillard's first formulation is:

> The mass realises that paradox of not being a subject, but of not being an object either. Every effort to make a subject of it (real or mythical) runs head on into the glaring impossibility of an autonomous change in consciousness. Every effort to make an object of it to treat and analyse it as brute matter, according to objective laws, runs head on into the contrary fact that it is impossible to manipulate the masses in any determinant way, or to understand them in terms of elements, relations, structures and wholes. All manipulation plunges, gets sucked into the mass, absorbed, distorted, subject to reversion
>
> (Baudrillard, 1983a: 30, trans. mod.)

His second formulation is as follows:

We are face to face with this system, in a double bind situation, an insoluble 'double bind', exactly like children face to face with the adult universe. They are simultaneously summoned to behave like autonomous subjects, responsible, free, and conscious; and as submissive objects, inert, obedient, and conforming. The child resists on all levels, and to a contradictory demand he also responds with a double strategy. To the demand to be an object, he opposes all the practices, disobedience, revolt, emancipation, in short a total claim to be a subjecthood. To the demand to be a subject, he opposes just as subbornly and efficaciously with an object's resistance, that is to say, in exactly the opposite manner: infantilism, hyperconformism, a total dependency, passivity, idiocy. Neither of the two strategies has more objective value than the other.
(Baudrillard, 1983a: 107, and see the discussion in 1988b: 218)

This is an important displacement. In the first statement the ambivalence is recognised as neither subject nor object from the point of view of the elite which wishes to manipulate the masses (this runs into practical impossibilities: *de facto* failures of manipulation). The second displaces the neutralisations: first, the form is one of struggle, or resistance, as either subject or object, the second is to judge neutrally the effectiveness of these forms of resistance – neither is more effective than the other in principle.

The theoretical importance of this example is considerable, for it should lead to the classification of key elements of substantive theory, for now it is possible to see that there is in fact a substructure to the analysis of subjects and objects:

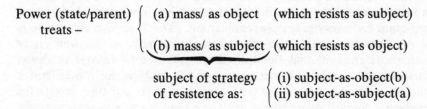

Power (state/parent) treats –
(a) mass/ as object   (which resists as subject)
(b) mass/ as subject   (which resists as object)

subject of strategy of resistence as:
(i) subject-as-object(b)
(ii) subject-as-subject(a)

It is thus possible to return to the question of the meaning of Baudrillard's conception of being in the 'Shadow of the Silent majority', which far more subtle than first appears. Chang has argued that the masses are silent because they follow a strategy of hyperconformism 'and it is by this hyperconformism and form of refusal and nonrecognition . . . that the masses are able to renounce the position of the subject' (Chang, 1986: 172); and Chen notes this means the masses 'are beyond the imaginary control of power'. But Chen then upbraids Baudrillard for his own fatalistic view that the masses will inevitably bring down the system in a catastrophic collapse (Chen, 1987: 86). This perhaps should be inverted, since Baudrillard is also suggesting something about Marx here. For Marx becomes intelligible in the light of Baudrillard's apparently regressive problematic. It implies perhaps that Marx himself was in this sense in the shadow of the masses, which is where Baudrillard wants to be: close to the masses' fatal strategies. The question for Marxists is: to what extent does this strategy form a substructure of ritual attitudes and orientations, and indeed its own fundamentally different epistemology within Marxism?

But there is a more subtle question which has been raised against Baudrillard, that suggests the victorious strategy of the masses cannot be claimed quite so quickly. Lash and Urry say:

> the implosion of meaning, subjectivity and the real world or the social is not primarily a way for Baudrillard's 'silent majorities' to resist domination, but instead a way that the 'masses' are dominated . . . cultural producers, in for example today's cinema of the spectacle, are aware of this change in the audience and produce films that cater to it . . . the dominant culture operates itself through the delinkage of meaning from images.
>
> (Lash and Urry, 1987: 290)

This raises the question of the mirror form of the object's strategy in the order of power itself. This argument, in fact, would simply make the masses dupes of the ruling class. But there is a more basic theoretical issue which suggests that all these interpretations – Chang, Chen, Lash and Urry and others rather miss an important point: hyperconformity is a strategy and it can always match an escalation of stakes. The masses are not beyond the control of the imaginary, they live in its shadow. A strategy of silence (the silent majority) is not the only strategy of the masses and this is recognised explicitly by Baudrillard.[13] It is because Baudrillard has in fact relativised the question by saying that it is now a period of cultural implosion that everything changes meaning. The masses' strategy becomes silent. Therefore there is in one sense considerable justification in the criticism (Berthelot) that Baudrillard has returned to a phase of theory dominated by fantasies of the mass, but the problem for Baudrillard is still different: the masses are now cool, implosive and this 'inverts the received scenario'. As he claims, the strategy of the masses now is remote from fascism, or rather by implication fascism is a non-silent strategy of hyperactivity in an explosive period. The inward implosion of meaning in the masses, therefore, is a popular negative fascism in a sense – one drained of drive and energy, become melancholic. Cool fascism seems a contradictory concept, but we are not far from it.

8   The object's seduction

we live in radical obscenity.
Baudrillard (1988b: 163)

On Seduction (De la Seduction) was published in France in 1979 and is a
hugely paradoxical attempt to outline the theory, principle and effects of
seduction in all its forms.[1] One of the targets is psychoanalysis, but a major
target is modern feminism. Its real target is again western culture, but this
time the critique is aimed at its obscenity. This has given Baudrillard's
reputation a major inflection: the accumulation of targets now embraces
ecology, socialism, human rights and feminism, as well as peace movements.
It is difficult to imagine that here we have a writer on the left of the political
spectrum. But his critiques suggest that he envisages a highly radical critique
that tries to get to the root of things. Certainly his critique of Marxism did
not follow the many efforts at revisionism of a liberal kind. His critique
of feminism can be seen as parallel, but his idea of what constitutes the
structures of the symbolic order of the feminine are not here located
explicitly in the same terms. The basic notions of 'symbolic' exchange
are decisively displaced by those of strategic reversibility and the duel.
Whereas a writer like Michel Serres attempted, against Althusser to
replace Prometheus with Hermes (the god of communication), Baudrillard
replaces Prometheus with Narcissus (Baudrillard, 1990a; 67).[2] The depth
of Baudrillard's opposition to western culture can be seen in his hostility
to western art since the Renaissance. And whereas Max Weber saw the
evolution of perspective in art as a triumph of rationalisation, Baudrillard
thinks 'all art since the renaissance has been rot' (Baudrillard, 1988b: 157).
According to Baudrillard, there has been an eclipse of the principle of
seduction, the play of the duel of appearances around significant stakes.
Eventually, western cultures have evolved towards an erasure of all
oppositions and referentials so that social relations engage at the level
of ludic pursuits without significance or consequence.

A GENEALOGY

In the discussion here, it is necessary to outline Baudrillard's brief genealogy of seduction which will provide a framework for the analysis of his theoretical arguments. The genealogy is presented towards the end of the work in a section entitled 'The political destiny of seduction'. He arrives at the genealogy by means of a long discussion of the principle of the game, which now replaces the concept of symbolic exchange in this work. This discussion of the game involves a consideration of Borges's story 'The Lottery in Babylon'. If the Babylonians developed the lottery, says Baudrillard, it was because it 'completely seduced them' and 'enabled them to challenge everything worth existing, including their own existence – and their own death' (Baudrillard, 1990a: 154). Baudrillard takes this as a possible ideal first social order, dependent on the rule; it is followed by a state dependent on law, and then on the norm:

1   the rule is a form which dominates through the ritual, and which cannot be transgressed, it establishes a logic of the duel. Here there is strong seduction and the stakes are high.
2   the law and the social contract is entirely different and is the age of history, of meaning and referentials, the age of mastery. The logic which dominates here is that of the dialectical polarity, contradiction. This is the period in which transgression and transcendence is possible. Seduction is altered in form around polar opposites.
3   the norm arrives in the age of 'the death of the social' and the neutralisation of oppositions. It is the culture of the signal. The logic which dominates is that of digitality, an order of connections, binary opposition and the electronic pulse. Seduction here is soft, in keeping with cool ambience, low stakes and low intensities.

This genealogy is really articulated around the process of the transition from hot, intense seduction, where the forms of involvement are vertiginous, to that of cool, ludic seductions of the soft culture (there is nothing to be lost in its games). It is not, then, that strategies derived from, or based on, games are ever abandoned. But the world has become safe, it is totally assured.[3] The game has descended to the level of the television game show, a world of playful combinatories, of infinite intersubstitutions: seduction's form engages our fascination. In the end the genetic code is a thing which can be played with, as aleatory in its nature and perhaps even the product of a cool game. All play becomes ludic play, as in play school and play time. All the elements of life can be played as if they were a stereo system with sophisticated control panels to adjust tonalities and timbres (Baudrillard, 1990a: 163). Here, even the social contract passes into a 'simulation pact'; it is 'sealed by the media' (ibid), it does indeed operate as seduction 'but such seduction has no more meaning than anything else, seduction here connotes only a kind of ludic adhesion to simulated pieces of information, a kind of tactile abstraction (Baudrillard; 1990a: 163). And at this point narcissism becomes narcosis (as already forseen by McLuhan as a pathological narcissism).

For Baudrillard this is no longer a mirror relation but a narcissim of the formula, a new and 'monstrous parody of the myth' (ibid: 168). Cold narcissism everywhere as *pars totalis* of the system in its software, soft seduction as diffuse and tensile (ibid: 174). This inaugurates large-scale mass seduction where the masses self-manage their own oppression: since the masses themselves have been developed psychologically in the system, they have been given inner complexity of desiring agents so that they can enter into a field in which they are coolly seduced (ibid: 175); it is an age fit for a new order of Jesuits (ibid: 176).

His argument, is both disarmingly simple and subtle. In primitive cultures the world was never, as we believe it, viewed as under (pseudo) magical controls of social practices. It was a cruel theatre of charm and enchantment, not in a sentimental sense but rather in a directly objective sense that the world could be and usually was seduced by (benign or evil) forces. Modern cultures have tended to downgrade these active, seductive forces dramatically; it has switched emphasis to mastering the ways in which the world is produced, as both truth and reality, it has sought to tear off the veil. Even in sexual relations the liberation of desire is now the goal. Radical seduction has been eclipsed in this process as if 'productivity', 'science', 'truth' has always been its enemy.

Since the Renaissance, then, there has been a series of attempts to end the fabulous seductiveness of appearance, to bring to an end and to abolish mystery of the veil. These critical efforts have been aimed at the elimination of the strategic significance of artifice, of the sign, of ritual action. There have been, what can only be seen in retrospect, a series of violent displacements: in production, sexuality, in the cultural domains, the totality of which have had a profound effect on the very meaning and value of the play of seduction: with a certain type of 'feminisation' of society has come not a triumph of the principle of seduction in the strong sense, but a form of seduction in, says Baudrillard, a weak sense (a '*seduction molle*'). An immense diminution of the power of seductive forces and a collapse of its social meaning.

MASCULINE AND FEMININE

It is evident, he claims, that there have been vast changes in the field of sexuality in western cultures: 'sex' has become generalised throughout the culture and yet at the same time, he suggests, a profound desexualisation has occurred within sexual relations themselves. As culture appears to become 'feminised' the feminine and the masculine become indeterminate. This process has to be distinguished carefully from that of a structural inversion of terms or forces. The lifting of the general law of sexual differentiation has been replaced by new mechanisms of oppression. Baudrillard suggests that the rise of the feminine has entailed the emergence of two important new features. First, the rise to an overwhelming value of the significance of pleasure (*jouissance*), and second, the emergence of a catastrophic nature of modern sexuality and sexual reality (sex is only the 'remainder' of a higher mode of seduction).

Analysis here, says Baudrillard, should, however, follow Freud to some degree. As Lacan has shown, Freud's notion that there is only one sexual drive, structured around the phallus, castration and repression is fundamentally correct. This is masculine and all sexuality articulated around this structure is masculine in nature.[4] Today, there is a widespread collapse of this structure, a tendency towards indifferentiation and erotic polyvalency. The basic trap of the 'sexual revolution' is the neutralisation of the fundamental distinction between masculine and feminine, in the direction of soft-edged feminisation, which arises because the structure of modern alienation is misrecognised.[5] The rationalisation of this movement is to be found in the idea of overcoming the age-old oppression of women. But this concentrates on the (largely physical) misery of women in past societies, to the exclusion of other levels and activities in which women had both power and sovereignty.

Actually, he suggests, it is this account which is accepted, continued and deepened in psychoanalysis which bases its whole strategy around the theory of the 'sexual'. But, Baudrillard suggests, this neglects the very nature and basis of power of women in the realm of the feminine, which is precisely where psychoanalysis fails to look: not in production (desire) but in seduction. The power of women is not in 'sex' itself. So, relations at the level of seduction are not and cannot be reduced to a process of repression and the the action of the unconscious. If this critique is correct, and seduction should be seen, in its strong form, as involving the challenge, play, strategies of appearance, reversibility, etc., the feminine is not strictly speaking an opposite of the masculine at all. Rather it is what 'seduces the masculine' (Baudrillard, 1979: 16; 1990a: 7).

In this perspective the feminine is not a marked or unmarked term; it is not in an order of productivity. It is not to be found where production is a dominant term. It has always, says Baudrillard, been located somewhere else. Thus the tendency of modern culture is to move to a pattern of the dominance of the bisexual; but this involves the collapse of the previous symbolic order itself. This other order of culture is always, in fact, based on the symbolic exchange and this is never understood or grasped by psychoanalysis, which, on this point is always reductive. Like Marxism, psychoanalysis produces explanation in the form of distinct and relatively autonomous instances. The sexual is postulated itself as such an instance. If power represents an attempt to master 'the real', seduction is a mastery of the world of symbolic exchanges. The 'immense privilege' (Baudrillard intends no double meaning here (1990a: 8)) of women, then, for Baudrillard, derives from a specific relation to this order (the symbolic), which is not that of truth, but of appearance and the strategies of appearances. The feminist movement, looked at in this manner, that is when it begins to align itself with production, productivity, science and even reality, forges a new system of complicity which can only end in the unwonted undermining of its own cultural base: the 'immense privilege' will be lost, and with it the challenge of the feminine. Baudrillard notes 'one must be incredibly blind to deny the sole force that is equal and superior to all others' (Baudrillard, 1990a: 8).[6]

Baudrillard examines the attempt by Luce Irigaray to talk of a specific and unrecognised feminine sexuality, and he cites the following passage:

> woman's pleasure has no need to choose between clitoral activity and vaginal passivity. The pleasure of the vaginal caress doesn't have to substitute for that of the clitoral caress. Each contributes, in an irreplaceable manner, to the woman's jouissance. Amongst other things . . . the caress of the breasts, the vulval touch, the prying open of the lips, the coming and going of the posterior wall of the vagina, the gentle stroking of the cervix of the womb, etc; to evoke only certain of the most specifically feminine pleasures.
>
> (Irigaray, 1985:18)

Baudrillard is quick to note: this account is dominated by the question of anatomy, which has an astonishing correlation with the Freudian concerns. It is consistent with certain currents of contemporary culture more generally, but it is particularly noticeable that here it leads to an erotics of diffusion, a diffraction of zones, it is decentred sexuality, a diffuse polyvalency of erotic values, *jouissance* and a transfiguration of the body as a whole by the forces of desire. Thus, in this perspective, it is the functionality of the body which is predominant, and pleasure is conceived as the manifestation of supposedly 'natural' forms and relations. In fact, he complains, nothing in this account is in principle at any great critical distance from Freud's formula that 'anatomy is destiny' (and Freud here was quite mistaken, anatomy is not destiny).

In all the accounts of this type, but particularly that of Irigaray (1985), it is not a question of artifice, or the effects on the body of seduction, but always the notion of driven desire. It is always the problem of the incarnation of sexuality which dominates discourse. There is only one force or perspective which really questions the Freudian doctrine that anatomy is destiny and the doctrine of phallic value, that is seduction – and this, he maintains, is the radical alternative to all such reductionism.

In relation to this opposition, it is apparent that seduction as a strategy is not at all interested in models that construct a difference between an infrastructure and superstructure, a strategy of overturning. Seduction plays in another register, and this has nothing to do with the anatomy or topography. The strategy of seduction is only ever a strategy of appearance (antagonistic to the principle of the real). Nothing, in this perspective, is gained by posing the real against the real, being against being, or truth against truth. This is always really a trap. The feminine is, on the other hand, only appearances. It is precisely this fact which enables the feminine to checkmate the profundity of the masculine. Once the feminine tries to throw against the profundity of the masculine a counter-profundity of the feminine, the secret power is lost. In fact the feminine can be seen to challenge the depth model, just as it challenges the difference between the authentic and the artificial. Joan Rivière, says Baudrillard, was right in a famous article (interest in which was revived by Lacan in 1977) to say that the feminine is artificial and authentic: she asks the question of the difference between 'genuine womanliness' and the 'masquerade' and answers to the effect that 'whether authentic or superficial it is fundamentally the same thing' (Rivière, 1986:38, cited in Baudrillard, 1979:21; 1990a: 10). There is, says Baudrillard, a striking resemblance between the feminine and simulation itself. And a paradox, for 'femininity provides radical evidence of simulation' and the possibility, the 'only possibility' of overcoming it (Baudrillard, 1979: 11).[7]

Baudrillard turns next to consider the situation of the transvestite. This is not to be confused with homosexuality or transsexuality (a position he alters in 1990b: 30), he argues.. Transvestites play on the possibility of breaking down sexual distinction. What happens, he suggests, is that as the signs of sexual distinctiveness become primary, transvestites are seduced by them. Their charm, then, even as far as their own situation is concerned, is not derived from a sexual polarity, but from everything which revolves around make-up, theatre and seduction, as if there was an obsession with the play of metamorphosis. The game of sexuality becomes total, but ritualised and ironic. This, in fact, is no latent homosexuality, he claims, and no 'symptomatic reading' is possible. It is rather the play of signs and the transubstantiation of sexuality in them which is the secret of all transvestite seduction. This often comes close to parody, and in historical terms approaches the ritual and theatre of Athens, where similar (but sacred) forms were evolved.

One could say, he suggests, if the logic of transvestitism were generalised, that women only exist in so far as they are created by men, or again, the existence of women is dependent on the imagination of men. But as has been said, women do not exist: they have no specific libido, nature, no writing, no feminine *jouissance*. It is possible to argue that it is out of this very situation that the power of women arises. Yet there is a more subtle argument. Take the symbolic use of make-up by women. It might be thought that this amounts to a resolution of the problem of sex through parody: that is through an excess of signs which puts an end to biology. However, it is really the symbolic law of castration which is suggested here, a transsexual play of seduction (Baudrillard, 1990a:15). This is above all carried off in the ironic mode, since what is attempted is to throw the false against the false, an irony which arises in relation to the woman as idol and object: to 'incarnate the peaks of sexuality while simultaneously being absorbed in their simulation' (Baudrillard, 1990a: 15). It is, too, ironically, the power of the object here which sends the male into the realm of the imaginary. In fact the only way out of male power is via this route, the route of seductiveness.

But what is male power then? There are, too, he suggests, some important misconceptions on this problem. Take one important one, the objection to the theory of the exchange of women in primitive societies. This theory becomes simplistic if it is thought that women are objects here, or that this is the first stage of commodity exchange. Virtually all of the modern discourse on inequality is a gigantic misunderstanding since the nature of exchange as duel is unrecognised. In fact, the inverse hypothesis is just as plausible and far more intriguing: that the feminine has never been anything but dominant. But this thesis has to be correctly interpreted. The feminine, not as a sex, but as the 'transversal' form of all sex, and all power, has, as its secret, a virulent form of non-sexuality: the challenge (*défi*).

It is in this sense that the masculine has always only ever been residual, as a secondary and fragile formation, such that it has needed a vast intellectual, institutional and religious fortress to defend itself and to survive. This has to be stressed: the phallic order has all the appearance of a fortress; this can only mean it is weak and fearful at its heart. Indeed it is just as possible to argue that the feminine is the only sex, or more accurately, it is only with the most extreme difficulty that the masculine can escape the grasp of the feminine: 'a moment's distraction and one falls back into the feminine' (Baudrillard, 1979:27; 1990a: 16). And if this is the case it is only derisory that one sex should attempt to move towards and simulate the character of the other as a 'liberation', certainly in the case of the feminine which might wish to approach a masculine which is only paranoid and paradoxical. It is the feminine which is primary, and the masculine only becomes a possibility by becoming an exception to it. All mythology has to be questioned on this point. Bettelheim (in *Symbolic Wounds* (1954)) expressed it well: it is not penis envy which is the motor of development here; on the contrary it is more likely that it is jealousy of the power of the fecundity of women. This is, says Baudrillard, the privilege which is so difficult to counteract. Indeed it could be argued that it is only the immense array of institutions created by men that have been able to balance it. At the level of signs, this balancing is realised in the profusion of practices such as the male confinement (the *couvade*) and of various modes of mutilations which parallel it (as artificial vaginations).

But Baudrillard attempts to distance himself from this extreme thesis to some degree, simply by posing it as an interesting and curious idea for, in the end, however, it is simply an inversion, and basically founded on the same set of terms. The basic structure of irony is lost, just as it is when femininity founds itself simply on physical sexual characteristics, even when it denounces oppression. These demands for reversals of oppression are simply the face of heroic humanism stemming from the enlightenment, and, the call to liberate the downtrodden – related to little or no understanding of the social relations or structures involved. In fact, here the feminine is not an order, a value: it is in its very strategy ungraspable as such. It is not even subversive, it is fundamentally related to the reversible. Power (masculine power) is, however, completely soluble in the reversibility of the feminine. In this sense then, the feminine is of the same order as madness. This, too, carries a threat, a secret, which must be normalised. In fact, the process of sexual liberation can be seen as an attempt to control and normalise the threat of the feminine. Its secret must be revealed, unveiled, controlled and contained.

It is often today advanced as a fact, he notes, that sexual pleasure is denied women and that the sexual revolution has as one of its aims the reparation of this inequality. This comes close, he remarks, to arguing that sexual pleasure is a human right, an argument which tends to ignore the fact that *jouissance* is itself secondary.[8] There is a superior structure, something which can arise in the absence of *jouissance* and can be more intense: seduction or pleasure (*plaisir*). *Jouissance* can be a pretext for this other game, a game which is more passionate, more vertiginous, and passion is far more than a sexual drive (it can, for example, play equally well on the refusal of *jouissance*). *Jouissance* is, in fact, not a strategy. It is only an energy in search of release. As such it is subject to any strategy which can direct it (and this is the theme of much discussion from the eighteenth century up to Kierkegaard). In this field, sexuality is ritual, is ceremony and has absolutely nothing to do with human rights or any revealed 'truth' of sexuality.

In the sexual revolution today, the challenge (*défi*) is no longer strictly possible, and all 'symbolic' logic is exterminated to the profit of male erection (and no doubt, he claims, wryly, its falling rate of *jouissance*). In fact, in the final analysis, the 'traditional woman' was not repressed and not probihited from participating in sexual orgasm, for woman was whole, not conquered, not passive. This is a notion to be jettisoned with all comparable theories of the masses as deeply mystified. All these ideas, says Baudrillard, are absurdly oversimple, and an expression of a patronising sympathy which, in the last resort, is based on sexist assumptions. The feminine has never been remotely like this image in any society, it has always been alive with its own strategy, distinctive and always victorious. Seduction is one of the principle forms of the challenge, which in the present situation the feminine seems in danger of losing.

Baudrillard's analysis maintains the new demand on women's equality, (of pleasure, of sex, of productivity, etc.) is therefore actually a strategy of the imposition on women of a new contract and duty. It involves the very creation of women as a sex, and orgasm as a proof of the sexuality of this sex. Pornography is only this idea served up in an exacerbated form where all feminine physical *jouissance* must be made visible: no more secret, the end to the uncertainty of the feminine. From this point radical obscenity becomes the dominant mode of 'sexual relations'

But the argument has to acknowledge also, he notes, that the feminine is not to be thought of as simply the process of 'seduction'. It is more fundamentally a form of challenge to the masculine to be a gender. It is a challenge to assume the position of primacy, to establish its hegemony and to exercise this to the limit (till death) (Baudrillard, 1979:34; 1990a: 21)). A specific pressure is exerted, and as a result, the masculine accommodates it and tries to contain it as if this negative was simply subversive. But the deadly form is that which is reversible not invertible and effectively seduction is the challenge of reversibility. This is not the seductiveness of the narcissistic 'mirror stage' of femininity, of the sexual ruse, but of seduction in the ironic form, as that which even 'breaks the reference to sex' and to desire, and moves to that of play and challenge.

There is more to seduction than any physical desire. What carries the day in the long run is a passion and engagement at the level of the sign, and this initiates a kind of sovereignty. Baudrillard puts this in the personal form: 'I shy away, it is not you who give me pleasure it is I who will make you play, and thereby rob you of your pleasure (*jouissance*)' (Baudrillard, 1990a: 22). The law of seduction is thus a continuous ritual, a play on who is seducing and whom is being seduced: the line of victory and defeat is illegible, there are no formal limits to the challenge. As against this, the sexual has only a banal conclusion, the accomplishment of physical desire.

If we return to the notion of modern sexual liberation, this is seen now as highly paradoxical. If the process is one of a feminisation or even a pornographisation of society as a whole, it is both a catastrophe for women but also for the entire symbolic order. In men it gives rise to a state of panic as men are faced with the liberated 'feminine subject' (Baudrillard, 1990a: 26), equalled only by the male fragility when faced with the 'alienated' feminine subject in sexual pornography. Whether 'liberated' or 'alienated', subject or object, sexual consummation assails the masculine. It is thus no accident, Baudrillard suggests, that pornography revolves around the feminine sex: there are here no scenes of weakness, fragility or loss of power for men. But sexuality generally has become a problem because it seems to require proof of capacity, and this has rendered the masculine sex vulnerable. The feminine sex is now available, in its degree-zero mode. But the power of continuity of the feminine is in marked contrast to the intermittance of the masculine.

At this point in the argument Baudrillard rejoins his analysis of consumer society: for the outcome is a society of sexual affluence. Society itself, he claims, no longer knows how to tolerate a scarcity of sexual goods (goods which only the feminine can provide). Society in its turn becomes feminised, and sexuality in the diffuse feminine mode proliferates.[9] It is advertising above all which generates this explosion of sexualisation, not to add sex to an object but rather to confer on the object this imaginary quality of the feminine, to be 'available at will' (Baudrillard, 1990a: 26). In this way society becomes monotonous. This is not just any monotony but very specifically the monotony of sexual pornography in which the masculine has a derisory role. The masculine is the marked term, it is too determined, and at the same time too fragile. The form of fascination goes into the neutral focussed on a sexuality that is both diffuse and active: the historical revenge of the feminine? Baudrillard's answer is: perhaps; but more certainly it is the continuation of the marked term in another form as an obsessional simulation of all the themes which have previously dominated this field: erectility, verticality, ascendance, growth, production. Behind the mechanical objectivication of signs the weakness of the masculine is all too clear, and degree-zero femininity carries it through.

OBSCENITY

But it is certainly important to consider the nature of the pornographic in more detail: if the *trompe l'oeil* facade challenged space itself to give more dimension, the pornographic seems to add in its way a dimension to the sexual: it is more real than real. But the former seduces, while the latter cannot. The more real than real, the hyperreal, fascinates. It is not sexuality on display in pornography, as many think; it is the absorption of reality into hyperreality. This accounts for so-called voyeurism; it is precisely the breakdown of the sexual scene and the eruption of the obscene. The sexual appears so close to the subject that it confounds itself. It is the end of illusion and the end of the imagination. If pornography of the traditional type still maintained a sexual content and continued the challenge through perversion and provocation, this has altogether passed away with the sexual revolution. Culture in the west passes into a state of new obscenity.

Modern irreality, then, is not in the imaginary, it is in the order of greater and greater exactitude and realism, heading as it were towards absolute reality. This is precisely the way in which art is now hyperreal, where even the pores of the skin are presented. It is the same in music with quadrophonic sound: in an air-conditioned room, music in four dimensions, ambient space, a technically perfect reconstitution of music by Bach and Mozart, which in this form has never previously existed is realised. Such music was never intended for this total ambience, which deprives the listener of all critical perception and the music of all charm. There is a confusion of the real with multiplication of dimensions. It is an obsession with technical perfectability, thus instead of improvement of quality of music, these systems constitute its definitive degradation. It is the pornography of music, just as pornography 'is the quadrophonics of sex' (Baudrillard, 1990a: 31).

The extreme realism of sound, has, as its equivalent in Japan, the 'vaginal cyclorama' at which men stare at prostitutes with their legs apart. They are 'permitted to shove their noses up to the eyeballs within the woman's vagina in order to see, to see better – what? . . . Obscenity has an unlimited future' (Baudrillard, 1990a: 31).

Thus culture has become obscene in all the full force of the word (ill-omened). Highly ritualised sexual practice has been displaced in favour of a naturalisation under the impress of the immediate gratification of desire. In former times it used to be: 'you have a soul, and therefore it must be saved'. Now, it has become, 'you have a sex, and you must put to good use' (Baudrillard, 1979: 57). All this is rather different from the sexuality as symbolic exchange (cf. Baudrillard, 1970: 236). It is seduction which operates an articulation in the symbolic order, a dual affinity with the structure of the other: indeed seduction should be seen primarily in this field as a challenge to the order of the sexual, and it triumphs. This is a profound triumph of ritual which reveals all revolutions and liberations are essentially fragile. Seduction, on the other hand, is ineluctable but changes its form. Take this example from an American film (*Capricorn One*, 1978) says Baudrillard, as an example of a new cynical mode of discourse, but one full of challenge and provocation, amorous inflection and complicity. A man eyes up a girl provocatively, and the girl responds 'What do you want?' And continues, 'Do you want to jump me? Then change your approach. Say you want to jump me!' The man replies 'Yes I want to jump you!' And the girl replies 'Then go fuck yourself.' Later, however, they reach the car together and she says 'I'll make coffee, and then you can jump me' (all the quotations in English in Baudrillard's text, 1979: 62). This, says Baudrillard, is a new form of seduction, one without nuance, functional, brutal, almost anatomical. In the writings of Philip Dick a parallel can be found which indicates that there can be a play on the very seductivity of obscenity – obscenity as a challenge.

This is a more general phenomenon, the undermining of apparently factual and 'true' discourse by other strategies and games. Pornography is an abstract form like science. It is a disenchanted form of the body (just as the enchanted form of use value is abolished in exchange, and the real is a disenchanted form of the world). The fact is, however, he insists, that in the end the ritual process is stronger than sex itself. This is revealed in the film *The Empire of the Senses* where sex is challenged at another level by death. There is nothing morbid or perverse in this, it is but the realisation of ancient tragedies. It is not a play on an affinity of life and death (thanatos) which is in question here, but sex as a ritual, a ceremony of which death is an obligatory denouement (Baudrillard, 1979: 65; 1990a: 45), it is the archetypal form of the accomplishment of the challenge. In fact, all forms of sexuality, even the most obscene, are vulnerable to it; they can pass into a reversible order. This is true of the body; and it is true also of power itself. This is not to be understood in any vulgar sense (which, he says, tautologically places or founds seduction in the desire of others), but as an order of reversibility which maintains a minimal cycle of symbolic exchange (not of separated positions) where power is exchanged according to a relation of challenge and response. A challenge can only be exchanged according to its cycle, into which it simply disappears. For at base, power does not exist, it certainly never exists as a unilateral force, a distinct reality. Seduction is eternally stronger than power, especially as power seeks to become immortal. It is subject, further, to all the illusions of production, and the trap of the direct relation to the real. This means that seduction is not to be found there. Or, indeed, in any field of force. If today, says Baudrillard, there is lure to power, it is perhaps because, there is a void which now threatens power with the possibility of reversibility. (For Baudrillard the real has never ever been of interest to anyone, it is charmless, an accumulation against death. What makes it fascinating is perhaps the very catastrophe of the imagination which is involved in making it appear.)

AGAINST PSYCHOANALYSIS

The usual way of thinking about the problem of seduction as a play of appearances, he claims, in psychoanalytic reason in any case, is to oppose a latent to a manifest content of discourse. There is always the temptation to invent or resurrect a meaning, a meaning behind a non-meaning. There is always the temptation to find a determination where one is missing. And this is believed to lead to a truth. Thus, an interpretation will always be led towards making connection with what is not said. Seduction, on the other hand, has to be understood in quite a different way: it is that which diverts us from truth. In this sense the superficiality of the manifest cancels out any hidden meaning, and attempts to charm it away by the enticements of pure appearance. But these appearances are not frivolous, they put into play a challenge and a passion which is more significant than truth:

> we needn't search for some beyond, in a *hinterwelt*, or in an unconscious, to find what diverts discourse. What actually displaces it, 'seduces' it in the literal sense, and makes it seductive, is its very appearance: the aleatory, meaningless, or ritualistic and meticulous, circulation of signs on the surface; its inflections, and its nuances.
>
> (Baudrillard, 1988b: 148; 1990a: 54)

Thus, against interpretation, which wants to reduce discourse, the seductiveness of discourse wagers itself and is even seduced by itself: it both absorbs meaning, and empties itself of it in order to fascinate others. The problem for discourse, is not therefore the unconscious and the supposedly determining effects of a deeper level of meaning; but, on the contrary, the problem of the 'superficial abyss of appearances'. In this sense it is the possible play of 'non-sense' on the surface of discourse which is the problem, the problem that is of the 'sacred horizon of appearances'. Against this phenomenon, modern forms of analysis are nothing more than a generalised reduction of all discourse to another level of 'deep meaning'.

And this inaugurates the 'violence and terrorism of interpretation'. It may well be in the last resort that it is this activity which is fragile, not that of the superficial or manifest appearance. Indeed, its function seems to be to build another type of fortress of meaning against the challenge of seduction. And the problem here, claims Baudrillard, is serious: it is clear, for example, that the phenomena which are appealed to by psychoanalysis, that is the dream, etc. are those phenomena which are highly seductive. Psychoanalysis is both seduced and unable to express this to itself. Indeed, it is also the case that Freud's primary repression was the repression of the fact of seduction. Freud abandoned the notion in 1897, and this has always been understood as an important moment in the formation of more positive concepts. But, says Baudrillard:

> seduction is not simply dismissed as a secondary element in comparison to more significant ones, such as infant sexuality, repression, the oedipus complex, etc. It is rather denounced as a dangerous force, which could be potentially fatal to the coherence of the future system.
>
> (Baudrillard, 1988b: 151)

But in modern French psychoanalysis, dominated by Lacan, a new form emerges. It is a kind of scientific psychoanalysis (which is not one he quickly notes), under the very spirit of seduction itself. But the play, even hallucinatory, of the signifiers, indicates the imminent collapse of psychoanalysis. Lacan places the symbolic under the control of the law. But this is a specious form. Freudianism has begun to collapse under the immense weight of its own productions, despite being perhaps the greatest system of interpretation ever created. This has happened as the revenge of appearances over interpretation. In fact, Lacanian notions of seduction complete the circle which began with repression. Basically the problem revolves around the notion of truth. In religion, and in Stalinist states, an enormous apparatus is necessary in order to protect such systems against the realisation that God or socialism is dead. These are only ways of preserving the seduction of a god or the revolution.

It is necessary, says Baudrillard, to identify and discuss two basic kinds of seductivity, the secret and the challenge.

THE SECRET AND THE CHALLENGE

First, the secret. This must, from the outset, Baudrillard suggests, be distinguished from that which is as yet unknown. It is rather the double, that which is not revealed in the complicity of knowing silence. There is an important quality of the secret here, a quality that is 'initiatory' that is, a recognition that the secret is on the other side of initiation. A specific form of tension is created between the existence of the secret and its non-possession or non-revelation. It is a peculiar complicity. This particular quality is, says Baudrillard 'the opposite of communication, and yet it can be shared' (Baudrillard, 1990a: 79, the translation in 1988b: 159 is in error here). Unlike that which is repressed or hidden and which strives to manifest itself, the secret appears as an implosive form: one can enter a secret but not leave. The secret, then, seems to draw its strength from an 'allusive and ritual power of exchange'. This is how it appears in Kierkegaard's 'Diary of a Seducer'(1971). In order to seduce, says Kierkegaard, an enigma must counter an enigma; seduction is an enigmatic duel which never reveals the secrets which motivate it. And yet this 'unsignified' of seduction, 'circulates, flows beneath words and meaning, faster than meaning' but always remains essentially invisible to meaning as its 'secret circulation'.

This phenomenon, then, is quite different from any psychological relation. It is not based on the idea of a shared fantasy or desire, and it is not a relationship of participation. It is important not to confuse the exoteric form of that which is spoken (but elsewhere), with that of the esoteric form of the secret. Unlike other forms of communication, this form is not in 'time', yet it seems to have its own rhythm. It is in this rhythm that the 'joy' of the secret returns to itself. It therefore breaks down the active and the passive, since each can become seductive. Here there is no interior and exterior; and no one can seduce unless they have been seduced. This game is played according to unspoken rules (which have a ritualistic character), and as it begins, it starts a process of circulation (which remains secretive).

Seduction, therefore, is reversible. It is reversed by the challenge and the power of defiance: seduction can exhaust itself. It is therefore, quite different from any operation of instinct, which is determined by drive and original energy (though not by aim or object). It is without 'origin' and has no specific form of the investment of energy. It is a pure form, a game.

Second, the challenge. This, too, has the form of the duel and is not only capable of being reversed but its essential tensions arise from this very possibility. It is important, Baudrillard suggests, to ask the question: why do we ever respond to a challenge? We seem, he notes, to respond without much prompting. This has a mysterious element to it. In one sense there is nothing more seductive than a challenge. It seems inevitable that the other is caught and involved, in a relation which is vertiginous: there is an element of madness which differentiates it from all other forms of communication. There is, here, something of a secret rule which assures the connection of signs that have no meaning as such. A challenge is quite different from a contract or interchange governed by laws. Against these the seductive challenge offers a ritualised pact, an obligation to respond to a challenge by a counter-challenge on the basis of its own rhythms; the rule of this exchange is never explicitly formulated or communicated. A law, then, is explicit and controlled; the rule of the challenge is implicit, immanent, immediate and inevitable.

Thus, the relation which is established remains enchanted, reversible, based on a tension that springs from the replacement of the contract with a 'staggering openness of possible responses'. The challenge, however, tends to be on the ground of a particular strength, and assumes a possible escalation to infinity. A strategy of seduction, on the other hand, tends to play on a weakness. But a weakness or failure is also a challenge. Seduction therefore tends to adopt weak signs; it plays with fragility, not with strength; but it is through fragility that seductiveness derives its powers: 'we seduce with our death, our vulnerability, and with the void that haunts us. The secret is to know how to play with death in the absence of a gaze' (Baudrillard, 1990a:83). Thus one can conclude, he says, that seduction is merely an 'immoral, frivolous, superficial and superfluous process'.[10] But this, in the end, is all powerful, and the dead are only truly dead when there are no longer any 'echoes from this world to seduce them, and no longer any rites challenging them to exist' (ibid: 84).

This is the order the game, of the rule, of strong seduction. And the implications of this are profound. It is not the case that one 'believes' in the rule, as in the law or in religion. It is only necessary that the observation of the law exists. The basic effectivity here is the challenge, and even the idea of 'belief in religion' is a highly dubious formula, like belief in Father Christmas. These faiths only really make sense if they are regarded as challenges: for instance, God is challenged to exist, and in sacrifice and prayer He is seduced; He cannot but respond. But the rule does not generalise or universalise itself; it remains enchanted, unlike the law which is based on the equality of right. In the rule the basic tie is that of the duel, the players are partners in a kind of bond, and there is no solidarity here. There is no need either for structure, superstructure or psychology. The rule has no philosophical foundation, or referent, and does not require a consensus. It also excludes work, and personal quality; on the contrary it involves only obligation, equality in the duel. It revolves around the ceremony. And 'meaning' is abolished here, by ritual itself.

Most of the evidence which Baudrillard uses to discuss these ideas is literary, notably the stories 'Death in Samarkand', 'The Diary of a Seducer' (Kierkegaard) and 'The Collector'.

DEATH AT SAMARKAND

The short fable 'Death at Samarkand' concerns a soldier who comes across the figure of Death at a market crossing and believes he notices Death making a gesture towards him. He immediately goes to the King for a horse so that he can escape quickly to Samarkand. When the King summons Death to ask why he has frightened his soldier in this way, Death replies 'I didn't mean to frighten him. It was just that I was surprised to see the soldier here, when we had a rendezvous tommorrow in Samarkand' (Baudrillard, 1990a:72).

Baudrillard follows this with two other short fictions: the first concerns a boy who, after asking a fairy to grant his wishes, is told that this will indeed be granted on condition that he never thinks of the colour red in the fox's tail. In spite of himself he can think of nothing else (Baudrillard, 1990a: 74). The second is very short, but still powerful: 'If you were to see writing on a door panel. "This door opens on to the void" – wouldn't you want to open it?' (ibid: 75). Baudrillard tries to analyse these stories as eminently seductive stories of seduction: he suggests there is something arbitrary yet compulsive and indeed necessary in its working out. Everything appears as a result the operation of chance elements yet everything seems completely predestined. Everything is apparently insignificant yet there is escalation to ultimate stakes. In fact Baudrillard's analysis concerns itself exclusively with the play of signs: in the first story the key is an involuntary sign as Death's gesture 'acted in spite of itself as a gesture of seduction'. Death is a rule, an indecipherable complicity between signs. In the second story it is the absurd, insignificant signifier which reveals its power. Because the colour red in the fox's tail is an empty referent, its action is magical. It seems simply the power of the void. Here, nothing (the void) exercises the passionate attraction of non-sense.

There are some grave difficulties with Baudrillard's analyses, probably most in evidence in the interpretation of the second story. Baudrillard's suggestion that the hypnotic effect of the tail is due entirely to the insignificance of the signifier is doubly problematic. Certainly it is easy to see the very insignificance of the tail set against infinite pleasure makes it seductive, and it is possible to imagine that Baudrillard might think of this red tail as a black hole into which the boy's imagination might disappear: but this is only as a result of the tension between the terms as they have been set in opposition. But even then it is not simply this opposition between the terms, or its tension, but the injunction which is thrown down, indeed even as a challenge, as bar set in motion, that the boy must not think of the colour red in the tail. This opens, rather obviously, into conventional issues of conscience and guilt, since the boy's orientations are already structured to scarcity and law. The attraction of the perverse infinity of pleasure (elsewhere considered by Baudrillard, the collection), follows the discharge brought by the action of conscience, a discharge onto the tail (or any object which might be thrown against the possibility of infinite pleasure). This means that the insignificant signifier is not the issue. The fairy could equally have put a significant one (the boy's mother, or father), in fact it is quite possible to analyse this story in orthodox Freudian terms, which here are superior to Baudrillard's flat semiology.

This problem is evident in the story of the door and the void. There is possibly a parallel, or many parallel stories of this kind in the work of Kafka (e.g. Kafka, 1983: 194–5, a story called 'At the Door of the Law').[11] Kafka's 'At the door' is more powerful than Baudrillard's since the door is not simply marked 'void', but has a doorkeeper who says that the door to the law may be opened, but not just at the moment. After years of waiting, the 'man from the country', asks the doorman why no one else ever enters this particular door. The doorman, now facing someone who is very old, admits that 'no one else could gain admittance here because this entrance was meant for you alone', and adds 'now I'm going to close it' (Kafka, 1983: 195). Baudrillard's story even appears as a truncated version of this one (omitting the trap set by the law, the deferred effects which will arise if the door has written on it 'this door is for you, do not open it', or 'do not open it yet', or 'this door is for you, do not open it because it opens onto the void'). In other words the void is simply forbidden; certainly the chasm, the abyss, exercises its fascination, but would anyone open such a door without looking over one's shoulder to see if there is not a doorman, or even a red fox's tail, somewhere?

The story of 'Death at Samarkand', does not however, appear in the same light. Here Baudrillard again sees the story as an indication that death is not a 'brute' fact, and occurs 'only through seduction' (Baudrillard, 1990a: 73). The key events in this story revolve around Death's involuntary gesture towards the soldier: the surprise at seeing the soldier. Death appears a curious figure: he can be summoned by the King, he can be met by accident or by a rendezvous (which is known as such to Death, and by others, but not to the second party). Baudrillard says Death has no plan, no strategy, Death works by chance. In this sense there is no unconscious in the story. But, again, another reading is possible. This suggests that the key to the story is not the chance encounter in the market place ('not meant to frighten', which may cause us to smile indicating there may be some unconscious effects here after all), but the coincidence of the meeting in Samarkand (although it is a rendezvous). Why Samarkand? It may be the place to flee to, it is as far away as possible. If so it is not an arbitary sign, but highly charged and motivated, a likely place, in the unconscious, for a meeting. Thus in this reading the soldier is not 'seduced' but frightened by Death's gesture; he is seduced by Samarkand. Baudrillard forces his analysis in order to say 'Death's naive gesture . . . acted in spite of itself as a gesture of seduction' (ibid): it is difficult to think of anything less seductive.

DIARY OF A SEDUCER

There are more problems with Baudrillard's main example of the principle of seduction in his discussion of Kierkegaard's 'Diary of a Seducer' (1971: 297–440).[12] The fictional diary of Johannes, recounting his seduction of Cordelia, is analysed by Baudrillard as an exemplary account of the ironic strategy of seduction, its techniques and its dynamic. Again it is important to compare Baudrillard's reading with the story as given by Kierkegaard, for this is instructive in relation to what it will reveal about Baudrillard's own techniques. For Baudrillard, the key to seduction is the mirror, the seducer mirrors Cordelia without her being aware of it. This makes the strategy of seduction oblique to its object, it is like a flash of wit, or a dream, as it crosses the psychic structures to find a 'blind spot, the secret that lies revealed, the enigma that constitutes the girl, even to herself' (Baudrillard, 1990a: 107).

Seduction in this sense has two moments, says Baudrillard: Cordelia's feminine resources are mobilised and suspended. She becomes a free-acting agent, yet in this very movement she is eventually caught, unwittingly. The second state is one of grace, even sovereignty. A vulgar seduction proceeds directly, is persistent, repetitive. A 'true' seduction proceeds indirectly, by reference to an absence 'or better, it invents a kind of curved space, where signs are deflected from their trajectory and returned to their source' (ibid: 108). This is the space of seduction as the object mobilised into a game where everything appears fated. The moment of suspense, or as Kierkegaard calls it, the 'spiritual' is the moment between the throw and the reading of the dice. The seducer (Johannes) like a fencer, moves indirectly to form a field of illusion into which Cordelia will be attracted, even to the point where she will begin to take initiatives, in fact for the seducer it is only when she has begun to take initiatives that the game is interesting enough for him to be seduced, that is she herself must make the crucial initiative (ibid: 109). Baudrillard suggests that Johannes:

> knows how to let the signs hang. He knows that they are favourable only when left suspended, and will move of themselves towards their appointed destiny. He does not use the signs up all at once, but waits for the moment when they will all respond, one after the other, creating an entirely unique conjuncture of giddiness and collapse.
>
> (Baudrillard, 1990a: 109)

Eventually Cordelia is engaged to Johannes, which is analysed only as an ascetic moment in seduction, and a 'sort of humour' in the disappearance of the stakes of seduction. In this moment of nullity, says Baudrillard, Cordelia is predestined and 'all her fire of passion lies revealed, just beneath the surface, in its transparence' (ibid: 111). This is true, he notes, of all seduction, Its passion lies in its predestination, this is the place where the seducer triumphs. At this conjuncture Cordelia, for Baudrillard, is a mythical figure, an enigmatic but equal partner to the seducer, and the final 'seduction' is a sacrificial form, a form of murder, a work of art, a flash of wit, a duel and an erotic maieutics. If there is an ethics of the natural simplicity in Cordelia, the seduction works at a second level, that of aesthetics, artifice, the play of the sign. The specific, ironic seduction is an aesthetics in a non-transcendental mode, the mirror of deception. A vulgar attraction is transformed into irony. Yet when she is finally 'seduced', 'becomes a woman', she is for Johannes dead, and is abandoned. Johannes says, 'if I were a God, I would change her into a man' (in Baudrillard, 1990a: 117). Baudrillard comments:

> Merely to seduce is interesting in the first degree; but there is a matter of what is interesting in the second degree. This doubling is the secret of the aesthetics. Only what is interesting about the interesting has seduction's aesthetic force.
>
> (ibid)

How, then, has Baudrillard read this story? To grasp this of course it is necessary to return to Kierkegaard's text, and indeed others which also deal with the theme of seduction and with the responses of the seduced. His main figures in these games are those of Don Juan and Faust:

> Of Don Juan we must use the word seducer with great caution . . . he simply does not fall under ethical categories. To be a seducer requires a certain amount of reflection and consciousness, and as soon as this is present, then it is proper to speak of cunning and intrigues and crafty plans. This consciousness is lacking in Don Juan. Therefore he does not seduce.
>
> (Kierkegaard, 1971: 97)

For Kierkegaard, Don Juan is in great contrast to Faust, who seduces only once, but in a way which is very different from that of Don Juan:

> The power of such a seducer is speech, ie, the lie . . . he and his activities are extremely musical, and from the aesthetic standpoint come within the category of the interesting. The object of his desire is accordingly, when one rightly considers him aesthetically, something more than the merely sensuous.
>
> (Kierkegaard, 1971: 98)

The Faustian mode is examined at some length, both are daemonic figures, yet Faust is higher in the scale of sophistication for: 'the sensuous becomes significant for him only after he has lost an entire preceding world, but the consciousness of this loss is not erased, it is constantly present, and he seeks not so much enjoyment as diversion of mind', (ibid: 204). This is evidently the case with Johannes.

Kierkegaard stresses that for Faust, 'happiness is not his companion', and unlike Don Juan, but like the figure of Death, 'young women do not dance into his embrace; he frightens them to him. . . . Faust seeks an immediate life by which he can be renewed and strengthened. And where can this be found better than in a young woman.' And in Goethe's Faust, 'Mephistopheles shows him Margaret in a mirror. His eye finds enjoyment in the vision. . . . What he desires is the pure, rich, untroubled, immediate happiness of a woman's soul, but he desires it not spiritually, but sensually.' For Faust, everything depends on Margaret's 'innocent simplicity' (Kierkegaard, 1971: 207): she does not comprehend him, yet 'she clings to him' as a child, she vanishes into him completely (ibid: 209). He is like an acorn in a small pot which he will burst, he cannot be contained in this immediacy, he 'desires her sensually – and abandons her' (Kierkeguard, 1971: 209).

It is clear that in the 'Diary of a Seducer' Kierkegaard has developed a situation where Faust is raised to a higher power, where the principal objective is a spiritual desire, an interest in the second degree, but this is only to obtain, through the object, a sensuous pleasure of the same kind as Faust, and when it is achieved the object is likewise abandoned. The 'Diary' is prefixed with an epigraph from Mozart's Don Juan ('His ruling passion is the fresh young girl'), but it is clear that Johannes is not Don Juan, but neither is his object a character such as Faust's Margaret; here there appears to be a crossover, as if Margaret is replaced with Don Juan's Elivera (Kierkegaard, 1971: 188–202), (or a version of); that is, someone more passionate and active.

But who is Johannes? He is described in the presentation of the 'Diary' as obsessed with his own aesthetic, and as having great oscillations of character:

> in the first instance he enjoyed the aesthetic personally, in the second instance he enjoyed his own aesthetic personally. . . . In the first instance he constantly needed reality as occasion, as factor; in the second instance, reality was submerged in the poetic.
>
> (Kierkegaard, 1971: 301)

The judgement continues that Johannes was not a person overwhelmed by reality, on the contrary, 'he was too strong; but his strength was really a sickness. As soon as reality had lost its significance as a stimulus, he was disarmed, and this constituted the evil in him' (ibid: 302). The introduction hardly presents a picture of exemplary seduction, and this is complemented by the conclusions of Cordelia herself, who says 'sometimes he was so intellectual that I felt myself annihilated as woman. At other times he was so wild and passionate, so filled with desire, that I almost trembled before him . . . always I was carried away by him' (ibid: 305–6).

It is, however, Johannes who speaks in the 'Diary', and his encounter with Cordelia is first as she is shopping, and she is mirrored in the very objects on sale; the real mirror, which Baudrillard acutely notices, is, like Johannes, at the the counter. There is no doubt that we are placed within Baudrillard's basic problematic of consumption (it is curious that in 'Seduction' this only emerges indirectly). It is also clear that this mirror has its parallel in Faust, as Margaret is first revealed in the mirror. There is further allusion probably, to the story of the Prague student (see Baudrillard, 1970: 301–3), where the devil buys the student's soul (in the mirror) in exchange for success. But the mirror for Johannes is, like him, a slave, a mirror which also catches her, but 'does not embrace her' (Kierkegaard, 1971: 311). It is also an unhappy mirror, says Johannes, it cannot retain the image, it must pass it on, it must be shared. It grasps appearances.

But Johannes has already reached a high level of reflection himself, and has a strategic reason for choosing this particular object:

> I constantly seek my prey among young girls not among young women. A women less natural, more coquettish; an affair with her is not beautiful, not interesting; it is piquant. This year I may not collect much; this girl absorbs too much of my attention.
>
> (Kierkegaard, 1971: 320)

Men have need for others, they are reflective. But young girls should 'never try to be interesting', and that means that in their youth 'she needs to be alone' (ibid: 335), for above all she needs to be self-contained. This intensifies the pleasure of the ritual, of initiation into the secret, so: 'A man with true aesthetic appreciation always finds that a girl who is innocent in the deepest and truest sense is brought to him veiled' (ibid: 336). And this kind of seducer is not interested in the artless, and the stolen kiss; if the art and the pleasure is controlled it is to: 'so arrange it that a girl's only desire is to give herself freely . . . when she almost begs to make this free submission . . . but this always requires spiritual influence' (ibid: 337).

What the 'Diary' presents, then, is an exemplary case of a perfect seduction in this sense, which, if we are to place this in the context of Baudrillard's own theory (and this is even pronounced in 'Seduction' itself), is a seduction which works by producing a liberation, a free subject, but only on condition that this subject is already formed in a specific way, out of specific kind of raw material, developed into a space which is already curved well in advance so that everything leads to a duel (in which there will be a crime, a murder, in the aesthetic mode). This parallels precisely Baudrillard's thesis of the liberation of the proletarian, the liberation of the consumer, the liberation of women in advanced affluent societies (the 'masses will be psychologised in order to be seduced; they will be rigged up with desires in order to be distracted. . . . The poor, seduced and manipulated masses! Where once they had to endure domination under the threat of violence, now they must accept it by dint of seduction' (Baudrillard, 1990a: 175); but, says Baudrillard, this is quite different in its form from 'aristocratic' seduction in the form of the duel; mass seduction is a soft form, diffuse, tensile, and arises from the oppressed themselves in their very liberation, as the masses manage its own servitude.)

Johannes' problems revolve around his assessment of Cordelia's character: is she proud, is she so feminine she will become reflective? Is she only to be enjoyed as natural? Baudrillard here says some surprising things. The seductive strategies followed by Johannes, he says, are in fact learnt from Cordelia; seduction 'originates entirely with the girl.' This is why it can be said that 'she has already played her hand before the seducer begins to play his. Everything has already taken place; the seduction simply rights a natural imbalance' (Baudrillard, 1990a: 99). Thus the righting of this imbalance leads to a particular form of warfare (for Johannes). The 'strategic principle' he says, 'is always to work her into an interesting situation. The interesting is the field in which the battle must be waged, the potentialities of the interesting must be exhausted' (Kierkegaard, 1971: 341).

There follows a campaign in two stages, the first is prosaic, the second enters into the poetic. (At the end of the 'Diary', it is noted that there is a third, the possible poetic disengagement; as it is it is clear that Johannes makes a most prosaic unpoetic, departure from the scene of the 'crime'). The first phase is determined by an attempt to challenge and neutralise Cordelia's femininity, partly by ridicule, but certainly by 'colourless intellectuality', so that she turns against herself and 'throws herself into my arms . . . still quite neutrally' (ibid: 342); the second phase is the awakening of femininity to a high intensity, and then a play with the formalities of the relationship, which she turns against, so that finally Johannes claims 'she belongs to me with the force of a world passion' (ibid).

As this works out, Johannes has to encounter and put to his own use, Cordelia's aunt, and a friend of Cordelia's, Edward, who is in love with her but lacks anything, says Johannes, but the most banal and hesitant strategies. Johannes takes up the role of confidant of Edward, advising him as part of his own plan, (he even at one point thinks of himself a possible Mephistopheles in relation to Edward, but, he reflects, 'Edward is no Faust'), and the role of conversant, with the aunt, whom he charms as possibly the decisive influence on Cordelia. First he ignores Cordelia, appearing purely uninterested in her, as he pursues his conversations with the aunt; but once he has gained a foothold, this changes into a series of provocations to Cordelia's femininity. Finally, he circulates a rumour that he is in love with 'a young girl'. His move, which ends the first phase, is a proposal of engagement which successfully passes through the aunt to Cordelia. He has made it appear that this 'confirmed batchelor' has succumbed to the charms of Cordelia. Now, using Hegelian notions, Johannes suggests that she has been sublated, she has had to perish in order that she could be transformed (Kierkegaard, 1971: 348).

The next phase involves the poetic art of developing Cordelia's feelings erotically, in view of the 'ultimate enjoyment' (ibid: 364). In this new phase there are two parts, the first is an art of disappearance, in which she will be taught how to triumph in pursuing him: this will bring her strength and liberation (ibid: 379). The second begins when she already feels free, feels her own power and passion, so that for him the struggle at last becomes worthwhile: it will lead to conquest. The aim, in this last phase, is to engage the erotic and then to withdraw it, so that Cordelia will want to use it as a means to win him back:

Erotically she is completely equipped for the struggle . . . there is a power
in her . . . she must not be held too long at this peak.
She will become the tempter who seduces me to go beyond the usual
limitation. She will do this consciously.

(Kierkegaard, 1971: 420)

Indeed, he leads her to her end by breaking off of the engagement, to
show that the 'informal bond' is strong. This is followed by a long (guilty)
reflection on the cruelty of women, which leads to the final act of the drama,
preceded by a number of 'significant omens', and self-congratulations on
the part of Johannes: 'her development was my handiwork. . . . How much
I have gathered into this one moment' (Kierkegaard, 1971: 439). Finally,
he reports 'it is over now, and I hope never to see her again. When a girl
has given away everything, then she is weak, then she has lost everything'
(ibid).

Before commenting on Baudrillard's analysis it is necessary to look,
quickly, at Baudrillard's analysis of the film *The Collector*, which tells
the story of a kidnap of a young women who is kept in a basement. The
collector will spare her if only she 'admits herself defeated and seduced'. He
will spare her if she 'loves him spontaneously'. One evening he invites her to
dine upstairs. At this meal, says Baudrillard, she 'genuinely tries to seduce
him'. This, however, provokes a panic reaction and he re-incarcerates her.
She dies. She is buried. Baudrillard comments, this is about the need to
be loved, and the refusal to be seduced. Thus we enter the world of
perversion, the spell of dead objects, where the dead sex object is
as beautiful as 'a butterfly with fluorescent wings' (the collector has
his butterfly collection).[13] The logic of the collector is perverse, it is
irreversible since the Other 'is immortal and indestructible'. But this is
only another lower form of seduction, says Baudrillard, who here reaches
a basic theoretical problem: since all objects can become seductive, in this
light, the specificity of his problem is in risk of disappearing: even 'the
odious and the abject can seduce. Where does the detour of seduction
stop?' (Baudrillard, 1990a: 127).

Baudrillard's discussion leads to the following conclusion: essentially
there is a profound difference here, for the pervert is radically suspicious
of seduction; he codifies it and therefore breaks the rule of the secret. He
changes it into a law. 'Perversion is a frozen challenge; seduction is a living
challenge' (Baudrillard, 1990a: 128). Essentially this is realised through an
effort by the pervert to seek a mastery 'over the fetishised rule and absolute
ritual circumscription. The latter is no longer playful'.

If we return to Johannes, it is clear that indeed Baudrillard can only
have presented a perversion in the guise of an exemplar. Johannes, in fact,
never disguises the fact that he is a collector, blaming Cordelia, incredibly,
for taking up so much of his time. It is surely the exercise of mastery in
aesthetic seduction that is his object, a mastery over the rule and ritual of

seduction. In the end there is no attempt to allow the seduction of Cordelia, at the stage of the aesthetically interesting, to play into reversibility. His two options only appear as escape through direct abandonment, after the conquest, or to make a 'poetic disappearance'. The third possibility, the one which Cordelia herself had anticipated now that she was a player in the game, was denied.

In fact Baudrillard seems to realise this, 'in effect she was robbed of her own seduction' and was turned into a 'trophy in some very intimate and devastating plot, the object of spiritual abduction' (Baudrillard, 1990a: 118). This is only another way of saying that she was given false pretenses, that the real secret of the story was in the plot, that is, in the intention that she be abandoned, that she be manipulated into a situation where she could be abandoned (after being conquered). An intention which, at root is not interested in reversible seduction, but in seduction as revenge for an inequality in nature. Baudrillard says of the collector that 'his love of the object, the amorous stratagems with which he surrounds it, display a hatred and fear of seduction. And not just the seductiveness of the object: he is just as repelled by any seduction that might emanate from himself' (ibid: 122). The difference between the collector and Johannes is more to be found in the fact that the former uses direct violence and intimidation, the latter uses intellectual means and the manipulation of situations and agents, to set up the victim as self-sacrificing, as if 'the ultimate enjoyment' was indeed an absolute, an absolute annihilation of 'everything' Cordelia possessed.

9   Fatal objects

Everything happens as the result of unwarranted predestination.
Baudrillard (1988e: 85)

The final phase of Baudrillard's work to date moves to the analysis of the object in its purity (or impurity), in its fatal passion, in its destiny. It is clear that Baudrillard has attempted to develop a remarkable epistemological reflection in order to make this investigation possible. Previously his analysis of the symbolic order has focused on gift exchange, seduction, anagrammatic resolution, on the rule; now the focus changes, and turns to epistemology, where the key term becomes that of the object's fatal strategy. The principal idea here is that the modern epistemologies, epistemes, centre on the notion of individual rational causation, voluntarism or structural causality, or indeterminism and probability. These, he argues, are all part of the same intellectual world. That which opposes this matrix is the epistemology of predestination, the fatal destiny of the object itself. It is clear from his own journal writings that he himself has also begun to live in this modality, a poetic form which radically opposes the Sartrean notion of the project, and the Althusserian notion of theoretical practice as dominated by its means of theoretical production.

IMMINENCE / *ÉMINENCE GRISE*

The key section of the discussion of the new epistemology has been in English for many years (Baudrillard, 1981d), but since the form of the appearance of the article gives no clue as to its wider significance it is probably unremarkable that no discussion has taken place around its propositions. (The article, called 'Fatality or reversible imminence' does not explain these terms. Curiously, key discussions are found in the adjacent sections of the book from which this is taken (*Les Strategies Fatales*). Take, for instance, sections preceding the extract published in English in 1981, one of which is called *L'imminence grise*, and surely gives the clue to the interpretation of the curious phrase 'reversible imminence' which otherwise would remain completely obscure (1983b:

186–7). This section contains the story of 'S' in Venice (a story which reappears many times in Baudrillard's work, (1983e) and again in 1990b: 162–6).

The two key terms reversion and imminence/eminence are themselves to be approached carefully. The insistence of the term reversibility ensures we are still on the ground of the problem of non-accumulation, with the idea of annihilation and transposition. It is clear that Baudrillard wants to insist that for him transsexuality is a hyperreal form, in which the possibility of reversibility is paradoxically reduced. Yet transvestism appears, at face value, as if it is a primary form of reversion. However, Baudrillard insists there is a key difference since reversibility depends on the prestructured existence of positions in the duel or the polarities in the dialectic. For Baudrillard one of the key myths here is that of Tiresias, who has experienced being both male and female.[1] Tiresias is asked to provide an opinion in a dispute between Hera and Zeus as to which sex obtains the greatest sexual pleasure. Tiresias proclaims that it is women by the power of nine (Baudrillard, 1983b: 186). For this remark taken as an offence by Hera he is blinded, not, says Baudrillard, because he has revealed a secret, but in the provocation to the desire of men (ibid: 183). This is a testament to the power of the challenge, of an outbidding, and not to a merging and fusion of the sexes. It points to the importance of metamorphosis and of the fatal. There are, in this myth the two sides to sexuality, as there has been in the eternal dream of eros, just as there are two sides to time (Baudrillard, 1983b: 186). It is, however, women who metamorphose into themselves, while the males metamorphose towards the feminine. Metamorphosis is never symmetrical, but it has to be understood as equally reversible.

The story of 'S' (which appears under the subheading 'L'Imminence gris'), is a story of a woman who follows a stranger (very slightly acquainted) in the streets as if removing all traces of his movements. In this way, says Baudrillard, she became his destiny. She wanted to create a kind of void around him, a vacuum, into which he was intended to fall. In this, however, it is not true to say that she had any specific desire: although she follows him to Venice, she doesn't herself desire this. She is not interested in his subjectivity, but nevertheless her existence alters the shape and curvature of his space (ibid: 187).[2] This void and the effect it produces on the subject is what Baudrillard calls the *éminence grise*: the art to make the other disappear (ibid: 186), and this is what 'S' does. The very idea of following a person, by chance, in the street, of following an aleatory route (it seems to go nowhere), becomes in its own way fascinating. It is to enter a network, into which the subject and the object are to disappear, since the subject exists only in the traces of the other. This must not be interpreted by the idea of drift (a popular current notion though for Baudrillard, one which does not seduce). What is seductive is the effect of doubling the course of the other (as in the Johannes' mirror (Kierkegaard)): it is the sense which arises when (for the subject–object) there is someone behind who knows that the route chosen leads nowhere. This is an uncanny feeling which can be experienced in the intense form of being shadowed.

'S' follows a virtual stranger to Venice, she searches a hundred hotels before finding him. She rents a room opposite the hotel in order to be able to follow his movements. She is not attracted to him, and has no desire to meet him. Because she might be recognised she disguises herself. Armed with binoculars and camera she tracks him and documents his movements. Even though it is Carnival in Venice she is only interested in his movements. She asks after him, and finds out about his projects, even the hour of his train to Paris. She takes an earlier train so that she can photograph his arrival.

In the 1990 version the story stops there. In 1983 it continues, with 'S' keeping to the track a little longer: she contacts the people who work with him . . . but the story is cut short, for although she has tried to avoid direct contact he now has become aware of her presence, and 'he becomes violent, the charm is lost and she abandons him' (Baudrillard, 1983b: 188).[3] Such a sense of being followed, says Baudrillard, can easily lead to the feeling of persecution. This is not at all the goal of 'S', which is to remove all traces of movement, but no one can live without leaving traces: the *éminence grise* (or *éminence blonde*, 1983b: 189), is that which steals the traces. Here the photograph which may appear to capture a presence, in fact marks an absence: he is followed and has no knowledge of having been 'present' to her. It is not in itself interesting to know that someone actually leads a double life. What is interesting is that which has the effect of a doubling, the uncanny 'intuition' that someone, the Other, is one's own double. An objective seduction transfigures a banal reality. In this case there is a transfiguration in the sense that an existence is indeed given a destiny (of the Other). It is parallel to the story of 'Death at Samarkand' where Death knows the appointed place of the rendezvous. In the story of 'S' destiny is in fact nowhere. It is not enough that a story be illogical for it to act seductively, the signs must work in a certain esoteric fashion. It is the same in theory.

EPISTEMOLOGY

The key sections of the discussion of epistemology consider the nature of chance, chaos and probability, and evidently we are not far from the story of 'S' as she has chosen her object by chance (virtually). But chance can also be posed in relation to the enchanted world: what is chance to God? Hölderlin, imagined the turning away, the disillusionment of the gods with human society, as a form of disenchantment. But in the face of the world of chance they have, says Baudrillard, become simply tired:

> If we suppose that an energy is necessary to animate the universe, to create signifying interconnection, fragile islets of anti-chance, then, sooner or later this energy will be wanting, even God will no longer

have enough strength to prevent the annihilation of meaning . . . God himself has ceased to struggle, turning away before the irruption of an insane universe. God is not scandalised, ulcerated, wounded by chance: he is tired.

(Baudrillard, 1981d: 275)

In order for it to operate, chance requires a certain kind of space. It permits the liberation of things and bodies as random phenomena only if the space is neutral, indifferent, for meetings which occur must do so without the slightest obligation. If this space is turned around back onto the human subject this subject introjects a kind of indetermination into all the spheres of existence: Brownian motion becomes human motion. If objective, structural causation accounts for a small portion of the human domain, the rest seems appropriately conceived by factors which can only be assessed through probabilities. But in theory chance requires that two orders, two series, two objects must encounter one another, just as causality requires the meeting of the two ends of the chain: cause and effect. This idea of connection of contact is very specific, and this is rarely noticed. Compare the meetings in the sacred world of ceremonial: here things 'interconnect' but they do so without coming into contact. The sacred movements enact a ceremony, a ritual, and objects move together, challenge each other, but do not touch. In the modern world this order of interweaving has been eclipsed, and the new space of things is impure, obscene. The action of chance is a form of obscene contact.

Even this idea can be subverted in a naive gesture: it is said that God produces chance (Stewart, 1990). For chance, with its possible beneficent outcomes provides the possibility of hope. It also has the dramatic effect of relieving huge burdens of guilt from human affairs. It could be said: 'Primitive people believed in a universe . . . of the omnipotence of thought and of will, without any trace of chance, but precisely, they lived in magic and cruelty. Chance allows us to breathe' (Baudrillard, 1981d: 276). In effect, Baudrillard suggests, the God who ordains chance and who therefore holds the world apart so that chance events can occur is 'ironically yet more extraordinary than the God who rules all things by his will, more extraordinary than the God of universal predestination' (ibid). The Promethean God has a 'fantastic' task, that of isolating all things, breaking all sequences, a God of almost infinite energy who can shatter all the natural affinities and attractions. In this light, says Baudrillard, how little chance there is that chance exists. But this immense expenditure of energy can also be seen to be a weakness, for it is the sign that a God of infinite energy cannot govern the universe directly. It is a better hypothesis to imagine the death of God, and blind chance is the action of things in his absence.

But there is an even more strange outcome. This is that the events which happen by chance seem to be more interesting or more significant than those things which happen as a result of the action of well-tried causes. These chance events are the 'special effects' of the universe, and they have a charm unmatched by the operation of rational forces. But it was the work of an 'ironic and diabolical' mind to have invented the operation of 'causal interconnections', and the mind that did so can rightly be described says Baudrillard as 'the devil of his time and should have been burnt alive' (Baudrillard, 1981d: 277). Yet it is the other possibility which is more interesting and mysterious. The mysteries of the world of attractions, interconnections, sequence, that is – where the indifference of chance does not exist – have more charm. The real problem in this universe is not to make contact, but to prevent the 'total correlation of events, to stop this vertigo of seduction' (ibid: 278). In this wwworld there is an ineluctable order, a destiny, as in speech where 'words have the same compulsion . . . to come together as if destined', not certainly at random, for it has a high degree of order, like poetry and theory, a high degree of self-regulation. Chance is never destiny, and destiny is a higher order.

Reason certainly has its effects but it is important to note that it does not establish a rational project of making connections, meanings, significance. It is, on the contrary, the introduction of a specific form of *neutralisation* where there was previously a magnetism. It breaks the eternal cycle of appearance. Thus rationality has therefore an obscene dimension, the promotion of an emptiness into the heart of things. Yet even the apparently rational ordering of things produces its ironies. For example, take the game of chance. Chance is paradoxically and radically denied in each participant for luck is not found on the ground of probabilities, but is a sign of election, of seduction. Luck is never neutral, it can be wooed, forced, encouraged. It must be challenged, just as God is challenged. Luck escalates, it has the form of the snowball, it is catastrophic. It is a challenge to God to enter into the game, and he must allow things to follow their destiny, to permit the order of secret conjugations to be made apparent.

This is the course of the fatal. In lifting the causal contract itself things become fatally convergent, not divergent. This is evident in poetry, and theory: arbitrary devices where things are 'caught in their own fatal development'. And this is only another form of exponential logic, a logic of excess. It is the same with the concatenation of minor misfortunes which through amplification, take on a different, and fatal dimension; even dreams and words, drained of their heavy meaning come to exercise effects as pure events on their own. Take a dream:

> I have just experienced a solemn though enigmatic bereavement. Someone tells me that this bereavement . . . happened very simply. I answer that it is always like that. And everyone around breaks into an immense burst of laughter. I have released a kind of laugh catastrophe.
>
> (Baudrillard, 1981d: 283)

What has happened, according to Baudrillard, is a massive but unintended interconnection, relating only to what was exactly uttered. It is, he says, the effect of a gesture which takes on meaning which was never intended. These are dreams, but they are found in the basic material of everyday life. Even seduction works by these unforseen conjunctures a strategy tries to reproduce. This only means that catastrophic conjunctures are never as such caused, they indeed abolish cause.

The way that the catastrophic event unfolds says Baudrillard wickedly is very pleasurable; things interweave in a way which is vertiginous, as though through an immediacy of seduction. And this process works towards its destiny:

> I remember an episode in which, having been saved miraculously from a fall in a car, the Spaniard stopped at the side of the road in order to touch us religiously, saying 'Suerte, Suerte.' The sign of the appearance of things is also that of their disappearance. The sign of their birth will be that of their death . . . that is destiny.
>
> (Baudrillard, 1981d: 286)

Destiny is revealed within the mysterious sequence, the doubling of signs (which are therefore not arbitrary, but attracted, seduced by an enigmatic fatal interconnection, for 'nothing is less accidental than the sign at the beginning which reappears at the end' (ibid)). It is the fatal meeting which is common, the chance event that is rare. As it is thus necessary to develop from prediction to prophecy, and this is the order of destiny, the world is comprehensible only as the precession and return of the sign. It is in the course of a ceremony that the course of events in the world can be grasped, he says in a voice which is itself prophetic, the ceremony of the world follows the same order.

Again Baudrillard presents what is an apparently personal instance. The events are obviously significant for Baudrillard, and certainly it is significant for what it tells us about him. There are two disconnected events some 10 years apart. In the first, Baudrillard has abandoned someone; in the second, someone has abandoned him. These people were important, he dreamed of them often. He had made no connection, but perhaps there was a sort of reversibility here, since the two were one day suddenly 'resolved' under a single sign, which fatally linked the two events. This coincidence was not chance, and there was no atonement in the conjunction. The coincidence had not been worked at psychologically, but altogether in a different modality, that of predestination of the sign. The conjunction and reversibility was intelligible without the secret having been revealed (Baudrillard, 1981d: 287–8).[4]

Something here seduces precisely because it is not wanted. This world is cruel, however, and it suggests the immense relief that entered the world with the invention of chance. But it is interesting to ask, says Baudrillard, which of the two systems is ultimately the more powerful. In the cruel universe of the omnipotence of thought, no one is innocent, and responsibility rules supreme, the subjective seems to pass to the object, and to the event, so that the world appears wanted, loved, invented. In this world it is necessary also that even the death of a friend should 'not have escaped from our thought and from our will' (Baudrillard, 1981d: 289).

The first characteristic of destiny is quite different from the process of meaning and law, which as Kafka rightly points out, says Baudrillard, always involves a delay. Rilke adds something here: destiny, he notes, is that which arrives without having been produced, it is the precession of effects over causes, the effects often disappear before the labour of the cause has finished its work. It is just the case with the secret, which travels faster than causes, and the secret of seduction which is always ahead of time. Even writing moves more quickly than conceptual connection, which is its secret.[5] A catastrophe does not wait, it is on the contrary, ahead of its appointed date.

The second is the insertion of reversibility into the causal order. The normal course of causality is the action of the cause on the effect, but in the process of predestination this is reversed so that the effect triumphs over the cause, and seduces it. This is felt and experienced as a dangerous situation, since there is no place for chance. Thus the movement towards uncertainty in western epistemology is equivalent to the movement into the hyperreal, or as Baudrillard calls it the hyperrational. Yet there is even here a certain 'presentiment' of a reversibility of the laws of science, quite contrary to its own logic and intuitions.

The third is the importance of the structure of the ceremonial itself, which as he shows with reference to a long quotation from the Hindu *Book of Manou*, has the shape of a destiny, in the concatenation of signs which mark out the necessary trajectory of an order, not a sociological order, or a subjective order, or evidently a random order. This order is minutely disciplined by signs and the rule which govern the process of metamorphosis. But the essential theoretical point is that this structure is not ordered by a system of simple statuses or differences, or even distinctions. It is through a system of discriminations that the structure unfolds: these are sacred distinctions, in a kind of theatre of cruelty, where each instant is marked by a necessary sign. Everything revolves around a process that is at the same time initiatory and ineluctable (Baudrillard, 1983b: 237–40). Baudrillard notes with a staggering irony that theory itself must also play this role: its struggle against the obscene mingling of things, like a ceremony it proceeds in terms of its own discriminations: in order to re-establish discriminations where they have been confused (ibid: 254).

FATAL STRATEGIES

The paradox of Baudrillard's discussion is that it does not lead to complete passivity or to simple compliance with a predestined universe. Clearly for Baudrillard the universe is active, passionate, and exists as a response to the challenge that has been made to it, just as the human is a response to the challenge from things. Thus if there is fate – Kismet, it is also a strategy alive in things. Perhaps he says, there is only one fatal strategy, theory itself (Baudrillard, 1988b: 198). This is, without further discussion, difficult to interpret, and it would be incautious, at this point, to link the symbolic order and theory. What occupies Baudrillard here is the distinction between banal and fatal strategies, for it is the relation between these two processes that the object becomes the dominant and active moment in the latter. But this really only begins to make sense if the terms are extended.

Banal strategies are those which emanate from the subject, and are posed with all the assumptions of the superiority of the subject in its apparent mastery of the world, it can set up a ruse for the world and outmaneouvre it. But for a fatal strategy it is assumed that the subject as object is mmore subtle, more ingenious, than the subject. When the object fails to reveal a rule of the game, the strategy of the object becomes ironic. Certainly there is subjective irony, since the subject can attempt to establish an enigma and set it against the world. But objective irony works through the very passionate indifference of the object, and this has a unique form of the violation of the symbolic order. It is precisely diabolical as it leans towards the subject and seduces it.

The object: 'I am referring to all of us and to our social and political order' (Baudrillard, 1988b: 199). A banal strategy is that which tries to manipulate the object directly, thus obedience is a banal strategy, but beyond a certain point one which often 'contains a disobedience fatal to symbolic order'. The object, on the other hand, becomes immanent, enigmatic, works by a logic of its own, and thus is a 'good conductor of the fatal'. The object characteristically outbids the subject, it contains more 'radical negativity', and this means that as things go from bad to worse in a catastrophic spiral of collapse it is the object which leads the descent. Yet there is an even worse form, which is the immediate diversion of the trajectory of the object at its very origin. The good is always the mirror of human intentions, the attempt to steal away from the double, from the shadow, reflected in the other. But this can never be resolved, since the double, that which magically reduplicates the banal, always haunts the subject. Thus, Baudrillard notes, 'when I speak of the object and its fatal strategies I speak of people and their inhuman strategies' (1983b: 283).

Baudrillard offers a curious example of the fatal logic which moves to excess:

> people in their holidays look for a boredom more profound than that experienced from day to day – a boredom redoubled, made out of all the elements of happiness and distraction. There is, importantly, a predestination to boredom in holidays, and a bitter premonition that it cannot be avoided.
>
> (Baudrillard, 1983b: 263)

The movement of excess is a redoubling of the banal. The banal strategy itself is perhaps a moment of obedience, and contains within itself a fatal strategy that moves into excess, into overbanality as a fate. In this way it moves to the second degree, the more banal than banal, a spiral of the worst, curiously, then, an ecstatic form. As the banal, the 'voluntary servitude' of everyday life is surpassed, it is in the solution of an 'amplification of negative conditions' (Baudrillard, 1983b: 264).

What interests Baudrillard, then, is the order of the second degree, and there are two more examples which he discusses: the first is the instance of redoubling, the second is the instance of the return (the second chance).

The first is again another curious example which starts with the proposition that it is the drive (pulsion) to the spectacle which is the strongest drive, a cynicism 'in the hearts of the people' (Baudrillard, 1983b: 201) that is in the strategy of the object. It is a drive to the catastrophe: 'the passion of a passion . . . a seductive passion, a diverting passion, where things are meaningful when transfigured by illusion, by derision, by a staging that is never representational but in a form which is prodigious' (ibid). This prodigious or exceptional form has always been condemned by moralists he notes, since it is an echo of original diversion, original sin. But this is wrong, for it is precisely in this eccentricity of things that we are protected against the 'real' and its disastrous consequences. This fetishism is a lesser evil. The greater evil is the project of a perfect world, made ready for the last judgement.[6] Rational liberation, revolution, is only possible at the price of the spectacle of the revolution. And, ironically the media have helped here, for they have put an end to the possibility of the real even[7]. Paradoxically, even though the drive to the spectacle is a more powerful instinct than self-preservation, it is the end a more preserving force, but only ironically. The nuclear war will not happen because this would deprive us of spectacle.

The second, concerns the nature of the return of the sign. If a sign occurs only once, we are indifferent to it, if it returns it becomes inevitable. In this perspective it is only if the sign of our birth makes its return are we really alive, since the return of the sign has abolished chance. When things are doubled they are complete; if things are never given a second chance they are finished even before they have begun to live. This order is immanent in human life. The return, or doubling has the effect of predestination, which is higher than the freedom of the will, since it endows a life with the depth of a former existence. A first encounter is always banal, always a field of misunderstanding. The fatal comes later, as the effect of an anterior existence. The recurrence of fatal episodes in a life is what makes the event of life.

Finally Baudrillard returns to the question: how can there be fatal strategies, perhaps they are paradoxes? The basic enigma is that fate is at the heart of every strategy, and a fatal strategy exists within all banal strategies (Baudrillard, 1983b: 269). The object plays the game, it redoubles it, outbidding strategic constraints, in a strategy which does not have its own ends or objectives, but induces the subject to collapse into a fatal logic which encompasses, paradoxically, its own objectives. This is what diverts: the unexpected, the surprise, the workings of an unknown rule, hence the effect of jokes, wit, irony, in an objective denouement, outbidding and redoubling. Chance can be ironic but is only an inferior form. Fatal irony is more tragic. To pass to the side of the object is not easy. It is not an alienated delirium of the subject projected onto the object. It is a different axiomatic, and there is a risk even in describing it. If the symbolic has indeed been passed into history (Lévi-Strauss), and history itself has been withdrawn (Canetti), what is left but the object and its fatal logic?

This idea seems to furnish the basis for a conception of the world beyond the dialectic as such and it is here he claims (following ideas that were promised in the earlier phases of his work) a formal 'pataphysics of systems' commences (Baudrillard, 1983b: 19).

This conception is squarely situated in Baudrillard's new conception of the world as pure object. But instead of existing in a dialectical struggle, the world and, therefore, the new relation to it has to be on the same terms as that of the object itself, it is itself to be combated 'with its own weapons': truth more true than true has to be opposed with a false more false than false. In other words, it is necessary to oppose not the beautiful and the ugly, but the more ugly than ugly (the monstrous); and not the visible and the hidden, but the more hidden than hidden (the secret); not the fixed and the mobile, but the more mobile than mobile (the metamorphosis). And that which is more rapid than communication, the challenge. At the other end, it is not the slow which must be sought, but the inert (the more slow than slow). The consequence is that out of this catastrophic spiral is born the fascinating, exemplified in the fascination with the hyperreal, the more real than real. It is a spiral of redoubling and of the superlative. Its logic leads, however, to the recognition of perverse goals, and to the principle of evil. And above all to the spiral of the worst.

At the level of the social, for example, that which is more social than the social is precisely the mass which absorbs all energies around it: inertia, resistance, silence. Where this logic begins its 'extermination' it touches the ecstatic point, and so in this perspective, the masses become the ecstasy of the social: 'the ecstatic form of the social, the mirror in which it is reflected in its own total immanence' (Baudrillard, 1983b: 14). In other respects, too, the real does not disappear to the benefit of the imagination. It is, on the contrary, to the more real than real that it passes. And that which is more real than real is simply hyperreal simulation. Again, it is the void. But here the empty is not to be understood in relation to the full. What occurs is the more full than full, the obese, or the more sexual than sex, obscenity and pornography: forms of saturation and overplenitude.

When this point is reached, claims Baudrillard, we are at the point of the eccentricity of all things. It is here that it is necessary to face the upsurge of change, indeterminacy and relativism, in the system. The general responses to these escalations have not been to return to old values, but curiously: 'rather to a crazy overdetermination, and exacerbation of referential values, of function, purpose, causality' (Baudrillard, 1983b: 15). Again the novelty here must be recognised. It is not an opposition anymore between determination and indetermination, but now to a 'hyperdetermination'. Purpose, finality, is not opposed to the aleatoric, but to the hypertelic. Functionality to hyperfunctionality. What always happens is a rapid expansion of the mass, in one direction, like cancer. There is an obesity in modern systems and this is for us their fascination and their weakness: 'it is in the void, and in order to avoid it, that plethoric, hypertrophic, and saturated systems emerge' (Baudrillard, 1988b: 188).

Hysteria, on the other hand, is the opposite of the telos. The hysteria of causality 'corresponds to the simultaneous effacement of origins and causes', for what happens now is an obsessional search for origins, the delirium of trying to explain everything and to reference everything. The mass expands and becomes a fantastic encumbrance, a growing mass of interpretations which has little relation to any objective. Growth immobilises growth after a certain point. It leads to gigantism in certain animal species just as it can in certain cultures (for example, the statues on Easter Island). This is the realm of the hypertelic, and it is the inert destiny of all growing systems which reach saturation point. It appears like short circuits in overloaded networks. It is the case with the world's demographic situation. At a certain point, there is a passage of the system into another entirely new space. This point is specific and mysterious: a point of no return. It is impossible 'to regress, turn back or decelerate'.

10 America, the desert and the fourth world

I was trying to get beyond theory, to find an object that was in some way visionary. *

                                                                Baudrillard (1988a)

We have seen how, from the end of the 1970s, Baudrillard altered his styles of writing, inaugurating a new unification of the personal and the formal aspects of his writing. This eventually lead to the publication of his journal *Cool Memories*, and to the broad project of the analyses of cultures in their very specificity: it is in effect the discovery, for Baudrillard, of new objects, complete cultures. Playfully he muses that his visits to America are like the undertakings of a 'missionary of the silent majorities' (1988a). His objective: to find 'the finished form of the future catastrophe', a result of his remarkable 'nostalgia for the future' (1988a:5).

THE PROBLEM OF KELLNER'S READING OF AMERICA

Although this short book, *America*, has been widely reviewed, it is clear that discussions of its ideas have been generally negative, and it has not generally enhanced Baudrillard's reputation as a social analyst. Kellner's own judgement, as a social theorist who works in America simply notes that the analysis is 'ludicrous' (Kellner, 1989a: 234), and finds Baudrillard's notion that capitalism has actually never existed in the US completely absurd. Yet this again perhaps is more of a problem than Kellner will admit, since Baudrillard calls the US the bastion of capitalism at precisely the point Kellner cites (1989a: 90). Kellner is not, and as yet Baudrillard has not found, a reliable guide to this particular work.[1] How is it to be read?

Certainly not as one might read Kafka's *America*, with its interminable problems of arrival and of settling. For Kafka's Karl Rosmer is an immigrant, someone looking for a home. Baudrillard is more of a tourist, and we know that for Baudrillard the allure here is the temptation of super-banality (Baudrillard, 1983b: 263). But Baudrillard is not interested

* Quoted in advertising blurb for Baudrillard's *America*.

in this ecstatic form, and he attempts to find another in the remarkable idea of 'pure travelling' and speed. In fact this throws considerable light on the nature of the developing complex epistemology, and the reflection Baudrillard establishes between the subject and the object in the advanced phases of modernity. Even this, however, is set in a marked continuation of Baudrillard's own project, since in a way, it is a return to the themes of *The Object System* (1968) with which Baudrillard's sociological career began, as it is clear that what interests him – though he uses another vocabulary, and the term now has a different meaning – is the ambience of this new total object. It could be read, and no doubt has been sold as a superior kind of travelogue, a specifically French interpretation of the American experience. Its vignettes casting a certain brilliant light on the catastrophe of American culture in its massive deculturation (a theme which can be found in Baudrillard's early reviews, 1962–3). It can certainly be read as the notes of a philosophically oriented French intellectual, of one of the most bitter and ferocious critics of modernity and postmodernity, allowing us to glimpse something of the curious character of Parisian values, fears, anticipations, prejudices. For even Kellner reads it as a 'pataphysical projection of his [Baudrillard's] own fantasies' (Kellner, 1989a: 170).

Kellner's reading, therefore, is that America is simply a part of Baudrillard's dangerous postmodern carnival (ibid: 168), a product of decadent French Nietzscheanism. But certain aspects are a great puzzle for Kellner, for is it Baudrillard's conception, he asks, to present America as model for the rest of the world? Kellner concludes hesitantly that he 'suspects' it might be, and fails to notice the paradoxical way in which Baudrillard presents his idea of America as both a model, and yet one which cannot be exported: it is both a vision of our future in Europe, and yet one which will never arrive. Kellner regards the book as a pale version of films such as *Vanishing Point* (1971) which present a crude notion of America as a cultural desert: the disappearance of human values, the pure object in its fatal indifference, just like a desert. Kellner reduces any poetic charge the book might have to a simple 'account' of the desert, where the human being is an 'intruder' (Kellner). For Kellner this hardly amounts to analysis, and he puts the term in quotation marks. But of one section of the book Kellner does attempt what he calls a 'symptomatic reading' (Kellner, 1989a: 169) of this 'melancholy' work. This reading simply finds that Baudrillard ignores what is interesting and important, and concludes that Baudrillard is completely defeated by his new object. Baudrillard's final conclusion, according to Kellner is that here indifference triumphs over meaning, and America simply fascinates in the period of the 'end of desire'. It is the final collapse in Baudrillard's project, the ultimate 'decline of Baudrillard's theoretical powers and the collapse of social analysis and the critique – as well as politics' (Kellner, 1989a: 170). The writing collapses into banality, and becomes utterly 'essentialist' (Kellner): the conception of America as primitive is racist, the desert image is cliché, his description of Americans is condescending, even possibly written when Baudrillard was 'leavened with whiskey', it is also sexist in its provocative suggestion of offering a woman in sacrifice to the desert. Gone is any effort to engage in social criticism of American racism and patriarchal domination. Kellner's explanation for this is that the turn to metaphysics in Baudrillard inevitably produces essentialist forms, and these issue in a 'tunnel vision' of essentialising theory: sexism, racism are its immediate products. Kellner sums up his reading of America by saying that Baudrillard's version of California is one that is 'Reaganised and yuppified': 'There are no migrant workers, no Chicano barrios, no Central American refugees, no Vietnamese refugees or Asians, not even any blacks . . . (and) to reduce Reaganism to dentifical effects is to miss many aspects of this complex phenomenon' (Kellner, 1989a: 171–2). It is difficult to imagine a more damning and dismissive account than Kellner provides here.

Yet there are severe difficulties with Kellner's reading, and many of his observations are not supported by a reading of Baudrillard's text, let alone a symptomatic one. This is perhaps not to say that Kellner has never read the book, but that his reading misses its theoretical structure and denouement.

First, it is quite wrong to suggest that when Baudrillard conceives America as still a primitive culture that this is 'racist' in some way. Kellner really offers no argument; he is content to cite a comment from Lyotard, who in any case is talking about something else. It is certainly highly surprising given the reading that Kellner has covered of Baudrillard's work that he fails to pick up any trace of irony in these terms, as if he thinks that the idea of the 'primitive' can be used by Baudrillard in a naive and pejorative way; certainly this tells us more about Kellner than Baudrillard. Second, Baudrillard does not claim that the image of the desert is in any way original (he refers to Reyner Banham *et al.*), the only question of any interest is precisely what Baudrillard achieves with this image. Third, it is clear that, risking the expression that it might be appropriate to sacrifice a woman to the desert, Baudrillard none the less so veils the occupation of such a divergent 'axiomatic' from readers like Kellner that he was almost certain to be misunderstood, for Kellner can only imagine sacrifice precisely as primitive (with its implication that primitives are indeed savage sexists and racists).[2] But Kellner has not grasped the text as a whole and therefore completely misses the ironic denouement as it strikes (1989a: 111). And, finally, does Baudrillard actually downplay racial oppression in America? Even on the very first page of *America* there is an awareness of the existence of the problem, to the Chicanos, and to the 'Americans who stole their lands' (Baudrillard, 1988a: 1–2). It soon becomes clear within the space of a few pages that at least in part, Baudrillard becomes Indian, Chicano. And the effect, the irony, that America is an achieved utopia, means, he says, that the Indians, the Vietnamese, the poor do not exist. They must disappear. It is only bad taste if they continue to show themselves, for the Last Judgement has already happened (ibid:111). How did Kellner and others miss this? For, instead of this text indicating the collapse of all theory, all analysis, all integrity, it is paradoxically Kellner's own practice of reading which is seen in disarray. Instructively it indicates more profoundly the devastating effects of Keller's ritualistic contempt for Baudrillard, against which he appears to have developed not the least form of restraint, even the normal forms of minimal intellectual rigour: he reads Baudrillard's description of Reaganism as having not the least degree of wit or sarcasm seeing only the reflection of Reagan's smile.

If there is a recognition of these, still simple, problems, at least there should be a more adequate assessment of the text, and this will ensure that a possible critique will engage with its object, for Kellner's critique appears irredeemably dogmatic, even frantic in its despairing disillusionment with an erstwhile theoretical hero now fallen into failure and defeat. First of all it is necessary to respect Baudrillard's intention to provide a certain critique of American culture, but this critique is not itself simply modernist (as the jacket of the book proclaims) or postmodernist (as Kellner insists), it is quite the opposite: counter-modernist and counter-postmodernist, as its content surely makes plain. It is not part of the carnival, is not eclectic. Yet on the other hand, as is made clear in the text, this work is not Marxist, and does not aim to make a socialist critique, which is surely what frustrates Kellner's orthodox Marxism.

Marxism, Baudrillard insists, in the American instance, is an unhappy transference from a European situation. Marxists like Mandel, like Jameson and also like Kellner, some of whom want to use Baudrillard's theory as an account of late capitalism, are, he suggests, unfortunately always one step behind the evolution of capitalism. Certainly, it is quite inappropriate to apply a simple Marxist analysis to the American situation for it misses precisely that which is original to it. Kellner here scarcely able to contain his anger judges this to be 'ludicrous'. If it is not a Marxist analysis, it is also, in Baudrillard's terms not a sociological analysis either, as there is an explicit rule that he avoid a consideration of 'deep America of mores and mentalities' (Baudrillard, 1988a: 5).

Baudrillard later commented: 'at the end of the seventies I was trying to get beyond theory, to find an object that was in some way visionary, in some way miraculous. And that for me was America – a bloc of light, modernity in the pure state, neither dream nor reality, but a primitive hyperreality, an achieved utopia' (ibid). Clearly Baudrillard's own conception of the project connects the writing in a wider trajectory of his changing analyses of the object form.

It is perhaps interesting to try to discover just what Baudrillard's intentions were in his own terms in writing this work. If we turn to *Cool Memories* (1987b), there are references to the book which indicate something of an answer. In one significant passage he refers to the writing of *America* as requiring one single method. He states that there exist a number of fragments and observations, writings which have the unity of having been written in a certain period of time: all these, he remarks, must be integrated, 'even the most banal', without addition or omission. The process of writing must adopt the view, he reflects, that these are the only and the best materials since they are given by a secret order of a certain obsession. 'The work takes off from the certainty that everything is already there and it is necessary only to find the key' (Baudrillard, 1987b: 273). This passage is interesting, not so much because it indicates a form of fatal writing, but more that it seems to indicate a problem. Perhaps the writing or the composition of *America* was not easy, and was not simply the co-ordination of notes. He has to insist on two things: there is sufficient material, but it is also necessary to find a key, as if there was a need for 'a solution which integrates it all'.

This at least suggests a possible mode of reading *America*, which must be done not symptomatically (actually this is never really attempted by Kellner), but as a mirror of Baudrillard's own form of writing, that is fatally, or poetically, for the text of *America* is perhaps close to that of *The Beaubourg Effect* (1977a), a specific form of cultural criticism, not here of a work of architecture but the architecture of a whole culture. It does not aim at depth or at a dialectical analysis. The problem for the reader is to find, therefore, an appropriate superficial form of reading.[3]

BAUDRILLARD'S NEW PROJECT

A starting point is also that of Baudrillard's 'vanishing point' (the title of the first section (1988a: 1–12)). From where is Baudrillard writing? From where should this be read? Critically, Baudrillard wants to attain a position from which he can see the disappearance of America culture, which means to go beyond it and perhaps, in Kierkegaard's terms, poeticise out of it as an aesthetic experience. It is evident that Baudrillard is placed in an intense bind here, since America is both highly seductive (but what is it that seduces? he asks), and repulsive, so that he wants to make sure that he can escape. This was also true of the Beaubourg, yet there the evident power of the seduction was far weaker, and we do not find any equivalent episodes of rapture. The Beaubourg was charmless, catastrophic, horrific. America is the ecstatic form of a future catastrophe. But how can this become the object of a fatal theory?

The strategy certainly involves the presentation of maximal paradoxes. These are given in terms of the drama and the charm of place: the Mexican Chicanos show American visitors the El Alamo where the Americans took their land; at Salt Lake City the Mormons ('puritanical conquistadores' (Baudrillard, 1988a: 5) keep their immense genealogical archives and the Bonneville speed track for cars; the Alamogordo, where the blinding light of the atomic tests was reflected in the white desert sand; at Torrey Canyon where the Salk Institute (of DNA fame) in its white marble buildings overlook the immensity of the Pacific Ocean. In the face of these striking combinations Baudrillard devotes himself to the search for 'desert speed, motels and mineral surfaces', to find as if in continuation with the writing in *Crash* (Ballard, 1985) that he had marked as the significant breakthrough appropriate to the current phase of simulation, to find the 'future catastrophe of the social in geology' (Baudrillard, 1988a: 5). This passage is a key formulation:

> Disaffection finds its pure form in the barrenness of speed. . . . Here in the transversality of the desert and the irony of geology, the transpolitical finds its generic, mental space. The inhumanity of our ulterior, asocial, superficial world immediately finds its emblem, its aesthetic form here, its ecstatic form. For the desert is simply that: an ecstatic critique of culture, an ecstatic form of disappearance.

> (ibid: 5, trans. mod.)

To find the point of disappearance it is necessary that the writing finds its form as a voyage, the effect on the subject of travelling at speed as it undergoes anamorphosis enables it to see the form of the mental desert, which is perhaps the pure form of the social desert. Baudrillard at this point specifically speaks as a Parisian: he knew about the desert form in theory, here it becomes visible as a form 'before your very eyes'. Instead of contrasting European culture in depth against the superficiality of American modernity, Baudrillard wants to see America from a position in which deep, luxuriant America disappears. But there is irony here since it is from the vantage point of the beauty of this ecstatic form that Baudrillard turns back on Europe to criticise its weight, density, history.

The invocation of American culture is one fused into minerality: the aridity of the humours, silence, the purity of the air over the crystallised intelligence of the desert. Travelling at speed has the effect of creating objects, it 'cancels out reference points', there is a loss of depth in vision, no traces are left behind, it leads to the triumph of surface and the possibility of reversion. If things, like the vase in *The System of Objects* (1968), are containers, driving empties the world of content, as speed outdoes the vegetal and becomes mineral. Here there is void, no seduction. In this way the picturesque sought by the tourist disappears into the metaphysics of speed (Baudrillard, 1988a: 9).

There is, he notes, the violent contrast: between the desert, the nuclear universe, the abstract universe of forms, and the vitality which arises from a lack of roots (no rhizomes here). This makes America, he suggests laughingly 'the only remaining primitive society' (Baudrillard, 1988a: 8). And so it is interesting, for Baudrillard, to travel through 'as though it were the primitive society of the future'. But its primitive is not simple, it has passed into a second degree, into the hyperbolic, it is a universe of such inhuman character 'that far outstrips its own moral, social or ecological rationale', the result of a puritanical obsession where everything must find its correct place, yet where everything is indifferent to place. In order to see this it is also necessary to enter a voyage which has no goal, no end as such, and to become aware of the fact that the deserts have no end. And to travel in great heat is to enter a form of disconnection and an evaporation of meaning (Baudrillard, 1988a: 9). This leads away from the social, and beyond good and evil, into a pure immorality the other side of the familiar, customs and morals. Driving vast distances produces amnesia, which is the spell of the unknown on memory. America becomes a woman, unfamiliar and destined to disappear. Driving induces a certain fatigue which also lightens things and leads to a rarefaction culture. This culture is to be grasped in its seismic break with Europe, it is 'tactile, fragile, mobile, superficial' (ibid: 10). But how far should one go? To the point of no return, he concludes, this is the key, for beyond a certain point movement changes its form, and one enters a true vertigo, and potential collapse, an 'irreversible advance into the desert of time' (ibid: 11). This radical experimentation 'is the only thing which enables me to get through and produces that astral quality I have not found anywhere else' (ibid: 28).

But what is astral America? This is evoked in a number of very contrasting ways. It is the extraordinary exhilaration that Baudrillard experiences in the face of 'the lyrical nature of pure circulation' (ibid: 27), which, though obscene, is nevertheless passionate and indifferent, it is the American joy in the 'collapse of the metaphor', quite different from the European melancholy and 'chasms of affection'. It is the exhilaration of the primitive, and of simulation, even though the Americans have no sense of it themselves. In fact only a European can see this:

> since he alone will discover here the perfect simulacrum – that of the immanence and material transcription of all values. The Americans, for their part have no sense of of simulation . . . they are the ideal material for an analysis of all the possible variants of the modern world.
>
> (Baudrillard, 1988a: 28)

But Baudrillard's conception of this world and of the method which can be applied to it is that of the hologram, the form in which each fragment contains the essence of the whole: each element is scanned by a certain kind of light, and in this light all the elements contain a single principle, even the smallest place in the desert, any street, any parking lot, any Studebaker, any house in California. Even the things, the materials themselves appear to be made of a 'more unreal substance', as things suspended in a void and made visible only by a special light.

It is not really surprising, then, that Baudrillard felt in need of a fatal sense that everything is present and already complete in his diaries and text of America. It belongs with the diary *Cool Memories*, and was published first. In this sense it was a departure from anything Baudrillard had published before, and as it turned out *America* (1988a) and *Cool Memories* (1987b) have been in publishing terms his most successful ventures. But in terms of the diaries themselves, the immense flood of observations, comments, reflections, aphorisms, criticisms, recordings, both splinter the everyday experience into a million fragments and yet here in America there is a formidible attempt to make each fragment into a *pars totalis*, apparently in the classical essentialist fashion as Kellner has remarked. Yet this is an effect which cannot be claimed for *Cool Memories*, and no critic has made the claim. Examined in this way the question is precisely what kind of unity is produced here? Does it come from the objects themselves or from the particular light which is thrown on them by *America* itself?

If we look at some details in *America* some surprising characteristics emerge. For example, immediately after describing the effect of desert light and holograms, Baudrillard introduces diary sections on the district of Santa Barbara. Suddenly Baudrillard begins to talk of the gardens and the houses in this area: 'the fake serenity is complete' he remarks, in a section that could well have come from *The Object System* of 1968:

> the proliferation of technical gadgetry inside the house, beneath it, around it, like drips in an intensive care ward, the TV, stereo, and video which provide communication with the beyond, the car (or cars) that connect one up to that great shoppers' funeral parlour, the supermarket, and lastly, the wife and children, as glowing symptoms of success . . . everything here testifies to death having found its ideal home.
>
> (Baudrillard, 1988a: 31)

This is not an untypical passage, it is followed immediately by one which notes: 'the microwave, the waste disposal, the orgasmic elasticity of the carpets: this soft, resort-style civilization irresistibly evokes the end of the world'.

If this is hologrammatic, then we do not need to read any further, for the only things that can follow are other particles of the hologram. Yet this leads us to the question of the complexity of objects here, for despite the astral light, there is also the principle of selection to be considered and the form of language which evokes them. Baudrillard introduces semi-poetic formulae into the text (some in English in the original):

Western Digitals
Body Building Incorporated
Mileage unlimited
Channel Zero (Baudrillard, 1988a: 31)

No doubt these were words and phrases which he found interesting and jotted down in his notebook (they are far more extensive in *Cool Memories*). Driving across America he picked up a collection of signs, and became completely converted to their enlightening effect: 'The point is not to write the sociology . . . of the car, the point is to drive . . . you will know more about the country than all the institutes of sociology and political science put together' (ibid: 54–5). But what, exactly, is learned? The end of the world is summoned by reference to joggers, to religious sects, to Marxists in the universities, to mentally disabled on the streets, to obesity, to the existence of an oil platform, and so on. 'My hunting grounds are the deserts . . . the freeways, the Safeways, the ghost towns, or the downtowns . . . I get to know more about the concrete social life of America from the desert than I ever would from official or intellectual gatherings' (ibid: 63).

The appeal to the desert is insistent (it can even function as a 'mythic operator' in the style of Lévi-Strauss), it is the key to the reading of America.[4] It is not part of nature. It is the void, the metaphor (ibid) of emptiness and continuity. The essence is to be able to read the desert of the sign (its mobility and immobility), it is outside desire, set against excesses of cultural pretension. But it is also used, following Reyner Banham as the central void around which the cities of Salt Lake, Los Angeles and Las Vegas group themselves. It is the astral light of the desert which radiates round as if it were a part of the ambience of the American culture itself.

Baudrillard spends a great deal of time in the desert: it is for him a sacred experience, it is:

> a sublime form that banishes all sociality, all sentimentality, all sexuality . . . caresses have no meaning except from a woman who is herself of the desert, who has that instantaneous, superficial animality in which the fleshly is combined with dryness and disincarnation.
>
> (Baudrillard, 1988a: 71)

Then he returns to the comparison with Europe: it is after this experience of modernity an unbridgeable gulf: 'You are born modern, you do not become so . . . what strikes you immediately in Paris is that you are back in the nineteenth century' (ibid: 73) It is as if each country, like each individual, has a destiny: in France it is the decadence of the model of 1789.

What is the American destiny? It can be seen, he suggests, in the very relation to facts. It is a culture of the fact, but Americans know nothing of facticity. Things are accomplished pragmatically, there is 'total credibility of what is done or seen', there is no ambivalence in the universe, their religion is the *fait accompli*, they have no conception of the evil genius in the working out of things, and this is their utopia. This means that it is a culture without the sense of heresy, sense of superstition and the power of appearance. 'Here there is no dissidence, no suspicion'; it is as if 'the irony of the community' (the principle of seduction, the feminine) is absent. (ibid: 85). The American is factual, thinks by use of statistics, or what is experienced 'thereby divesting (thought) of all conceptual value' (Baudrillard, 1988a: 87). Religion has simply become 'a way of life', and 'can no longer be challenged or questioned' society has become one-dimensional (ibid: 91), in the end the American 'suffers from a kind of infirmity when it comes to abstraction' but this is a kind of glory: the 'empirical genius which so amazes us' (ibid: 95). It is the 'ideal type of the end of our culture' since it does not know or experience irony. (ibid: 97–8).

Baudrillard's conclusion could be said to suggest that American culture never amounts to an aesthetic object of the second degree. It is seductive, like the desert; it is in a sense the ecstatic form of this seduction, but it is of the primary orders: primal, primitive: 'it sacrifices all intellect, all aesthetics in a process of literal transcription into the real' (Baudrillard, 1988a: 99), and this is realised in complete authenticity. American society and culture are not alienated. The implication of this is that the Beaubourg effect could not simply exist in America, it is specific to a European country like France (it could not exist even in Italy), and this for a host of reasons: 'not only does centralisation not exist but the idea of a cultivated culture does not exist either, no more than that of a theological, sacred religion. No culture of culture, no religion of religion' (ibid: 100).[5] In this culture everything can be turned around into its opposite, and this is the specific power and attraction of this culture.

In terms of Baudrillard's own theoretical matrix, what fascinates him is precisely this apparent unity of a world of seduction of appearances in the symbolic orders of primitive peoples, which for him is the greatest of all forms of seductive powers which operate in a world of doubles, of evil, of reversibility, and that of this third order of the 'absolute simulacrum' where again there is the absolute domination of appearance, but one altogether different from the first order, since here all effects of the double have evaporated. The second order, that of the historical culture in depth has never evolved.

So compelling or pervasive is Baudrillard's evocation of the desert and its strange beauty that readers have failed to notice the dramatic denouement of Baudrillard's text. Douglas Kellner is simply transported, Baudrillard 'does not see the homeless, the hopeless underclass, so evident in the Reagan era, and does not mention that it is very specific policies that have produced this suffering' (Kellner, 1989a: 172). Yet the central, and key chapter of *America* is precisely on Reagan and Reaganism, which leads up to the consideration of the new 'fourth' world, the poor within the heart of the first world. The generation of the orgy itself has thrown up, he says, not a disenchanted elite, but one which is 'mobile and enchanted'. In the context of the new ideology:

if utopia has already been achieved . . . the poor are no longer credible. . . . While frequenting the rich ranchers or manufacturers of the West, Reagan has never had the faintest inkling of the poor and their existence. . . . The have nots will be condemned to oblivion, to abandonment, to disappearance pure and simple. . . . That poverty was until recently being relieved, which was still within the orbit of subsidised socialisation, has now fallen within the scope of providential (presidential) decree. It is as though the last Judgement has already happened.

(Baudrillard, 1988a: 111)

This world has a new character, and the era of Reagan and Thatcher is an epoch of a new form of disenfranchisement, for now 'entire swathes of the population are falling into oblivion. . . . This is the fourth world. Entire sectors of our modern societies, entire countries in the Third World now fall into this Fourth world desert zone' (Baudrillard 1988a: 112). The argument here, though brief, draws Baudrillard's whole theoretical project back into a point of contact with critical theory: 'This new phenomenon has a special character for whereas the Third World still had a political character (even if it was a resounding world-wide failure) the Fourth world has none. It is transpolitical' (Baudrillard, 1988a: 112). Is this a return of a latent Marxism in Baudrillard's thought? He compares the situation of the *de facto* excommunication of the 'fourth world' with the burning of surplus goods to keep the price high, and the disappearance of tribal peoples who are 'surplus to requirements'. Despite Kellner's remarks about Baudrillard's avoidance of the responsibility of 'specific policies' Baudrillard refers to the fact that:

The policies of governments are themselves becoming negative. They are no longer designed to socialise, to integrate, or to create new rights. Behind the appearance of socialisation and participation they are desocialising, disenfranchising and ejecting. The social order is contracting . . . entire zones are 'disintensified', becoming . . . dumping grounds.

(Baudrillard, 1988a: 113)

The problem is, says Baudrillard, there will be no revolution, since 'enfranchisement, emancipation, and expansion have already taken place' (1988a: 113). The buffer zone, the desert zone around the Beaubourg is here identified as a crucial social dimension of modernity and now connected with fundamental alterations in social structure and social order: it is into a zone of this type that the 'fourth world' are dumped. The new inner desert.

In a final section, 'Desert for ever', Baudrillard returns to a superb poetic evocation of the American experience (for a European). The implosive Californian sunset:

It is a kind of suspended eternity . . . with the guarantee that it will always be like this each day, that every evening will be that rainbow of all the colours of the spectrum in which light, after having reigned all day long in its indivisible form, in the evening fragments into all the nuances of colour that make it up, before it finally disappears. Nuances which are already those of the instant rainbow catching fire in the wind on the crest of the Pacific waves.

(Baudrillard, 1988a: 121)

The overall shape and structure of America is now completely visible as a dramatic event in its own right, with its own tensions, feints, denouement, finale. It is in six parts.[6]

1   The epistemological theory of the work, the theory of the way in which the object can make its appearance and disappearance, the practice of invocation of a poetic object and the preparation of the poetic mode of disappearance in the final act. This object has a special beauty, has a dramatic scene which is not at all theatrical, but its beauty is cruel. Its main location is the structural space:

Salt Lake
[Ocean] (desert) California – (desert) – Las Vegas [NY]
San Antonio

Around this series of structural positions Baudrillard constructs and locates his voyage.[7]

2   The recounting of events, the banalities of the voyage, is given a unity from the light which Baudrillard casts on them: the reflection of desert light.

3   A return to the voyage, to Porterville, Death Valley, Santa Barbara, in further reflections on the desertification of culture, but in the mode of ecstatic formations.

4   The move towards an ironic theory, the achieved utopia which is articulated around an immense series of contrasts between Europe and America. America as constructed out of the dreams of utopian pioneers retains this modernity in its character, but in the form of an anti-culture, thus a possible table of differences:

US	*Europe*
modernism	historical culture + modernism
eighteenth-century capitalism	nineteenth-century capitalism
twentieth-century capitalism	
escape from history (Paz)	historical depth
multi-racial	racial
federalist	universalist
realist–utopian	metaphysical melancholy
paradox	dialectic
facts	facts and facticity
ecstatic banality	obsolescent charm
hyperreal	surreal
desert	mountains

5   The move towards an ironic denouement: the theory that the realised utopia revived by Reagan has begun to fall apart. The idea was dominant in the 1950s when it had a certain validity, and Reagan used it to throw a factitious credibility over his reign, as if pure signs, the advertisement the image was all that counts, but American power is fading and has need to bolster itself with manipulated successes

(Baudrillard, 1988a: 109). The true support of the Reagan government is a new yuppie generation, but only on condition that the social order itself contracts leaving a new zone for the specific transpolitical object of this society: the new 'fourth world', the excommunicated in a world of communication, the inner desert.

6   The return to the desert, but its meaning has been transformed. It began in the mode of the hyperreal, (of J.G. Ballard's *Crash* (1985)) a fusion of minerality and deculturality. It was one-dimensional, planar (in contrast with European culture with historical depth), a triumphant revolution never completely understood by Europeans or Marxists, since it is not a decadent culture, nor a culture of alienation (these belong only to Europe). But now it is clear that, for Baudrillard, this triumph attained its utopian realisation in the 1950s. Since the 'orgy' of the 1960s and 1970s there has been a growing realisation of its failure, and with it, the beginnings, with Reagan, of a simulation of the utopian form, yet at the same time the creation of a completely new social order, conceived by Baudrillard in zonal terms: the new transpolitical inner desert of indifference.

Part IV

Where are the blinding insights of yesteryear? Around me I see nothing but groundless hysteria and unscrupulous vitality.

(Baudrillard, 1990c: 38)

11 The double spiral

*This double spiral . . . – a spiral swerving towards a sphere of the sign,
the simulacrum and simulation, a spiral of the reversibility of all signs in
the shadow of seduction and death.*

Baudrillard (1988c:79)

It is easy to become enchanted and bewitched by Baudrillard's poetic
theorising, yet some have found this oppressive: 'the disagreeable thing
about being with someone who is always right, is that it leaves you
with nothing to say for yourself . . . Baudrillard is popular but disliked'
(McDonald, in Frankovits, 1984: 27). On the other hand, nothing is
more easy to dismiss than a writer who suggests replacing the apparent
solidity of a theory of the mode of production with a theory of modes of
seduction. The difficulty, however, is that Baudrillard's desparate search
for a principle of critical reflection on our societies leads in directions and
situations which are undeniably uncomfortable. He has, very briefly talked
about this in an interview. Discussing his own relation to theory, he said:

> For a long time I was very 'cool' about producing theories. Of course
> there had to be an obsession behind it, but I didn't think it had very
> much to do with anything . . . I'd always kept my distance from culture
> – as well as theory. I maintained a position of distrust and rejection . . .
> Several years ago all that changed. Somewhere along the line I stopped
> living, in Canetti's sense. . . . The giddiness I'm talking about ended up
> taking hold of me . . . I stopped working on simulation.

> Finally, by various paths, all this came to have extremely direct
> consequences on my life. . . . There is in theories something that does
> away with the feeling of being 'unstuck'. But what theory brings back
> on the other hand, to reaccentuate it, pervert it – in the full sense of the
> word – I'd rather not know about.

(Baudrillard, 1987c:81–2)

HÖLDERLIN IN NIETZSCHE

We are not really given enough information to grasp precisely what happened. Some have suggested that Baudrillard decided himself to become a 'model', others that his *Cool Memories* is a form of 'schizo-autobiography'. Yet what Baudrillard hints at is more complex, in some senses quite the opposite, a kind of repairing of the breach that the separations in life had opened. In another interview he remarked: this new episode 'is the consequence of a return to origins . . . After this immense detour through ideology, radical critiques, Marx and Freud, there is in my thought a return to the authors from which I started, Nietzsche and Hölderlin' (Baudrillard, 1983d: 83).

Before this return, his writing, he reflected, had been something artificial, unconnected with his life as such. Now he said, 'it is not as if I live to write but everything is involved at once. There is no longer a critical and analytical distantiation which allows you to "explain" things'. When the previous mode was left behind, so was the difference between interiority and exteriority. Now the world is the exterior, there is a 'kind of schizophrenia which may be complex and rich'. Whereas previously there was a doubling up, this changes altogether so that now what is written describes what you are. 'With Nietzsche this mixing of things is striking. At this moment a book becomes something else. It is no longer a cultural process . . . it becomes a sort of rule of life' (Baudrillard, 1983d: 85).

These moves make Baudrillard's writings difficult to assess on a single dimension, and his works, like the works of Nietzsche and Canetti, will remain on the margins of social analysis, and even adopt a hostile attitude to it. It is as though there is a change of register, from social analysis to a rich inmixing of metaphysics, ethics, literature and poetry, as well as cultural criticism. What counts is no longer only clarity and rigour of critical conceptualisation, but on the contrary the effectiveness of poetic affinities in the very texture of theory itself. But some questions immediately come to the surface: is this Baudrillard's attempt to capture an original unity, perhaps conceived as an eternal basis to human life? Or is it a special sort of contact with the object which will allow a closer understanding?

These are crucial problems, and they have to be resolved in order to assess the structure of Baudrillard's work as a whole. Certainly in his own reflections on his intellectual trajectory he suggests that it has to be seen as a double spiral, a movement along two threads of enquiry which encircle each other. Interpreting this spiral is the central question here. The first thread is the deepening investigation of the symbolic cultures, through the symbol, reversibility, the anagrammatic, seduction and the principle of evil. The second is the analysis of modern ambience, consumption, simulation, mass culture. Baudrillard thinks in terms of absolutes, the first is treated as sacred, the second as fallen, as catastrophic. At some time Baudrillard made his own pact with the symbolic order, yet the culture of simulations is only attractive in so far as it radiates with the power of evil. It is indeed important to see that Baudrillard's analyses all begin with this set of divisions and values already in place, and that even the very forms of semiological analysis used may, in the end, have been used against themselves (as Lefebvre once clearly advocated). And if there is black and white here (a constantly recurring opposition in his works), Baudrillard is on the side of the black mass.

Yet there are, inevitably, positions of a more complex pattern which begin to emerge, making it possible to begin to identify what might be called his complex component positions: his violent 'pataphysical' distrust of 'culture', yet his commitment to rich syntactical culture of meaning; his search for principles of critical opposition to bourgeois and petit bourgeois culture even in critical theory and structuralism, yet his rejection of situations where critical theories begin to interact to form a general critical problematic. His relation to the status of the symbolic order is not altogether without hesitations: is it nostalgic or not (Baudrillard, 1988c: 63,80)? Evidently his initial writings were developed in relation to a debate with Marxism and at one period he was involved in an attempt to work within a Marxist framework, suitably modernised. In this period his work was explicitly oriented to forms of practice and class struggle, a matrix which had long-lasting effects. After his break with Marxism on the grounds that it is compromised by its utilitarian pact with capitalism, he works towards a situation where it will be problematic to ask what could be said to be the function, purpose or practical aim of his own theory. Yet again, the earlier contempt for the situation of parasitic and decadent classes, passes into the pathos for the decline of the intellectual or more precisely the critical intellectual. His vision becomes a melancholy one: we are left, he says, with a whole baggage of 'badly digested rationalities, of radicalism without social bases, without enemies, and without stakes' (Baudrillard, 1983d: 85) and, 'the intellectual has no future'. Baudrillard was bitterly contemptuous of the rising nouveaux riches, the new petit bourgeoisie; yet in the end this class disappears, it merges into the mass. On the other hand, there are new forms of resistence in the contemporary society, now dominated not by the triumphant, responsible or revolutionary, subject, in a positive resistance against injustice, but on the contrary, a specific kind of negativity in the subject become object in a more general revenge of the object in its secret fatal strategy.[1] Here Baudrillard's malicious enjoyment of the misfortunes of the fortunate becomes pure *schadenfreude*. His ultimate enjoyment is the success the modern system can bestow on himself as the embodiment of irrationalism in a society geared up in all its educational and cultural institutions to the triumph of rationalism.

THE MIRROR OF SEDUCTION?

There is, nevertheless, a strong sense in which Baudrillard's own analyses and criticisms, are themselves caught, ironically, in their own net; that his own writings reflect more about his own predicament than about the fate of objects. He has ventured out on a voyage only to find a return to origins within himself, the construction of a system of involutions: is his writing not in its totality a gigantic collector's gallery? Is he not, in his writings a personality who has made, in the most contradictory simulation of all an attempt at cultural metamorphosis: to become woman, a transvestism in writing? In the end this has brought considerable problems, for he has been taken as a postmodernist, despite his ardent denials. He has tried to place the modern world in a bind, to confront it with enigma and with ambivalence, but perhaps he has only confronted and lost himself in the double bind posed by the world itself.

He has also attempted to develop his own position by launching savage critiques against his former allies, particularly Marxism, Saussurean linguistics and psychoanalysis, an attack which sought to find their weakest points in unexamined, or uncriticised assumptions. But then Baudrillard's own project has its own assumptions and without doubt a similar form of criticism can be developed against him. For example, he criticised the Saussurean notion of the referent as a concession to the determinant notion of 'reality', yet in his arguments around the process of seduction, he constantly refers to the possibility of natural, feline, spontaneously produced charm and seductiveness, apparently innocent of all cultural determinations. More and more his positions attempt to leave behind social analysis as such, and embrace the world of appearances with such a degree of naiveté that his thought enters a purely non-theoretical simulation of its object:

> It must become excessive and sacrificial to speak about excess and sacrifice. It must become simulation if it speaks about simulation, and deploy the same strategy as its object. . . . If it no longer aspires to a discourse of truth, theory must assume the form of a world from which truth has been withdrawn.
>
> (Baudrillard, 1988c: 98)

This epistemology is quite rightly stigmatised as a drift to a theoretical descriptive empiricism by the Althusserians: it is to enter the world of ideological doubling, it can 'explain' nothing, which of course can never break out of its mirror relation (and that is why for the Althusserians it remains eternal in its very structure).

But at the same time theory has another role, quite different from this role of mirror: it is he says 'to seduce, to wrest things from their condition, to force them into an over-existence which is incompatible with that of the real' (ibid). Here theory is far from being passive, yet it, in a sense is again only a mirror of the fact that the real itself challenges theory. The object has its secrets, its secret strategy: theory becomes, as far as possible the image of the object, it becomes the fatal challenge, evidently this form of the challenge is a simulation. But what is the object? 'When I speak of the object and of its fatal strategies I am speaking of people and their inhuman strategies' (Baudrillard, 1988b: 200, trans.mod.); presumably then, this has to be grasped as in opposition to the principle of the subject's human strategies. Baudrillard reiterates the example: of parents' attitudes to their children – to treat them as both subject (and the response is passive, where the child 'becomes object'), and as object (the response is active). The object can resist through over-simulation, hypersimulation, infantilism, total dependency, pure dumb idiocy, overacceptance (ibid: 218–19), in a period when the outright form of direct oppression (inducing the positive action of the subject) has been transformed into the gratificatory mode. Is Baudrillard's own theory of the object, a simulation in its own way of this mode, i.e. object-like in this sense? Is it Hölderlin's bind: 'the primitive equilibrium attained between the first artist and his world no longer holds. The child is now dealing with men with whom he will never . . . be familiar enough to forget their superiority. And if he feels this superiority he must become either rebellious or servile'? (in Girard, 1977:158). Is it a challenge in the Nietzschean form of *ressentiment*? Nietzsche gives the case of what he calls 'Russian fatalism':

> who knows how much I am ultimately indebted, in this respect also, to my protracted sickness! This problem is far from simple: one must have experienced it from strength as well as from weakness. If anything at all must be adduced against being sick and being weak, it is that man's really remedial instinct, his fighting instinct wears out. . . . Men and things obtrude too closely; experiences strike one too deeply; memory becomes a festering wound. Against all this the sick person has only one great remedy: I call it Russian fatalism, that fatalism without revolt which is exemplified by a Russian soldier who, finding a campaign too strenuous, finally lies down in the snow. . . . This fatalism is not always merely the courage to die: it can also preserve life under the most perilous conditions by reducing the metabolism, slowing it down. . . . Carrying this logic a few steps further, we arrive at the fakir who sleeps for weeks in a grave.
>
> (Nietzsche, 1969: 229–30)

The irony of *ressentiment*, says Nietzsche is that it is dangerous for the weak, since it burns up energies, but superfluous for the strong. If Baudrillard reacts against the loss and pointlessness of the revolt of the object (masses) in a new social situation (post-1968), French fatalism is even more logical and philosophical than Nietzsche's. Nietzsche says that during periods when things were going against him 'I displayed "Russian fatalism" . . . by tenaciously clinging for years to all but intolerable situations, places, apartments, and society, merely because they were given by accident: it was better . . . than feeling that they could be changed' (ibid: 231). Baudrillard realises that this was no accident, and develops a whole new epistemology to prove it: an enormous theoretical energy diverted from active *ressentiment* (against the system) towards what Nietzsche calls 'great reason': 'accepting oneself as if fated, not wishing oneself "different" (Nietzsche, 1969: 231), except that Baudrillard wants this elevated to the second degree. 'carrying this logic a few steps further' we arrive at the fakir in his grave at Baudrillard's (and Canetti's) 'I have stopped living'.

In other words Baudrillard is not content to simulate the object passively, to try to trap it in a fixed mirror image, as if in some simple empiricist reflection (the truth of the object). Ultimately, it is the second degree that interests him: 'it is not enough for theory to describe and analyse, it must be an event in the universe it describes' and this means, that theory must 'take on the power of the fatal sign, even more inexorable than reality' (Baudrillard, 1988c: 101).

Now this is a problem in all of the variants of the anti-rationalist position, from versions like Baudrillard's, right through to that of the theoretical non-rationalism (Balibar, 1978) of the Althusserians, for if people are not motivated or moved by scientifically calculated reasons, or by the flights of ideological circumlocution, how are they moved? One answer is the Pascal–Durkheimian–inspired mechanism of ritual; that is, they are not moved by ideas, by its ideological formula, but the action of ritual itself, or as Althusser put it, in his own pataphysical mode, 'kneel down, move your lips in prayer, and you will believe' (Althusser, 1971: 158). Of course this is altogether very naive, for however much people can be mobilised to enact state rituals in this manner, if there are more effective attitudes and practices which undercut them they will appear as entirely artificial. But there are different kinds of ritual and they can coexist, for example, different forms of marriage (the civil and the religious marriage, the royal marriage) where a ritual, ceremonial action is deemed to produce a change of status, of self. The revival and elaboration of monarchical ritual at the end of the nineteenth century is, in part, the revival of a symbolic order, in Baudrillard's terms. It is possible to speculate about the symbolic metamorphosis of divine power, the magical transformations of the coronation, the investment of reflected glories in the aristocratic hierarchies, and so on. No doubt in this case a simulation during the latter phases of a productivist (second) order, on a basis perhaps of a *ressentiment* of the masses against the utilitarian bourgeois and petit bourgeois political formations (perhaps Tom Nairn's sociology of grovelling is also a form of *ressentiment*), or could it even be a form of monarchical *ressentiment* against them? Baudrillard suggests that these phenomena are not certainly sustained or to be explained by belief. Who believes in Father Christmas? he asks. (Perhaps someone should say: It is the children.) Against the immense construction of late–Victorian pseudo-ritual,[2] one which has become universally practised, in innumerable different ways: would Baudrillard treat us to a homily on the hypocrisy of Christmas? If so what would replace it? Druidic rituals, or Janus?

This is the crucial problem, for however much Baudrillard incites us to appreciate the functioning of symbolic orders, and the logic of gift and counter-gift, he would reject both the simulated forms which are realised in modern societies (the Christian forms – on which see the eulogy by Talcott Parsons (1978) in terms taken directly from Mauss, and the semi-pagan forms, Christmas, a gigantic effervescent potlatch, but for Baudrillard, in the grip of consumption panic). The problem is that these are not really extreme cases, and Baudrillard has made it a point to look for the extreme: this is where events occur, and where his theoretical events must also happen (Baudrillard, 1990b). They can occur in the very inertia of the slowing down, the 'Russian fatalism' (hibernation) within our societies, or as Baudrillard has found they can also over-react in hyperaction, in speed, velocity, in exhilaration, as is the case with his visits to America, and what we might call his 'American fatalism'. Yet this is made more complex by his very calculated invocation of sacrificial exchanges, of the seduction of beautiful women, of the seduction of racial types, at the level of pure appearance, (that is the immediate, the empirical, the innocent (that is never innocent)). Baudrillard is caught in his own snare: of trying to introduce his own simulations of primitive rituals, primitive symbolic exchanges into a society that not only has done it more effectively, but also will inevitably divert these symbolic powers into something else. Yet on one level, as his critique of Foucault shows, he is as completely aware of this as was Nietzsche: it is the genre of fascism. In his latest book, (1990b) he celebrates Ayatollah Khomeini's *fatwa* against Rushdie: a symbolic challenge, how modern! How is it that Khomeini's restoration of the powers of the mullahs is genuine? How is it the examination of *The Satanic Verses* (precisely in the ideal modality for Baudrillard, a literary–poetic challenge, the theory of the principle of evil) is overlooked?

NIETZSCHE IN DURKHEIM?

When Baudrillard's work is surveyed at as a whole there is the suspicion that he has simply rediscovered the same phenomena everywhere he looks, has himself created a collected world which is simply a gigantic kaleidoscope (where, as Lévi-Strauss notes, the 'patterns are produced by the conjunction of contingent events (the turning of the instrument by the person looking through it) and a law (namely that governing the construction of the kaleidoscope), which corresponds to the invariant element of the constraints' (Lévi-Strauss, 1972: 36)). There are two kinds of thinkers, says Michel Serres recently: those that always find the same thing everywhere, like Bergson, on each piece of his domain always digs the same hole; on the other hand there is the fox who goes in search of a different totality, one of great variety (Serres, 1990: 103). Baudrillard, despite his wish to invoke the value of difference, of radical alterity, and to live off this difference intellectually, finds it repeated interminably in each of the spheres of his investigations.

This effect is, no doubt, the result of complex causes. There are two which deserve consideration – theoretical and methodological. Theoretically, as we have seen, the temptation to view the world as homogeneous is always present in the Manichaean vision. And Baudrillard admits to it: 'For me the reality of the world has been seduced, and this is really what is so fundamentally Manichaean in my work. Like the Manichaeans I do not believe in the possibility of 'real-ising' the world through any rational or material principle' (Baudrillard, 1987d). But, second, there are deeper theoretical problems for the approach to objects departs dramatically from Marx in the direction of an unlimited semiology, or semi-urgy. Baudrillard inverts the conventional argument, which suggests that uniformity of reification extends out from the commodity form, by proposing that the commodity form is a derived instance of a higher law, of exchange, which is as wide in scope as the whole culture, affecting politics, sexuality, art. In other words he does not advocate, directly, reductionist Marxism, holding, for example, that all political strategy and practice can be explained immediately by the flow of money; but his position, nevertheless has the same effect, for in this theoretical reflection, the same principle is at work everywhere (the economy is not the generator of this code, but the recipient of it). The spheres of the society are distinct (each overdetermines itself – in simulation), but there is no reason in Baudrillard which could explain why they form a society since he has no principle of social reproduction (primitive societies dominated by symbolic exchange are given no societal rationale, in the simulated cultures society even exchange is absent). Baudrillard's conception of capitalism seems (after the death of the social, history, meaning) to be one which simply adds together utilitarianism, booty capital, and the 'ecstasy' of the circulation of finance capital. In all his many genealogies there is no place for the genealogy of contract (Durkheim, 1957) or the working out of co-operation between guilds or soviets (Mauss, 1984), if there is a genealogy of the state it is in the very unfamiliar form of a genealogy of ideological apparatuses which control death, dying and the dead.

In this general sense it is instructive to compare the Durkheimian and Baudrillardian perspectives. Both adopt a two-phase world history: segmental (symbolic) societies, superseded by organic (simulation) societies. Durkheim suggests that the culture of the advanced societies is formed around the process of exchange, specialisation and differentiation of function, but developing forms of social solidarity first around the guilds in the medieval period, but gradually entering into a general crisis in the Renaissance, which was partially resolved by the new disciplines of the catholic counter-reformation; the crisis intensified again in the eighteenth century (Comte's critical period) leading to the revolution of 1789. (There was within society said Durkheim, 'a void whose importance is difficult to exaggerate . . . a malady *totius substantiae*, affecting all the organism' (Durkheim, 1964: 29; see the discussion in Gane, 1984)). After that date there is a desparate series of attempts to restore a social equilibrium, which Durkheim himself regarded as the problem of the creation of a form of solidarity equivalent to that of the guilds. Modern science born in the Renaissance can be applied to the realm of the social, a move which will aid society's own attempt to heal its own internal sickness: its problem of solidarity. Thus Durkheim is a rationalist, but of a complex kind. His nephew Marcel Mauss developed the theory of the gift and the counter-gift as a non-utilitarian theory of primitive exchange at exactly the same moment as his critique of Bolshevism as a failure of the politics of soviet (guild) solidarity. (See Mauss on the Russian revolution (1984), and the important letters of 1936, and 1939:

> One thing that, fundamentally, we never foresaw was how many large societies, that have more or less emerged from the Middle Ages in other respects, could be hypnotized like Australians by their dances, and set in motion like a children's roundabout . . . I believe that all this is a real tragedy for us, too powerful a verification of things that we had indicated and the proof that we should have expected this verification through evil rather than a verification through goodness.

> (in Lukes, 1973: 339)

Baudrillard situated himself between a rationalism and irrationalism, himself between in the scientific and anti-scientific tradition. The tendency of his own work concludes that rationalism in science, in art, has had, since the Renaissance a series of catastrophic consequences for western culture. The basic consequence is the destruction of the symbolic order itself and the introduction of the notion of the 'real world'. Yet to understand this and to demonstrate it has meant the adoption of these very scientific instruments themselves. In the end science is part of the problem since it represents the operation of the structural code itself: it is accumulative, destructive of the symbolic order. At first it tears apart the symbolic world in order to possess the real, but in the progression of scientific development, as Nietzsche had pointed out, 'we have abolished the real world; what world is left? the apparent world perhaps? . . . but no! with the real world we have also abolished the apparent world!' (Nietzsche, 1968: 41). This is decisive for Baudrillard who theorises this process as the third phase of simulation, the culmination in the hyperreal. But the more fundamental values are those of the unattainable cultures of symbolic exchange, and it is from this base that devastating critiques can be made of the cultures of simulation.

The major differences between the two sociologists, lie in the divergence of theoretical position: Durkheim locates himself (not without some hesitations) in the flawed, unfulfilled, or rather incomplete project of the culture of organic societies, in the project for a sociology as a science of society; Baudrillard is based in primitive symbolic exchange, and develops a form of sociology which is best described as transtheoretical, a form of resistance *from* the irrational, a form of *ressentiment*, and a theoretical *fatwa* against the modern and postmodern system. If Durkheim developed a theory of anomie, of social pathologies of the structure (a teratology), in order to begin to define the norm, for Baudrillard, the norm is not that of medieval guild society but the generic symbolic cultures, of which the feudal society was one variety: the cultures of simulation are, virtually by definition pathological, since they break up the rituals of the eternal return of the symbolic exchange, and accumulation is death. If Baudrillard eventually, ambivalently, decamps from his base in the symbolic-exchange cultures as an impossible base, as an impossible nostalgia, it is to follow the logic of French fatalism, that is the impossible idea of a fatal strategy (not fatal and not a strategy) in theory. Durkheim wrote a sociology of suicide in order to show that society has a problem of insufficient solidarity; Baudrillard in a bizarre continuation, writes studies of terrorism and obesity to show that these are forms of resistance which follow the object's pathological logic (beyond the threshold; they are transpolitical). In effect, for Baudrillard, sociology is an attempt to unveil the real, and remains for the most part in a simulation of the second order (positivism), it was always a simulation of the model of other sciences, quite consciously so in the positive period. Baudrillard is engaged in the same project as Durkheim but inflected with Nietzscheanism (in the spirit if not the letter of Bataille) Baudrillard's version is more dynamic: suicide now becomes, not a classification, but a fatal strategy – the fatalistic suicide, curiously, would be a form of *ressentiment* against the future which is completely blocked (that is there is an antagonism between a subject and the cage of his or her future).

Durkheim constructed a table of the forms of suicide. Egoistic suicides are characterised by apathy, and 'indolent melancholy'; altruistic forms involve passion, a mystic enthusiasm, calm feeling of duty; the anomic form is supported by irritation and disgust, accompanied with violent recrimination against life in general (Durkheim, 1972: 293). It may seem a little harsh to treat Baudrillard in terms of a problematic of suicide, yet he himself stresses the importance of his having ceased to live, and the importance of his own aesthetic mode of disappearance. This is certainly not the simple index of the absence or excess of social regulation as in Durkheim's structural theory. It is in Baudrillard to be thought in (Nietzschean) terms of will, strategy, resistance, struggle and indeed authenticity.[3] It is as though the forms of suicide fall into two types: the active engagement of the subject (altruistic suicide), and the more apparently passive object form (apathy, melancholy). Durkheim defines the anomic form as a combination of anger and disappointment, exasperated weariness. It is the energy, the drive which is important 'the object upon whom the passions are discharged is fundamentally of secondary importance. The accident of circumstances determines their direction' (Durkheim, 1972: 285). Clearly Durkheim's own basic orientation is altruistic in form (calm duty), whereas Baudrillard is a very complex mixture but evidently dominated by the anomic in, perhaps a combination of egoistic–anomic fatal strategies, suitable for a world in which the subject resists as object.

This leads to the question of Baudrillard's relation to psychoanalytic theory for there is more than a hint that terms such as fetishism, perverse desire played a decisive role in the formulation of Baudrillard's general theory.

A PERVERSE DESIRE?

The crucial indications of Baudrillard's use of psychoanalysis are to be found in his early writings. One of the central themes of his work is a very special reworking of Marx's notion of the 'fetishism of commodities' which, in many different existentialist forms, was a dominant theme in critical thought in the 1950s as a way of approaching the question of human alienation. It came under severe attack from structural Marxism, and was eclipsed by a different, structuralist, problematic. Baudrillard indeed follows Althusser in rejecting the notion of fetishism in so far as it enmeshed 'critical analysis within the subtle trap of a rationalistic anthropology' (Baudrillard, 1981b:89). The basic problem here, Baudrillard emphasised from the start was the danger that the theory 'presupposes, somewhere . . . a non-alienated consciousness'. Even Marxism falls into this error, he noted, and as it does so became incapable of analysing 'the actual process of ideological labour'. But then Baudrillard's solution to the problems in the first phase of his work was to argue paradoxically (since it assumes precisely the importance of an anthropological postulate) that the 'fetishised notion' even of base and superstructure should give way to a 'comprehensive theory of productive forces' (ibid: 90). In a strange way this theory does emerge in Baudrillard in the sense that his spheres of cultural process overdetermine themselves in a world without apparent base and superstructure, having become however, not productive forces but seductive forces, en route.

What Baudrillard attempted to achieve was a very specific non essentialist notion of fetishism as a theory of the 'perverse structure that perhaps underlies all desire'; thus transformed it might become, he hoped a genuine analytic concept. In order to locate this object at the level of social ideology, it was to Lévi-Strauss and his radical critique of Durkheim's analysis of totemism that he turned. This, said Baudrillard at a crucial point in his development, 'was a radical breakthrough that should be developed, theoretically and clinically, and extended to social analyses in general' (Baudrillard, 1981b: 90). Objects are wrongly conceived here as reified, endowed with mystic forces such as mana. In the theory of objects as endowed with energy, what is forgotten is that they are first marked by signs, it is the sign which makes a talisman (Baudrillard, 1981b: 91), not as a positive meaning, but as that which can establish a system of differences. If fetishism exists, it is a fetishism of the signifier, leading to the manipulation not of the concrete but of the abstract code. The key he insisted from the beginning of his investigations was not to be found in the alienated consciousness, but in the structure. It is 'something like a desire, a perverse desire, the desire of the code is brought to light . . . by exorcising the contradictions spawned by the process of real labour – just as the perverse psychological structure of the fetishist is organised, in the fetish object, around a mark, around the abstraction of a mark that negates, bars and exorcises the differences of the sexes' (ibid: 92). What happens, then, in the generalisation of the code, is a reduction of these sectors to commutable sign values within a 'framework of a system of exchange value that is now almost total' (ibid: 93). In this way Baudrillard manages to find a definition of a social process that becomes totally all-embracing: not fetishism of the commodity but fetishism of the code. For example, money fetishism, is not a fetishism for substance, for the thing, for accumulation, but, says Baudrillard, for the abstract system in its systemic fascination, which like the collection allows the perverse desire to roam throughout.

Baudrillard doubles up this analysis with that of narcissism, and the two come together in the conception of the 'beauty fetish' and the beauty system based on the model. The work of pure signs attempts to arrive at a perfect artifact which escapes in the modern system the interior space of moral sublimation. A long labour of increasing sophistication is concealed in the final perfect object. Baudrillard's itemisation included, tattoos, stretched lips – indeed 'anything will serve to write the cultural order on the body' (Baudrillard, 1981b: 94). The essential thing is the perfection of the cultural sign system and this establishes something new and different from previous systems. The crucial characteristic is a system which can be completely autonomous, 'cut off from external determinations and from the internal reality of its desire, yet offered up in the same turn as an idol, as the perfect phallus for perverse desire' (ibid: 95). The body can be divided, into partial objects: even the whole body can be a partial object (a fetishised nudity). The crucial process is one of division, separation and then reassembly in a montage governed by a code. A perverse structure in so far as it 'substitute(s) the line of demarcation between sign elements for the great dividing line of castration. It substitutes the significant difference, the formal division between signs, for the irreducible ambivalence, for the symbolic split (*écart*)' (ibid). Thus, in place of anthropological essentialism, there is a psychoanalytic one.

The whole notion of seduction is, in this light, a modification of the Freudian notion of charm, in the passage cited by Baudrillard:

(women) who suffice to themselves, who properly speaking love only
themselves (and) exercise the greatest charm over men not only for
aesthetic reasons . . . but also on account of interesting psychological
constellations. . . . The charm of a child lies to a great extent in his
narcissism, his self-sufficiency and inaccessibility, just as does the charm
of certain animals which seem not to concern themselves about us, such
as cats and the large beasts of prey.

(cited in Baudrillard, 1981b: 95)

There is, Baudrillard suggests, an affinity between polymorphic perversity
of the child and that of the contemporary commercial system which
eroticises objects in a perversion that is embodied in the model. What they
have in common as systems of seduction is a ' "beyond" of castration' which
is consummated either in a natural harmony, or a perfectly closed system.
It is this which induces a fascination, like that for a perfectly smooth body,
'without orifices, doubled and redoubled by a mirror, devoted to perverse
auto-satisfaction' (Baudrillard, 1981b: 96). The modern beauty system is
an immense labour of signs which leads to the 'negation of castration' and
a 'negation of the body' (as divided complex whole), and the new order
liberates a desire without barriers.

Baudrillard used these key notions from Freud to generate a cultural
theory, involving both a theory of perversity (avoidance of castration,
fetishisation of the code), and a notion dominated by the theory of
narcissism attached to the feminine 'model' as that which breaks free
from the ambivalence of the sexual to create full, positive terms (male
and female) and their equivalent needs, and rights. There is a third concept
which is equally important, the notion of hysteria, and somatic investment.
Hysterical symptoms are displaced, and can appear as 'migraine, colitis,
lumbago, angina, or generalised fatigue: there is a chain of somatic signifiers
which the symptom "walks" along' (Baudrillard, 1970: 107). And in this way
the theory of the body is a crucial moment of the general theory, either in
psychoanalysis or in social analysis, since 'the body (is) a resumé of all
ambivalent processes: at the same time invested narcissistically as object
of erotic sollicitude, and invested "somatically" as object of anxiety and
aggression' (ibid: 296). It is here in this evocation of crisis, the theory of
crisis of modern society as developed in Baudrillard's early writings, that it
is possible to find the explanation to a question which many have found a
puzzle: why does Baudrillard find contemporary mass communication not
flat, dull, flaccid, but in a condition of ecstasy? The term ecstasy emerged
in Baudrillard's writing when his critique of psychoanalytic theory was
advanced: gone was overdetermination in depth. In its place the hysterical
symptomatology was the ecstasy of communication.

The first chapter of Baudrillard's retrospective survey of his work.
L'Autre par Lui-même ('The Other by himself' trans. as *The Ecstasy
of Communication* (1988c)), begins with the trajectory from the object

system, a problematic which still analysed the Object as it passed through the alienated subject, to the ecstasy of communication, or of circulation:

> let us call this ecstasy: the market is an ecstatic form of the circulation of goods, as prostitution and pornography are ecstatic forms of the circulation of sex. Ecstasy is all functions abolished into one dimension, the dimension of communication. All events, all spaces, all memories are abolished in the sole dimension of information: this is obscene.
>
> (Baudrillard, 1988c: 23–4)

We can recognise this as the perverse universe, the pure functioning of the code, the fascination of the code without barriers to desire, the cancellation of the structure of symbolic castration, but it is also the universe of hysterical symptomatology without the function of displacement (if that is conceivable). The structural law of the code has become the transparency of communication. In fact Baudrillard wants to baptise the new order:

> If hysteria was the pathology of the exacerbated staging of the subject – of the theatrical and operational conversion of the body – and if paranoia was the pathology of organisation – of the structuring of a rigid and jealous world – then today we have entered a new form of schizophrenia – with the emergence of an immanent promiscuity and the perpetual interconnection of all information and communication networks. No more hysteria, or projective paranoia as such, but a state of terror which is characteristic of the schizophrenic, an over-proximity of all things.
>
> (Baudrillard, 1988c:27)

The question is, is Baudrillard describing the world or his own theory? From hysteria/paranoia to schizophrenia/terror. The account describes the schizophrenic's descent into a world without limits, a world characterised by 'the absolute proximity of things . . . this overexposure to the transparency of the world'. It is tempting to suggest that this world only really emerges for Baudrillard after his critical period, after his critique of the Freudian topography, and may be consistent with the gradual fading of the base in the alternative, too simply conceived symbolic order. This latter idea is evidently very important from the point of view of Baudrillard's own complex theoretical make-up since the division between the symbolic and the semiological cultures represents both a division, and a value which prevents in its way the ideological delirium (which may come, as Althusser pointed out about Hegel, in any theory without a topography, where ideas simply produce their own existence, just as much as from a psychological breakdown of the difference between self and others (Deleuze, Guattari)). But if Baudrillard's topography is best thought of as linear, the temporal sequence of cultures (incidentally in Baudrillard's case a sequence which is closer to historical process than genealogy), the danger is that once this division fades, or becomes something more and more difficult to hold onto as a genuine Other as Baudrillard changes position (the hope for cultural revolution becomes a 'nostalgia'), his writing is drawn into the current synchrony, a culture defined by him as without a topography in depth of any kind. This temptation is brutally cut short in the final section of *La Transparence du Mal* (1990b), where he reformulates this opposition in terms of the basic notion of radical alterity.

THE PROBLEM OF EVIL

But there are complications here. It is notable that Baudrillard has also maintained a strong interest in the moral dimension, the problem of good and evil. His thinking on this theme was dominated by his reflection on the story 'The Prague Student', the story of a student who sold his reflected image to the devil, thinking he would have no need of it.

But the other image, the double, begins to intervene in his own life, and makes it impossible. He tries to kill it, and finds that he has only wounded himself, mortally. 'The object (soul, shadow, the products of our work become object) take its revenge' (Baudrillard, 1970: 305). His argument is that from the middle ages, and especially from the romantic revival, the myth of the pact with the devil reflected the engagement with the market and the breakdown of age-old moral controls over it. It is a form of radical alienation in the promethean age, but things are altogether different in affluent societies, which are 'hedonistic and regressive' (ibid: 308): no more malificent instance within society, only a beneficent ambience. Alienation is abolished, absorbed into the logic of the sign. This becomes a game of substitution in a general combinatory; paradoxically, the radicals who provide a critique of affluence over-reified objects and gave them a diabolic value, a response, Baudrillard remarked, that was perhaps more perverse than the spontaneous consumer order itself. It is clear that Baudrillard felt there was a trap here. The critique of the immorality, the evil in the system, would be absorbed, bringing the greatest of all dangers. This is indeed the conclusion of his own analyses: the principle of evil in fact becomes absorbed, so that the modern system passes from a chronic to an acute phase of moral crisis the fatal strategy of the object glows with an 'inverse energy' (Baudrillard, 1990a: 111). The problem of the shadow does not disappear, in principle it cannot. For Baudrillard, as for most moralists (see Midgley, 1984: 122) it is the shadow which is ignored, suppressed, unacknowleged, that disappears into the world of things, or into the world of objects.

Baudrillard himself then 'shadows' the object to that place where evil has its logic: the fatal strategy of the object. Baudrillard appears to take up the most uncompromising position of all. It seems to combine *schadenfreude* (a malicious enjoyment in the aesthetics of collapse) with cynical forms of irrationalism, and a fascination in the downward spiral of the worst outcomes into catastrophic outcomes. This strikes a rationalist mind, such as Midgley as another version of a 'superstitious acceptance of unnecessary evil, based on a false belief in human impotence', the model being she says that of Oedipus:

> True fatalism characteristically shows human effort as useless, indeed self-defeating. This comes out clearly in the story of Oedipus. Here disaster is foretold, but all the efforts which anybody makes to avoid it are futile; they only bring on ruin the sooner.
>
> (Midgley, 1984: 96)

This situation is compared with those which are comforting for the triumphant rationalist: the farmer, for example, who tries to control floods and water supply 'is not doomed to find, like Oedipus, that his efforts must always rebound useless on his head' (ibid: 98). But it is clear that these arguments may not be subtle enough, since the ecological catastrophe brings a continual stream of examples of the serious compounding of problems by well-intentioned intervention. But Baudrillard's position is not that of complete inaction, or that all action is counter-productive. It is that there is a world, perhaps poetic, which secretly ordains, through esoteric affinities, an order which is determinate, determined, but quite different from that of the physical or social universe defined by the sciences. It is in this sphere, now extended to the object world in general that the principle of evil is to be found. It is here that Baudrillard rejoins the world of the sociology of the sacred. Where Durkheim thought that sociology and rational sciences might even begin to replace superstition and even the very vocabulary of evil (which threatens all rationalist problematics), it is now clear that the belief that science could define unilaterally, a hierarchy of values and means will never be sufficient to replace the principle of evil. In effect, Mauss's judgement that Durkheim (the sociologist above all who stressed the pervasiveness of social disease) had ironically fundamentally underestimated the possibilities of processes triumphing in their evil not their beneficent form, the most telling indirect commendation of Baudrillard's project.

IMMINENT THEORETICAL CLOSURE

But the eventual effect of Baudrillard's own project is one of the most surprising ironies of modern thought, as has been discussed earlier in this book (Chapter 3). It is as if it were another 'verification' in the evil. For however much Baudrillard attempted to divert theory, at its origin, in a fatal strategy, it was too late: his oeuvre has been claimed by, oversimulated postmodernism (Kroker), undersimulated postmodernism (Jameson) and then attacked as postmodernist. This certainly indicates something of a problem. One way of posing it would obviously be to say that Baudrillard writes to challenge his readers to move into the present (though critics have pointed out that pataphysics is a paradoxical critical nostalgia, a recycling), the third order of simulation culture. Whereas almost all his readers to date seem to be, for him, hopelessly stuck in the second order, that is of Marxism and related forms of dialectical thought. From this perspective the major character of his writing appears as an immense display, as a series of affronts to rationalism, humanism, feminism, socialism, political ecology. Western art is 'rot'. 'Marxism is only a form of capitalism'. The social, constructed in the nineteenth century is in an advanced state of decomposition if not already dead. These are absolute assertions, without appeal. They are a challenge, but launched in such a way that there can be no response: there is no Baudrillard debate, the very idea is self-contradictory since Baudrillard's essential thesis is that this is no longer a real possibility. Perhaps his appropriation by postmodernism has confirmed this.

Perhaps the word challenge is wrong. Perhaps the most apt concept would be that Baudrillard has given up the intellectual challenge of the hypothesis which he began in *The Object System* (1968). Now his work is in a different modality: what Alice Jardine has called the gynema, the horizon of the feminine. For Baudrillard, all the productivist, masculinist imagery is being replaced with that of seduction and counter-seduction, that is the principle of the feminine. It is not as if Baudrillard as others have done, writes as a woman, and he certainly does not claim to be an intellectual transvestite let alone indulge in 'critical cross dressing'. This is perhaps difficult to grasp even for sophisticated critics such as Alice Jardine, who while recognising that Baudrillard's strategy is based on the superiority of ritual and ambivalence, and that is today realised in a principle of femininity as seduction, simply notes that 'according to him, it is women who are blindest to this fact; it is women who are working against the possibilities for true cultural renewal'. Instead of following up what this might mean for Baudrillard, she immediately jumps to the defence of feminism. (Jardine, 1985: 67).

But what would it mean? Baudrillard has considered sexual and gender relations at every stage of his career. There are sufficient indications to suggest that his view must be considered against his basic genealogy: symbolic exchange, gift, rule, strong seduction, through a period of polarity (and hierarchy), to that of the current system, which for Baudrillard is based on narcissism and soft seduction. The feminine is the principle of seduction, ambivalence, but it is also that of appearance, of the superficial, of the feint. In the current phases of simulation, it is precisely these characteristics which in the consumer society have become predominant: its complement, the loss of (a masculine principle) depth. But he insists, seduction is quite different from provocation, 'nothing could be less seductive than a provocative smile or inciteful behaviour, since both presuppose that one cannot be seduced naturally and that one needs to be blackmailed into it or through a declaration of intent' (Baudrillard, 1988c: 67). It is as if Baudrillard is aware that he provokes (he sometimes claims it as a virtue sometimes as vice, and realises that this is not seductive, as if he confuses challenge (in the macho style) with seduction itself (yet he also says 'challenge, and not desire, lies at the heart of seduction . . . is that to which one cannot avoid responding' (ibid: 57).)

What is seduction? It arrives 'only through empty, illegible, insoluble, arbitrary, fortuitous signs, which glide by lightly, modifying the index of the refraction of space' (ibid: 60). And here Baudrillard arrives at his basic rationale for a form of writing that does not aim to persuade: seductive signs are:

> without a subject of enunciation . . . they are pure signs in that they are neither discursive nor generate any exchange. The protagonists of seduction are neither locutor nor interlocutee, they are in a duel and antagonistic situation. As such the signs of seduction do not signify; they are of the order of the ellipse, of the short circuit, of the flash of wit.
>
> (Baudrillard, 1988c: 60, trans. mod.)

This order is not that of discourse itself, not that of debate or argument (this is presumably a phenomenon in depth). Across this strikes the flash of seduction, of wit, an idea, of beauty, and 'we exist only in the brief instant when we are seduced – by whatever moves us, a face, an idea, a word, a passion' (ibid: 69). This idea even finds its seductive forms in writing, that is a something which moves 'faster than conceptual interconnection, such is the secret of writing' (*écriture*) (Baudrillard, 1983b: 232); on the other hand, the strategic work of the sign mysteriously works in its own time, towards its appointed destiny.

But then Baudrillard wants to complicate this and turn it into a strategy or a technique of seduction which is highly calculated, a play on signs: he 'who attacks first is lost . . . never oppose one's desire to the desire of the other, but aim at the hollow spot of appearance, or trap him in his lure. For seduction does not exist any more than luck exists for the gambler' (Baudrillard, 1988c: 69). Turning back to Kierkegaard's 'Diary of a Seducer', he remarks that what was seductive was the enigma, and this is 'never revealed'. He remarks, 'had the secret been revealed it would have been sex, and sexuality would have been the the final point of the story, had there indeed been one. But there is none, and in this regard psychoanalysis has deceived itself' (ibid: 65). This is an important comment, suggesting as it does some degree of support (from Kierkegaard) for Baudrillard's interpretation of the world, for at this stage Baudrillard has long forsaken anything but literary evidence for the state of the world. The strategy of seduction developed by Johannes, and indeed interpreted by Baudrillard as such elsewhere, does not really begin until the aesthetic object becomes interesting in the spiritual sense, and this is already a work of preparation that is highly calculated psychologically. The object of Johannes' interest is certainly sex, and as soon as this sex is collected and added to his total, he abandons Cordelia hoping she would become a man. But this is not the central issue, which is why Baudrillard should want to *reveal* this apparent secret: his mode of discourse is as positive and unseductive at this point as any equivalent empirical study (its very empirical inadequacy is its very seductiveness). But Baudrillard does enter into the poetic: he presents the story of Brahma and Sharatuya and weaves it into the text of the discussion. It is undoubtedly a powerful, and seductive device. But it does not work as a flash of wit, but rather as a simulation of an exotic ritual. Remarkably, at one point he certainly hears the anticipated voice of criticism for he remarks 'I am not expressing any reactionary nostalgia' (Baudrillard, 1988c: 63).

In writing in this way, the force of his text is that of an obsession with signs, styles, modes, in an attempt to both challenge and seduce, yet the two simply collide. He wishes, perhaps, to collect persona, but also to provoke: he is the semiologist, the sociologist, economist, anthropologist, post-Marxist, epistemologist, poet, fatalist, theorist, prophet, art critic, media theorist, philosopher, tourist, journalist, diarist, genealogist of culture. He is a collector of objects, from the cigarette lighter in precisely the 'system of objects' to entire cultures (*America* (1988a). But in fact things have changed in the double spiral, and from the neat system, through a critique of the order of simulation, and into fatal theory, he has travelled also from the system to the heterogeneity of things with the paradoxes and aphorisms and humour of *Cool Memories* (1990c). This heterogeneity of things, however, is far from being accumulated by Baudrillard in an eclectic fashion. As is clear from the analysis of *America*, there are strange unities to be discovered in radical modernity: in order to find them one must learn to inhabit the spaces between the spiral of the Unifying Subject and the spiral of the Fatal Object, and to learn that it is the latter spiral which exercises a fundamental influence.

'Snow is no longer a gift from on high. It falls precisely at those places designated as winter resorts' (Baudrillard, 1990c: 144).

Notes

1 INTRODUCTION: READING BAUDRILLARD

1   See 1970: 116. It is also true to say that Baudrillard makes no claim that his work is strategically effective: 'I am not a strategist' (1989e: 17), he said recently.

2   The Marxist critique begins at this point, since the theory of the commodity very directly limits this object to the economic: 'an ideology of reification that sees "things" everywhere . . . confuses in this thing every social relation, conceived according to a money thing' (Althusser, 1969: 230).

3   This is presented in Carroll (1974). Dostoyevsky visited (in 1862) the futuristic exhibition at the Crystal Palace in London and was both fascinated and appalled at the naiveté of the religion of technical progress. Baudrillard's notion of the revenge of the crystal has something Dostoyevskian about it (Gane, 1990).

4   In fact, Baudrillard's terminology has changed over time, and in his later writings often talks of the destiny of the pure sign, as something which can be found in all societies.

5   Lukes, in his table of the difference between the mechanical and organic social forms (1973: 158) curiously omits to put science into the latter category. There is a latent problem in Durkheim concerning the relation between the contractual net of solidarities in the organic societies and the revolutionary, uncontractualist notion of science which he develops (see Gane, 1988).

6   This formulation is provisional here. If there is no class struggle, there is still a mass struggle in Baudrillard's latest works where the struggle is one whereby the subject resists as object becomes more object than subject.

7   Notably, for example, Meaghan Morris, whose writings on Baudrillard are amongst the most accurate.

8   Therefore doubled by a critique internal to the system, from the *mass-as-object*.

9   Probably not so surprising as it might first appear, since Bataille had already taken that path in the College of Sociology, 1937–9 (Hollier, 1988). This has always been a curious phenomenon, and widely considered a 'gigantic misunderstanding' (Heimonet, 1984). For Durkheim's notion of the sacred, and the reversibility of good and evil (see Caillois, 1959).

10   See Goffman, 1981: Chapter 4.

11   Popper often comes close to suggesting that a metaphysical research programme (1986: 150), is more than an intellectual relation to a problem, and it is clear that Popper's own relation to science and to the world it depicts is one

of wonderment. Baudrillard's work is often found offensive on the grounds of its evident moments of pure *schadenfreude* not wonderment.

12 Nietzsche: 'when I imagine a perfect reader, he always turns into a monster of courage and curiosity; moreover, supple, cunning, cautious: a born adventurer and discoverer' (1969: 264). Are these three stages? And for the bad reader:

> I can foresee the impatience of the bad reader: this is the way I name or accuse the fearful reader, the reader in a hurry to be determined, decided upon everything . . . it is bad to predestine one's reading, it is always bad to foretell. It is bad, reader, no longer to like retracing one's steps.
>
> (Derrida, 1987: 4)

13 If Baudrillard's reputation has been established on the basis of supporters such as Kroker and critics such as Kellner, it is not surprising that he has wanted to establish some distance from them: 'that is their business' (in Gane, 1990: 331).

14 Hegemony is not defined by quantitative generality but by its effective role as the leading edge over that which is simulated in the dominant sectors of the culture.

15 This could be expressed again in terms of strategic alliance, between the strategy of the 'subject as critical subject', and 'subject as fatal object'.

16 For Baudrillard, as for Mauss and Durkheim (see Gane, 1984). Marx's version of communism did not achieve the radical alterity from capitalism that he aimed for.

17 It is evident that Baudrillard plays with many of the key terms of Althusser, and in the process these terms change their sense. One important example is that of the dialectic and 'overdetermination' (Althusser, 1969). Fundamentally, Baudrillard rejects the operation of a dialectical process as the necessary logic of social formations in displacements of dominance by a determinant instance (a totality in which there are always internal contradictions in principle). These ideas are replaced by a notion of the cultural code (symbolic or semiotic), and it is this code which in its action made it appear at a certain moment that the economy was an independent and dominant mode. This was inverted by Marx. Marxist critiques of Baudrillard would reverse this reversal and argue that Baudrillard is himself the victim of the apparent death of political economy, it is this which gives the illusion that the mass media are the dominant forms of social integration (on the discussion of Althusser's notion of ideological state apparatuses, see Gane, 1983c). As for Baudrillard's notion of dialectical and non-dialectical processes, both would figure within the Althusserian conception of dialectical processes, since this conception (1) rejected the notion of dialectical transcendence as Hegelian, and (2) rejected the Sartrean-inspired notion that the dialectic was a social dialectic, that is constituent of social interaction. Baudrillard clearly makes the dialectic disappear from lived experience, but never displaces its domain from the social to the theoretical object. Most of Baudrillard's conceptions can be thought in terms of contradiction and overdetermination, which is not in fact surprising since the origins of these concepts are rooted in Baudrillard's psychoanalytic problematic (which has remained decisive), just as they were for Althusser.

2 ESSENTIAL BACKGROUND AND CONTEXT

1 This interview dates from the time when he had already begun to talk of the mass (and the collapse of the class struggle). It is clear that although

he does not develop an elaborate conception of the elite as opposed to the mass, his framework is only intelligible in terms of the struggle of the masses against the (political, cultural, intellectual) elite, and dominant social and cultural order, as this interview makes clear. The feint he adopts against sociology is to say that it must now be obsolete because the 'social'is now dead (classes have disappeared into the mass). But sociology is not to be confined to such a narrow object, nor is social theory. The problem identified in the interview is the collapse of the intellectual as an independent critical fraction of the elite in the face of cultural homogenisation. If there were no longer alternative independent ideological positions and values (this argument parallels the decline of marked gender positions) he was able to identify modes of resistance to the dominant elite in the form of subject as object becoming fatal object (again it is possible to find a kind of *schadenfreude* in his relation with women, see Baudrillard, 1987b).

2   It is interesting that Baudrillard makes a distinction which is also elaborated in Gouldner's thesis (1979) between intellectual and intelligentia. The difference is that together for Gouldner they not only form a class but a class with a future, as against the monied bourgeoisie which is now in decline. For Bauman (1987), the transition is marked by the decline of the intellectual as legislator (and there is no doubt in effect that Baudrillard is one of these). Thus another strategic component must be taken into consideration. Together with a basis in the symbolic order, and in the mass, Baudrillard's vision is also, as Bauman has indicated elsewhere (1986), inflected with the crisis of a section or fraction of the French intelligentsia and its loss of powers (or sense of). The decline of intellectuals is also discussed by Jaccoby (1987) and his 'The Decline of the American Intellectuals' in Angus and Jally (1989: 271–81): here the conclusion is: 'a certain kind of independent intellectual is on the eve of disappearing. A deathly professionalisation and academisation permeate society, draining public culture of vitality. Professional life and thought survive, but the larger culture turns grey' (ibid: 281). On the other hand, Foucault:

No, I don't believe in the refrain of decadence, the absence of great writers, the sterility of thought, the restricted and bleak horizon . . . we don't suffer from the void, but from too few means to think about all that is happening . . . one always complains that the media crams peoples heads, but there is a misanthropy in this idea.

(Foucault, 1989: 198)

3   Gorz (1966) provides a succinct statement of how Sartre's social philosophy was read at this time.
4   It is the deathly character of this world evoked by Marx which seems to be an exemplar for Baudrillard's own evocation of the end of the world.
5   For recent considerations of the relation of Sartre and Althusser, see Elliot, in Griffiths (ed.) (1988: 195–214) and Sprinker (1987).
6   It is clear that however much Baudrillard attacked Sartre from a structuralist point of view, he never relinquished entirely the definition of the dialectic as the action of historical transcendence. Like Marcuse (1968) he saw in the emerging one-dimensional society a society without the possibility of transcendence and, therefore, dialectic. This was not an option for Althusser. Baudrillard retained the notion of overdetermination, shorn of its principle of determination in the last instance and contradiction.
7   Baudrillard's version was the most ingenious of all; society-become-object, or 'totality without a subject', a kind of inversion of the Hegelian principle of 'absolute subject' (that is as 'absolute object'). In this perspective it is no

wonder that Baudrillard is an advocate of delirium.

8   There are even good grounds for thinking it a version of 'post-modern Marxism', if postmodernism is defined as the displacement of modern systems by asystemic intervention. In general, postmodernism is not approached this way (see Hutchinson, 1989 for a recent discussion of definitions).

9   Canguilhem's influence on Baudrillard seems indirect but powerful, especially the extention in Canguilhem of the concept of pathology into the genetic age (Canguilhem on genetic error, 1978: 171–9). This is quite a different direction of thought from that indicated by Forrester's suggestion in a discussion of Foucault on Freud that the concept of the abnormal, of pathology had become 'foolish' (1980).

10 Marxists in the Althusserian school always had difficulty with Marxism's rationalist elements, witness Balibar's essay (1978) 'Marxism is not a theoretical rationalism' (p.17). This presents a difficulty in the face of a challenge from irrationalism like that of Nietzsche or Baudrillard. Balibar's solution is to call it a secondary issue.

11 It may seem quite perverse to suggest that a writer like McLuhan has also stated theses of a similar kind, but see McLuhan in Stearn (ed.), 1968: 316, 320, 335–6.

12 It is highly instructive to compare these 'conversations' of Lévi-Strauss, with the 'Interview with Baudrillard', of 1984 (in 1987d: 37–54).

13 For an informative recent account of situationism see Wollen (1989). Perhaps mercifully Baudrillard has yet to be embroiled in this literature for it is clear that the situationists were in part an important outcome of the fusion of Marx, Nietzsche and Durkheim established in Bataille (Wollen, 1989: 89). Baudrillard has recently noted:

> I was very, very attracted by Situationism. Situationism is like a kind of primitive theoretical scene, a radical one. And even today if Situationism is past, there remains a kind of radicality to which I have always been faithful. There is a kind of obsession, a kind of counterculture . . . and that's why I am not at bottom a philosopher, it's because I have always had a kind of radical suspicion towards culture, or even towards ideas – a kind of barbarism, in fact. A barbarian position.
>
> (Baudrillard, 1989e)

14 In the early phases of Baudrillard's work he seems close to Veblen (1959) in many respects since they share a commitment to non-parasitic, non-hierarchical forms of work and workmanship (see Baudrillard, 1969b). Recent discussion of Baudrillard's relation to Veblen (see Rojek, 1990), runs into difficulty when the important changes of Baudrillard's position are ignored, especially in relation to the notion of work (important before 1969, afterwards the whole ideology of function, use, work, is associated with a problematic of production, and is rejected as a totality: Veblen, like Marx was part of that problematic).

15 This translation differs slightly from that given in Barthes (1984: 119).

16 It should be said that there is irony in this dedication, which is not to Sartre but to his essay 'L'Imaginaire'.

17 It is important to note how significant this is for Baudrillard, as can be seen specifically in the very conceptualisation of the movement from transgression to neutralisation in the mass:

> It has nothing to do with any real population, body or specific social aggregate. Any attempt to qualify it only seeks to transfer it back to sociology and rescue it from this indistinction, which is not even that of equivalence (the unlimited sum of equivalent individuals: 1 + 1 + 1 + 1 – such is the

sociological definition), but that of the neutral, that is to say neither one nor other (ne-uter)'.

(Baudrillard, 1983a: 5–6).

See the important discussion by Berthelot (in Zylberberg, 1986: 179–94, 'Les Masses: de L'etre au neant'). It is clear that Baudrillard is seeking the ne-uter of the mass, something close to the 'negative essence of transgression' in the absence of the very possibility of transgression.

18   In her essay 'Stabat mater' (1986: 161–86), Kristeva aims at a divided writing and its specific ambivalence, but somehow only juxtaposes two texts, we are led instead to 'an achievement of that which is irreducible, that of the irreducible interest of both sexes in asserting their differences, in the quest of each one – and women, after all – for an appropriate fulfilment. The text alongside says: 'love, here, is for the impossible' (p.184).

19   This process took millenia for Baudrillard, centuries for Kristeva, but only decades for Lefebvre.

20   Naomi Schor says: 'Much of Baudrillard's work is tinged with a scarcely veiled nostalgia for a lost or unattainable object that would not be disfigured by the industrial ornamental detail (Schor, 1987: 56). Schor probably underestimates the complexity of Baudrillard's argument, which goes much further than she suspects. Detail, which she sees as feminine, is located in ornament, and precisely ornament added to industrial goods in order to give them individiuality. For Baudrillard it is important not to reduce the symbolic to the semiological, and between the ornamentation which has meaning in symbolism, and ornamentation which decorates a commercial product, there is a world of a difference, and the difference is in a sense that of two forms of the feminine, one strong, seductive, the other cool, narcissistic.

21   Baudrillard's norm is certainly not that of Durkheim's conception. It is sometimes the 'primitive symbolic' order itself, but inflected by the Nietzschean norm: life. (See Kofman 'Baubo: theological perversion and fetishism' in Gillespie and Strong (eds) (1988: 175–202).

3 BAUDRILLARD, POSTMODERNISM, MARXISM AND FEMINISM

1   It is also remarkable that there is no discussion by Baudrillard in Ferry and Renaut's (1985) survey and discussion of the principal ideas generated around and in relation to the events of May 1968 in France, since Baudrillard is certainly one of the very few thinkers who developed an original analysis of it. They do in fact refer to the 'beautiful' (Ferry and Renaut, 1985: 17) even the 'original' analyses of Lipovetsky (1983), without realising the influence of Baudrillard on them, perfectly well acknowledged by Lipovetsky.

2   Hebdige tries to identify postmodernism with the following inventory, saying that the more 'contradictorily nuanced a word is' the more likely it is to be effective in focusing debate (a rather dubious argument which could and should be inverted):

> When it becomes possible for people to describe as 'postmodern' the decor of a room, the design of a building, the diagesis of a film, the construction of a record, or a 'scratch' video, a television commercial, or an arts documentary, or the 'intertextual' relations between them, the layout of a page in a fashion or critical journal, an anti-teleological tendency within epistemology, the attack on the 'metaphysics of presence', a general attenuation of feeling, the collective chagrin and morbid projections of a post-War generation of baby boomers confronting disillusioned middle age, the 'predicament' of

reflexivity, a group of rhetorical tropes, a proliferation of surfaces, a new phase of commodity fetishism, a fascination for images, codes and styles, a process of cultural, political or existential fragmentation and/or crisis, the 'de-centring' of the subject, an 'incredulity towards metanarratives', the replacement of unity power axes by a plurality of power/ discourse formations, the 'implosion of meaning', the collapse of cultural hierarchies, the dread engendered by the threat of nuclear self-destruction, the decline of the university, the functioning and effects of the new miniaturised technologies, broad societal and economic shifts into a 'media' 'consumer',or 'multinational' phase, a sense (depending on who you read) of 'placelessness' or the abandonment of placelessness ('critical regionalism') or (even) a generalised substitution of spatial for temporal co-ordinates – when it becomes possible to describe all these things as 'postmodern' (or more simply, using a current abbreviation, as 'post' or 'very post') then it's clear we are in the presence of a buzzword

(Hebdige, 1988: 181–2)

Hebdige has furnished his book with two apt epigraphs, one from Blake 'General Knowledges are those Knowledges that Idiots possess', and James Brown's 'What it is is what it is' (Hebdige, 1988: 4), and these precisely express the true lumpen character of the postmodern inventory.

3   Curiously Kroker and Cook herald Baudrillard as a 'new wave political theorist' (1988: 178). What this means is simply that, according to these authors, Baudrillard 'privileges' the punk generation as a 'new generation of rebels' who are 'hyper conformists' and turn the system's logic 'neutrally' against itself. It is difficult to find anything new in this idea, except that it has never before been called a 'new wave'; previously it was defined as ressentiment. The fact that Baudrillard's position is presented as the latest fashion is of course Baudrillard's ultimate failure, given his theoretical position on the catastrophic nature of the fashion cycle. It certainly became a buzzword and quickly a new organising principle: Harvey (1985) has no mention at all of postmodernism, yet by 1989 the same material (or much of it) was absorbed directly into the new frame (Harvey, 1989).

4   The extract is taken from Baudrillard (1988e: 86), where it is clear that the words 'Please follow me' come from the Other, from the woman, and not from Baudrillard. The critique of Baudrillard here perhaps should start with an examination of the irony that it is in the story of 'S' the woman who follows a man. In general, and in a way known directly to Baudrillard in the story of Johannes and Cordelia (Kierkegaard) it is the man who tracks the woman as prey.

5   Note that Baudrillard says 'seduction simply rights a natural imbalance by taking up the pre-existing challenge constituted by the girl's natural beauty' (1990a: 99).

6   It is here we encounter Baudrillard's own simulations, this time of the symbolic cultures, from a position which looks distinctly like critical theory (second–order simulation).

7   It is interesting to examine these criticisms, which suggested that Marcuse's conceptions were elitist, quietist and based on a fundamental misunderstanding of the nature of capitalist societies. Three such critics are worth discussing: Cohen, MacIntyre and Kellner. Cohen notes the drift of Marcuse's object from social to cultural criticism, and from social relations to objects. In the presentation of one-dimensionality, examples are no longer situated in a sociological framework, but listed in a way which makes any differentiated setting irrelevant. The arguments tend to ignore production altogether as a

topic of investigation, and the cultural analyses tend to dwell on 'freak' cases, and much of the analysis simply accepts the ideology of the modern capitalist society at face value, and therefore his theory provides an ideology for capitalism. Yet for Cohen, Marcuse's argument that 'contemporary society uses the instruments of liberation to contain, divert and defeat the struggle for liberation . . . is true, important, Marxist and new' (Cohen, 1969: 49).

MacIntyre found the writing of Marcuse pessimistic, and speculative. It was also elitist. In trying to go beyond Marxism it became pre-Marxist. The new society, permissive, happy, but based on the suppression of needs which could generate revolutionary criticism, finds its echo among right-wing writers who find modern, affluent, liberal society a form of cultural totalitarianism: the modern form of domination is through work, welfare, libido and a new language which flattens out reality. This is dangerous, said MacIntyre, since this blurring of differences makes it more difficult to identify the real totalitarians, rational debate and criticism should at all costs be defended, the welfare system is not a simple counterrevolutionary mechanism but a new terrain of political and social struggle. (As for the analysis of the function of permissiveness, MacIntyre seemed to show some sympathy.) Basically the whole conception has theoretical flaws: society is not homogeneous but a complex totality, and not everything becomes functional for the system (the universities struggle to maintain some autonomy), and society is not controlled by a single elite for it is simply too complex. In talking of opposition to the system Marcuse is always tempted by petit bourgeois bohemianism and the lumpen proletariat, and infantile leftism (MacIntyre, 1970: 88–9).

Kellner found Marcuse had developed a 'powerful Marxist critique' of modern society, and was an 'outstanding critic of contemporary culture' yet his theory was carried away with the appearance and not the reality of contemporary society, it exaggerated its arguments and was thus found wanting in relation to the actual historical process it tried to grasp, it also remained too abstract and failed to examine specific processes. But the overall contribution was a genuine attempt to update Marxism in an analysis of capitalist societies integrated more and more through consumerism and its ideologies (Kellner, 1984: 273).

In sum these critiques concurred that Marcuse was empirically suspect, did not identify key sites of continuing struggle, exaggerated his case to the point of misinterpretation which had potentially damaging political consequences. It also had an incipient cultural elitist tendency, and tendencies towards irrationalism. But there were, with Kellner and Cohen some high degree of support and praise on some points, both saw the attempt as a genuine continuation of Marxism, towards an analysis of a stage of capitalism in which cultural integration was greatly intensified. Kellner also defended Marcuse against Baudrillard's attacks, turning against Baudrillard's 'extremely vague' position, 'tinged with irrationalism'; and, specifically against Baudrillard's conception of symbolic orders as non-accumulative, Kellner suggested that Baudrillard's ideal was 'masturbation, or gratuitous violence and destruction' (Kellner, 1984: 404).

4 BAUDRILLARD'S ATTEMPT TO DEVELOP MARXISM

1 For instances of the failure to grasp this work and Baudrillard's work up to 1973 see Giradin (1974) who can only see in these essays a 'rewritten inside-out version' of Sartrean philosophy, or D. Miller, who is bemused by the subtleties of it (Miller, 1987: 47–9, 165), especially Baudrillard's

idea of commodities 'referring only to themselves and appropriating all other aspects of social relations to themselves through consumption . . . a complex (and dubious) point' (ibid:48). Harvey discusses, even begins his whole consideration of Marxist theory from the point of use value, but the discussion never resolves the equivocation over eternal needs, social needs and needs produced in relation to capital; he is happy with Marx's phrase that a use value 'is the object of the satisfaction of any system whatever of human needs', unwilling to pick up the problem of the utilitarian implications of such a conceptualisation and therefore unaware of the theoretical and political dangers of generalisation from his base (Harvey, 1982: 5–9). A writer with a more Durkheimian formation like Gouldner, on the other hand, was quick to see the significance of this question, and its subversiveness for Marx in particular (Gouldner, 1980: 199–214). A balanced discussion can be found in D'Amico (1978) and in Lipovetsky (1975). Particularly disappointing is Poster (1981).

2   Given that Baudrillard is a 'media theorist' it is remarkable that his reputation developed without any analyses of media content.

3   It is important to note this concern in Baudrillard for strategies of cultural exclusion as opposed to domination. It continues in the analysis of forms of excommunication in the later writings. It appears, however, to be situated uniquely at the cultural level in which these pure strategies can be identified, as against social exclusion of proletariat or peasantry.

4   This thesis is essential to Baudrillard's later writings, which emphasise the dual reponse of the object/child: as subject and as object. Here the (subordinate) petit bourgeoisie has to act as dominator (excluder) but also is, at the same time, compromised, humiliated. This is also the basis for the theory of simulation, which can be seen in terms of different rising, and blocked, class fractions. Rewritten in Marxist terms Baudrillard's theory would be one of bourgeois hegemony through its break-up of the symbolic order, the triumphant incorporation of the proletariat in a bad simulation of production, and the formation of a historic compromise in the ambient culture of the petit bourgeoisie – in the end the incorporated subaltern classes struggle through new forms of *ressentiment*, fatal strategies in the defeat of the social project. The strategy of Marxist critiques of Baudrillard is to question the dominance of the new phase of fatal strategies: many simply take his historical and theoretical position and add on a happy ending (the revolution is still on the agenda).

5   The ambient culture is overdetermined by both its social political ambivalent relations with the bourgeoisie, and its position of dominance in relation to the proletariat.

6   For the concept of 'mana' see Mauss and Hubert (1972) evidently an important reference point for Baudrillard.

7   The resentment here is in rationalist mode, and later becomes a strategy in the mode of *ressentiment*. He notes: 'The apparent passivity of long hours of viewing . . . hides a laborious patience' (Baudrillard, 1981b: 55). The discussion implies the affinity of high culture and that of the 'prelogical' culture of the African bush, as both are outside the base of utilitarian values (ibid).

8   This is a crucial formulation which makes what he later calls the symbolic order, the eternal basis of social life. There is still some ambivalence in Baudrillard as to whether this still exists or is superseded. It is clear that at this stage of his theoretical development society was complex not only in terms of its social and cultural makeup, but also in terms of the intercalation of the mechanisms of prestation and those of commodity exchange.

9   It would be possible to reconstitute Baudrillard's theoretical evolution from this proposition, showing how the symbolic cultures were intimately connected

with non-commodity social relations, and their metamorphoses; and that this growth of commodity exchange involved the dramatic change in the character of the lived world, towards that of reification of objects. But Baudrillard gives this thesis a revolutionary edge: the epistemological rupture of the symbolic world.

10   This proposition marks the point at which Baudrillard seems to treat symbolic exchange as increasingly annihilated by semiological exchange.

11   In fact, by 1976, Baudrillard had worked out a way of trying to analyse the persistent destruction (ideological, social, cultural) of the symbolic economy.

5 A CHANGE OF POSITION

1   It can be seen from this discussion just how far Baudrillard was at this period from a fully Nietzschean position, since he locates the discussion with respect to gift, not debt (see by contrast Deleuze and Guattari, 1977: 190). Arthur Kroker seems to overplay the Nietzschean elements in Baudrillard at this stage, with his suggestion that in the concept of the 'logic of signification' (*For a Critique*, 1981b), Baudrillard had 'succeed in teasing out the existence of the sign as the basic structural logic of the commodity form and what is more, in deciphering it as dead power'. This means, says Kroker, that Baudrillard's analysis 'does not stand in fateful opposition to Marx's *Capital*, but, rather, represents its perfect completion' (Kroker, 1988: 77). This argument simply erases a whole episode of theoretical labour in Baudrillard.

2   If Marx wanted a firm base of human uses from which to attack the private market system, Baudrillard wants a firm base in the symbolic exchange cultures: this allows him to be sufficiently concrete to attack consumerism, but also sufficiently abstract, indeterminate, to avoid having to explain why the gift-exchange system has been and still is being destroyed by market exchange and the structural law of value.

3   It is at this point that the use of apocalyptic notions of total revolution, total critique and total rejection of the system, reaches its peak in Baudrillard's writings. The Total Revolution which fails, evidently, will become a Totally Impossible Revolution and opposition to reform and ecology (Baudrillard, 1981b: 202). It also implies that the system, having become totally abstract, leaves precious little room outside itself: it abolishes symbolic exchange as such and everything is absorbed, even history (see Niethammer (1989) who weakens the credibility of his criticism by claiming without evidence that Baudrillard was a Communist Party intellectual. Niethammer seems to forget the existence of utopianism, and its persistence, opting for a simple process of overoptimism leading to overpessimism in Baudrillard's development). This is possible because Baudrillard concerns himself with the object in system, and this can be seen as a trap already waiting for Baudrillard himself. Critics have not been slow to point it out: 'He ultimately envisages a spontaneous, impassioned, almost mystical overthrow of the general code, but his previous delineation of political economy as master-device of mobilisation and co-optation renders this option paltry and improbable' (Valente, 1985: 62). Just as critics of Marcuse once claimed that one-dimensional theses could become the system's very own ideology, so Valente claims now that Baudrillard 'buttresses the code form'. But this would only be the case if Baudrillard definitively moved to the position that symbolic exchange was irredemiably lost.

4   The phrases indicate just how rationalist the critique of Marx was at this time.

5   This is a highly significant attack, but one which seems entirely hypocritical.

The base/superstructure concepts prevent, precisely, the mobility of theoretical objects. It is Baudrillard's own collapse into a theory without topography that allows such a circulation of objects and forms.

6 Post-modernism *avant la lettre*. The whole basis of Baudrillard's rejection of postmodernism as playing with the pieces, the leftovers, as radical, is grounded here in the rejection of ideology itself.

6 BAUDRILLARD: THEORETICAL CRITIC

1 In fact many of Baudrillard's orientations and 'obsessions' could be explained by reference to the division of labour imposed in the social sciences. If there is specialisation in the field of consumption, it is probably likely that eventually everything will be explained by reference to consumption, unless there are checks.

2 Kroker is quite wrong to suggest that Baudrillard's break with existentialism arrived in 1976 (Kroker 1985: 82).

3 His notion of 'smallest common multiples' for example, or the table of conversions in the general theory (Baudrillard, 1981b: 123) – Baudrillard's own rather naive simulation of structuralism.

4 A crucial weakness until his last essays, was the failure to identify just where the system actually was. In his later works it is clear that his focus becomes that of the system of different national cultures (America in the global order).

5 Why deprive others of this pleasure (said Nietzsche)?

6 Had Baudrillard wanted to develop a notion of seduction in the style of Kierkegaard at this point, he could have done so with direct connection with Marx's notion of the subject in the second degree. It is clear, however, that the principal concerns of Baudrillard here are not actually a critique of Marx, but a critique of a certain form of Marxism (quite a different thing).

7 There is a hint here of a continuation of Baudrillard's earlier note on simulation as a form of cultural defeat: Marxism as the repressive, ideological proletarian simulation of the social structure of capital, or rather the structure of bourgeois political economy, as opposed to the ambient culture of petit bourgeois simulation. Note this is previously Durkheim's position.

8 It is curious that Baudrillard cites Sahlins on the inapplicability of the concept of scarcity, just at the time Sahlins applied the notion of mode of production to primitive cultures (Sahlins, 1974).

9 Very schematic if compared with say the analysis of Keith Thomas (1984), but such a comparison is quite illegitimate.

10 This line of thought is developed extensively in Durkheim's critique of Saint-Simon and Marx.

11 This is the point at which the theme of the control of power of death begins to emerge in Baudrillard's work, developed at length in 1976.

12 Evidently a foretaste of the story of the good butcher Chuang Tzu (see Baudrillard, 1976: 187–9).

13 Baudrillard should perhaps if he is consistent say that the Copernican revolution was eventually established in anthropology by Marcel Mauss. c.f. Talcott Parsons (in Dillon, 1968: 6).

14 This discussion marks a major change from that of *For a Critique* (Baudrillard, 1981b: 143ff) which uses the idea of magic as mystique.

15 It is this confrontation which provokes Baudrillard to criticise the rationalist critiques of superstition and to attempt to rescue it, and to elevate it to the degree of the gift.

16 For background to Baudrillard's discussion see Descombes (1980: 156–67).

17   This discussion though brief is crucial since all the modern forms of emancipation are ambivalent processes. Baudrillard sees them as regretable aspects
of the destruction of symbolic exchange, and refuses to engage in working them
through.

18   Much hinges on this argument. Baudrillard's treatment of it here is short, sharp,
and glib. This weakness is surprising, but seems intimately connected with a
desire rapidly to find a way out of the conventional (Marxist) problematic.

19   A term developed in a slightly different context by Guattari (1984: 11–23).

20   See this idea in Barthes (1967b) and Marcuse (1968).

21   See Bataille (1985).

22   See Derrida (1981).

23   Here Baudrillard finds himself once again drawn back into admitting, against
himself, of Marx's identification that it is production which is the strategically
key mechanism in capitalist societies.

24   Latent in this discussion is the parallel between Baudrillard's notion of the
church and scientific Marxism which holds back, delays, and controls the
demand 'for paradise now'.

25   This discussion has been translated into English (Baudrillard, 1981c) and
has already become the focus of dispute, largely it seems as a result
of misunderstanding, and in one case (Kellner), growing ill will towards
Baudrillard's work. Lee Hildreth, the translator suggests this section from
L'Echange Symbolique et la Mort (1976), seems to circle around the theses
of the important French psychoanalyst Jacques Lacan, but this is never
acknowledged, it is a 'kind of invisible presence, a (the) repressed signified'
(in Baudrillard, 1981c: 87). This overlooks the fact that Lacan is discussed
elsewhere in the book (Baudrillard, 1976: 204–6), where Baudrillard
discusses the relation of the symbolic, imaginary and the real and surprisingly
perhaps defends Lacan against Lévi-Strauss. Douglas Kellner, however, has
used this translation to attack Baudrillard's intellectual integrity. He argues
(Kellner, 1989a: 23) that, suddenly, the phrase describing Baudrillard's intent
has passed from being 'revolutionary analysis' (Baudrillard, 1976: 342), to
'evolutionary analysis' (Baudrillard, 1981c: 83). Kellner leaps on this as a
possible unacknowledged, manipulative change of position between 1976
and 1981.

It is necessary to examine the nature of this (utterly fatuous) claim, briefly,
before looking at the arguments themselves. First of all what is the nature
of this translation? It is not exactly the text of the book, it has a paragraph
replaced (Baudrillard, 1981c: 75; 1976: 334), there is one paragraph omitted
(Baudrillard, 1981c: 69; 1976: 329), and there are some typographical errors in
the English and in the French, and it seems to have some minor amendments
and deletions (even in the first paragraph but notably in the penultimate
paragraph). One paragraph from very early in the book (Baudrillard, 1976:
7–8) is inserted in the article (1981c: 83) without an explanation – it obviously
serves the function of introducing the argument. In a note in the English (note
4, 1981c: 85), a phrase is omitted which must be an error since the point does
not make sense without it (see Baudrillard, 1976: 338) – but even in the French
there is a typographical error (an r for a t)). In the English version Leclaire
has become Lecalire, and even in the sentence previous to the case in dispute
(the missing r in 'evolution') there is a missing s. So it is difficult to identify
with complete assurance just what is a change and what is a mistake. Hence
what Kellner's remark ('an instruction to change the discourse by a writer who
had decided to polemicize against the concept of revolution and revolutionary
analysis?') tells us, is that Kellner's own ritualistic attitude to Baudrillard had
switched from admiration to one of contempt. It would be quite a simple matter

for Kellner to have made an enquiry of Baudillard directly rather than build a case on the weak foundations of a typographical error. (In fact only very occasionally has Baudrillard checked his English translations.)

Even so, there is an addition to the argument in the English version (Baudrillard, 1981c: 82; cf. 1976: 341): 'The hegemony of the (Freudian) primary process must be broken (through the attack of poetry first, but thereafter more generally, at every level)' a statement that does not seem consistent with a claim such as that made by Kellner that Baudrillard was now in the process of rejecting the revolutionary implications of the notion of the symbolic order, indeed, it is quite the reverse of this (thereby revealing not only a change of attitude on the part of Kellner, but more seriously a gross and fundamental misinterpretation).

26 Thus his attack, though similar to that of *Anti-Oedipus* (Deleuze and Guattari, 1977), is motivated by criticism of all productivist notions, psychoanalysis as the mirror of desire (conceived on the model of production).

27 In fact this comment, and Baudrillard's writing on symbolic exchange in general, seems strangely rooted in a rather limited notion of a single gesture and its return a counter-gesture which cancels the first. In order to understand the system of such cycles of obligation, Baudrillard in the end resorts to the explanation of the 'primitive', that is, fate. It is here perhaps we find the most serious theoretical weakness in Baudrillard's whole effort, and explains much about his preference for single seductions, for the strange, for the new, for excitement, for the superficial, for, it is here that his own image of the Other can dominate (narcissism), and when this image meets something else (the Other, the world, the mundane, reproduction) he abandons the scene for yet another strange encounter with himself. (cf. A. Carter, 1979: 145).

28 Again, it is a very positive notion of the symbolic order which is presented by Baudrillard, one which itself could be inverted so that the principal term would not be gift but debt.

29 Baudrillard was clearly hugely disappointed by Foucault's work. *Discipline and Punish*, published in 1975. For him it marked a decisive turning away from Foucault's earlier revolutionary works which were used by Baudrillard as exemplars for the analysis of basic genealogies.

30 This has been a repeated criticism of Foucault's work. See particularly Derrida (1978: Chapter 2) on Foucault.

31 If Baudrillard uses ideas from Foucault and Deleuze it is true that these borrowings do not necessarily convert into one another. The more basic issue is whether or not each sphere of analysis Baudrillard himself undertakes (sexuality, death, media, etc,) all reveal exactly the same forms. This, if true, would vitiate Baudrillard's conclusions (and turn his own researches into vast simulation exchanges, a definite possibility, which he must be aware of himself).

32 Paradoxically, Baudrillard seems to move to this position himself as if this confrontation had been a delayed effect. His later position suggested:

if hysteria was the pathology of the exacerbated staging of the subject – of the theatrical and operational conversion of the body – and if paranoia was the pathology of organisation – of a rigid and jealous world – then today we have entered into a new form of schizophrenia – with the emergence of an immanent promiscuity and the perpetual interconnection of all information and communication networks.

(Baudrillard, 1988c: 26–7)

33 This an extraordinary but basic proposition. Democratic structures, he argues, operate very much like the church, and the Marxist Party, in the sense that they

are capable of deferring effective challenge, and thus defusing it.

34   This was a direct provocation to Foucault, who in his introduction to Deleuze and Guattari praised the non-fascist life (Deleuze and Guattari, 1977: xii–xiv). As far as I know Foucault did not respond, though, he did encourage others to do so, without apparent success. There is a nuanced defence of Foucault in Racevskis (1980).

7 CULTURAL IMPLOSION

1   In fact it is surprising that Norris (1989) who has a background in philosophy and literature rather than social science does not grasp the sense of Baudrillard's poetic discipline, and completely underestimates the subtlety of his anti-rationalist epistemology.

2   A recent discussion by Baehr (1990) succinctly outlines the conceptions of the social mass in Max Weber's thought, which demonstrates the slippage towards a fear of the irrationality of the mass and its potential volatility. Baudrillard, on the contrary, regards the mass paradoxically as both non-existent, and as employing an intelligent silent strategy.

3   See Baudrillard, 1983a: 2. Interpreters immediately rewrite this word modernity, as postmodernity.

4   The change of position from 1972 is, then, dramatic, since Baudrillard then dramatically attacked 'magical thinking', ironically, the treatment of ideological content as 'a sort of mana that attaches itself to . . . representations that magically impregnate . . . mystified subjectivities' (Baudrillard, 1981b: 144).

5   Baudrillard even gives parallel formulations: the masses neutralise the radiations of 'State, History, Culture, Meaning' (Baudrillard, 1983a: 2). Carlo Levi invokes: 'that other world, hedged in by custom and sorrow, cut off from History, and the State . . . where the peasant lives out his motionless civilization on barren ground in remote poverty, and in the presence of death' (Levi, 1982: 11). No doubt Baudrillard would divest himself of the pathos, as condescension.

6   Note Baudrillard's own 'pataphysical' rejection of culture: 'I spit at culture' (1989e: 19).

7   Baudrillard is not quite straight here, for his position has long been in evidence. An excellent account of it can be found in Carroll (1974).

8   The evident theoretical problem is that the mass which is not 'subject or object' now has a practice. In other texts (Baudrillard, 1988b) he resolves this in the direction of the action of the object. But the argument does not essentially rest there, for what is aimed for is a 'subject-as-object'. It is also the topic of a long discussion in *Fatal Strategies* (1983b).

9   The genealogy then follows exactly the course of others derived from Foucault: particularly of madness, death, etc. Where eventually the object disappears into society or into every individual and society becomes haunted by this presence, as each individual is haunted by the madness and death it fears may be there in every other. The theme of the death of the social is now very widespread in social theory as can be seen in discussions quite remote from Baudrillard, for example, in Lash and Urry, who surprisingly opt for the following formulation: 'the disorganisation of capitalism and the theoretical dissolution of the social, appear – in some sort of elective affinity – to be proceeding hand in hand' (Lash and Urry, 1986: 109).

In 1987 Lash and Urry situated Baudrillard as the major theorist of this idea, and they comment 'we agree with much of (his) analysis, especially the idea of consumption dominated by sign-consumption, and a generalisation of consumption in the form of the spectacle (not meaning), and that boundaries between the cultural and everyday life have become obscured. But they draw the line at the idea of the masses waging a successful silent, fatal strategy (Lash and Urry, 1987: 290).

10   For a discussion of the the the pataphysics of Alfred Jarry, see La Belle (1980) who cites, in an awkward translation, Jarry's definition: 'Pataphysics is a science of imaginary solutions which brings into harmony symbolically the lineaments of the properties of objects depicted by their potentiality' (ibid:143).

11   Baudrillard wants the mass to be able to negate, to neuter, ne-uter the culture of simulations (it is not capitalism which is the problem here, since it is only one phenomenon of the simulation culture), by being able effectively to sustain an order of reversibility against it. If the symbolic order is conceived as essentially ambivalent, Baudrillard's basic project is to identify forms of resistance which can remain ambivalent in the face of simulations.

12   I owe this point of clarification to discussions with Dominique Lecourt. For recent discussion see the 'Introduction' to Rattansi (ed.) (1989), where some of the current complex problems are exposed. From Baudrillard's point of view it was Althusser himself who got trapped in an epistemological model that was soon superseded.

13   Baudrillard's contradictory doctrine of the social (which is dead, but still alive) is clearly evident in *Cool Memories*:

it only exists for its victims. Wretched in its essence, it only affects the wretched. It is itself a disinherited concept and it can only serve to render destitution complete. Nietzsche is right: the social is a concept, a value made by slaves for their own use, beneath the scornful gaze of their masters who have never believed in it.

(Baudrillard, 1990c: 113)

8 THE OBJECT'S SEDUCTION

1   Baudrillard's credibility to speak on seduction has been challenged by feminists. With violent provocations such as 'with certain women, we do not love them as we would wish or as they would wish. We prefer to violate them and lose them', his writings on seduction are probably the least successful of all his efforts to find a principle from the symbolic exchange cultures to attack simulation, precisely because his choice of and theory of seduction is derived from the eighteenth century.

2   Following on in the footsteps of Marcuse in *Eros and Civilization* (1955, Chapter 8).

3   One of Baudrillard's playful exaggerations, perhaps a pataphysical imaginary non-resolution.

4   See the interesting debate on this in Wollheim (1975).

5   There is a large debate around these themes especially the work of Lasch (1980, 1981) and Lipovetsky (1983), in a kind of inversion of the thesis of the 'authoritarian personality' in a previous period, as if each age mirrored its social mood in the individual.

6   One of the main contemporary sources for the thesis of the power of women in primitive societies and its decline with colonialism is Sanday (1981), but whose use of the terms power and dominance is the inverse of that of Baudrillard.

7   This argument seems confused: the primary simulation of seduction, or the primitive double, is quite different from the puzzle without a mystery, or a

simulation without a secret, characteristic of hyperrealism.

8 *Jouissance* is an important term, and very difficult to translate. For clarification see the note in Cixous and Clement (1987: 165–6) (cf. Gallop, 1988: Chapter 6.)

9 See the recent Baudrillard-inspired discussion in Barthel, (1988: 169–83).

10 It is interesting that Derrida has specifically referred to reading as seduction, and been roundly criticised by Bourdieu for so doing. Derrida reading Kant:

> Letting myself be led by pleasure, I recognise and, at the same time, I pervert an injunction. I follow it: the enigma of pleasure sets the whole book in motion. I seduce it: in treating the third Critique as a work of art or a beautiful object, which it was not meant simply to be. I act as if the book was indifferent to me (cited by Bourdieu).

> Bourdieu responded 'he never withdraws from the philosophical game. It is an exemplary form of denegation' (Bourdieu, 1984: 495).

11 See the use of this story by Derrida against feminism (in Jardine and Smith (eds) 1987: 189–203).

12 For an interesting recent discussion of Kierkegaard's aesthetic see Eagleton (1990). Adorno's essay (1989) discusses some of these issues in a completely different light. He sees the *Diary of the Seducer* as the key to Kierkegaard's work in the sense that it evokes in the description of formation of Cordelia's interiority: this

> constitutes the contours of his doctrine of existence itself. Inwardness and melancholy, the semblance of nature and the actuality of judgement: his ideal of concrete individual human life and his dream of a hell that the despairing inhabits for his lifetime.
>
> (Adorno, 1989: 42–6)

13 Note also that the butterflies make their appearance in Baudrillard's poems *L'Ange de Stuc*, 1978: Section 10.

9 FATAL OBJECTS

1 For discussion of this myth in the work of Baudrillard see Burchill in Frankovits (ed.) (1984). Tiresias is a figure who looms in the background of much of male French philosophy, menacingly (see Girard, in Macksey and Donato, 1972: 20; and Lacan, 1982: 90).

2 This analysis rejoins the aesthetic reduction:

> 'Follow me' she was told, I am more interesting to follow than the housewife on the corner. But that is a misconception and confuses primary interest with the aesthetic intensity of seduction. It does no good to discover, while shadowing someone, that he has, for instance, a double life, save to heighten curiosity – what's more important is that it is the shadowing in itself that is the other's double life. . . . It is this effect of doubling that makes the object surreal.
>
> (Baudrillard, 1988e: 78–9)

Sophie Calle herself writes:

> For months I followed strangers on the street . . . . I photographed them without their knowledge . . . . At the end of 1980, on the streets of Paris, I followed a man whom I lost sight of a few minutes later in the crowd. That very evening, quite by chance, he was introduced to me at an opening. During

the course of our conversation, he told me he was planning on an imminent trip to Venice.

(ibid, 1988e: 2)

She is a photographer and her photos are published in the same book with Baudrillard's text. The photos are unremarkable, even dull. But they are accompanied by a chronology and commentary by Sophie Calle herself, through which she recounts following the man and, unfortunately, being discovered. After this she is at a loss, dreaming, pathetically, of 'taking his room, sleeping in his bed' (Baudrillard, 1988e: 68). Baudrillard, then, has altogether missed the true irony of the story. This is a mirror image in fact of the *Diary of the Seducer*, a diary of a fiasco of seduction. Its real misery is not identified by Baudrillard, the ironic parody of the man who shadows women, one of the common forms of contemporary persecution. (Baudrillard says 'there is something murderous in the situation for the one who is followed. He can feel resentful and victimised'). Sophie Calle, as 'S' appears in *Cool Memories* as Baudrillard's partner, as one who is obsessed by objects and the object world: 'In the wretchedness of his New Delhi room, weeping hot tears (no doubt more for the personal offence he had suffered than for the lost object), 'S' still finds the strength to photograph his telephone' (Baudrillard, 1990c: 199).

3 Baudrillard hints, in the 1983e version (1988e: 83) that there is always the 'possibility of reversal'. Yet when 'S' is discovered, when she is 'unmasked' he says 'the game stops there' as if reversion was immediately impossible (1988e: 84).

4 These events, happenings, dreams, resolutions which enter Baudrillard's writings are all remarkably banal. The resolution which Baudrillard notes in his fatal unravelling of these two events 10 years apart was that these two people had the same name. He looks no further, and is content to have found a conjunction of signs.

5 There is here a theoretical key to Baudrillard's new way of writing: it is itself a transfinite form: an ecstatic form. Kroker writes of 'panic' reading in an attempt to catch it. But this misses its target and starts a spiral of its own which mirrors a spiral of delirium, the spiral of the worst, and becomes a parody of Baudrillard's own spiral.

6 Here Baudrillard rejoins the problem of the double, important in his early works, and the question of the shadow which dominates his entire work (the classic commentary on the literary background to this is Tymms (1949), a recent reflection in Midgely (1984).

7 Baudrillard could write at the beginning of 1991 'the gulf war will not happen' (Baudrillard, 1991)

10 AMERICA, THE DESERT AND THE FOURTH WORLD

1 But see the interesting and informative discussion in Zurbrugg who concludes that however much Baudrillard tries, his account compulsively reduces the present to 'paradigms of the European past . . . the terms of his imagination are a way of synchronisation with their subject . . . the camera of John Ford . . . and . . . Baudelaire and Jarry' (Zurbrugg, 1988: 55). Richard Poirier (1989) writes, *America* is 'replete with absurdities. The result is a more than average demand on the reader's leniency, as if surely the author must mean more than he is saying . . . Baudrillard pushes, alas, pushes his luck . . . all in the service of self-referentiality . . . as he says of video-stereo culture 'a surface intensity and deeper meaninglessness'.

Paul Buhl, incredibly, sees Baudrillard's America as an unironic celebration of paradise, his position says Buhl, now:

> substitutes for the messianic conclusion, a permanent continuation of the present, and changed the valence of our commodity fetishism. The realm of cruel deception has become the realm of enchantment . . . the socially disenchanted . . . now become part of an almost perfect spectacle . . . America = excitement.
>
> (Buhl, 1990: 168)

2   Others have followed the same line of thought. Zurbrugg: 'it is difficult to know what to make of such studiedly sexist, and sadistic, speculation . . . surrealist and Sadian values intermingle' (1988: 54). Yet this would conflict with all of Baudrillard's theoretical orientations: it is more likely perhaps a Baudrillard strategy, misconceived and spiralling downwards.

3   This is only one moment of a reading: that which follows an (apparently) regressive epistemology into the fatal and the *pars totalis*. It follows the ascent to poetic ecstasy. Yet this becomes perverse, in Baudrillard's own thought: a pure collection.

4   This is the site of the structuralist moment of *America*: it forces Baudrillard towards a new conception of the social totality, and it marks the second stage of reading, and of a shift in the problematic: for readings are here seduced by their problematic.

5   The violent return of the social totality. This major section on social and political America is so strategically placed that it forces a displacement in the meaning of terms (desert, culture, etc.).

6   Meaghan Morris has noted this in her own analysis of *Fatal Strategies* (Baudrillard, 1983b), but it applies equally to *America*: 'There are four phases . . . the laying of a decoy (here the feint of the poetic epistemology (author); the bait (degraded object); the purging of the scene (disappearance); the annunciation of a new scene (appearance); and the raising of the power (the dire object). (Morris, 1988a: 192).

7   The idea and model for this could well be Marin's analysis of Disneyland, a 'degenerate utopia' (1976: 60).

11 THE DOUBLE SPIRAL

1   This is a new growing thematic in contemporary sociology and social theory. For a key consideration of its significance see Lockwood: 'Fatalism: Durkheim's hidden theory of order' in Giddens and Mackenzie (1982: 101–18), and Stauth and Turner (1988). With these sociologists there is a groping towards a vision of the significance of a fatal social order. Baudrillard has already elaborated it and provided it with a stunning mix of primitive and ultra-modern finery.

2   See Hobsbawm's discussion in 'Mass producing Traditions: Europe, 1870–1914' in Hobsbawm and Ranger (eds) (1984: 263–307).

3   Baudrillard stresses that his discussion is never psychological, subjective or emotional. If there is a fundamental melancholy it is in the nature of objects in today's culture not in a personal orientation. Here he is more Durkheimian than Durkheim.

Bibliography

Note: I have kept these references strictly to the minimum. A more ample bibliography of Baudrillard's publications can be found in D. Kellner's *Jean Baudrillard* (1989a). But the bibliography here lists some further publications, and publications overlooked by Kellner. I have not sought to indicate all the existing translations where there is duplication, nor indeed all the French publications where there is duplication. The bibliography here is simply the working selection that I have used in the writing of this book.

Abercrombie, N., Hill S. and Turner, B.S. (1986) *Sovereign Individuals of Capitalism*, London: Allen & Unwin.
Adorno, T.W. (1967) *Prisms*, London: Spearman.
—— (1989) *Kierkegaard, Construction of the Aesthetic*, Minneapolis: University of Minnesota Press.
Allison, D. (ed.) (1985) *The New Nietzsche*, London: MIT.
Althusser, L. (1969) *For Marx*, London: Allen Lane.
—— (1971) *Lenin and Philosophy and Other Essays*, London: NLB.
—— (1972) 'Reply to John Lewis', *Marxism Today* October: 310–18; November: 343–9.
—— (1976) *Essays in Self Criticism*, London: NLB.
—— (1978) 'The crisis of Marxism', *Marxism Today* July: 215–20, 227.
—— (1982) *Montesquieu, Rousseau, History*, London: Verso.
—— (1990) *Philosophy and the Spontaneous Philosophy of the Scientists, and Other Essays*, London: Verso.
Althusser, L. and Balibar, E. (1970) *Reading Capital*, London: NLB.
Anderson, P. (1983) *In the Tracks of Historical Materialism*, London: Verso.
Angus, I. and Jally, S. (1989) *Cultural Politics in Contemporary America*, London: Routledge.
Angus, I. and Sut, J. (eds) (1989) *Cultural Politics in Contemporary America*, London: Routledge.
Aries, P. *Western Attitudes towards Death*, London: Boyars.
Baehr, P. (1990) 'The "Masses" in Weber's political sociology', *Economy and Society* 19 (2): 242–65.
Balibar, E. (1978) 'Irrationalism and Marxism', *New Left Review* 107: 3–20.
—— (1985) 'Marx, the joker in the pack', *Economy and Society* 14 (1): 1–27.
Ballard, J.G. (1985) *Crash*, London: Faber.
Barthel, D (1988) *Putting on Appearances*, Philadelphia: Temple University Press.
Barthes, R. (1964) 'Elements de semiologie', *Communications* 4: 91–135.
—— (1967a) *Elements of Semiology*, London: Cape.

—— (1967b) *Writing Degree Zero*, London: Cape.
—— (1972) *Mythologies*, Frogmore: Granada.
—— (1984) *Camera Lucida*, London: Fontana.
—— (1985) *The Fashion System*, London: Cape.
—— (1988) *The Semiotic Challenge*, New York: Hill & Wang.
Bataille, G. (1985) *Visions of Excess*, Manchester: Manchester University Press.
—— (1988) *The Accursed Share*, New York: Zone.
—— (1989) *The Tears of Eros*, San Francisco: City Lights.
Baudrillard, J. (1962–3a) 'Uwe Johnson: La Frontiere', *Les Temps Modernes*: 1094–1107.
—— (1962–3b) 'Les Romans d'Italo Calvino', *Les Temps Modernes*: 1728–34.
—— (1962–3c) 'La Proie des Flammes', *Les Temps Modernes*: 1928–37.
—— (1967) 'Compte rendu de Marshall McLuhan: Understanding Media', *L'homme et la Societé* (5): 227–30.
—— (1968) *Le Système des Objets*, Paris: Denoel.
—— (1969a) 'Le ludique et le policier', *Utopie* (2–3): 3–15.
—— (1969b) 'La practique sociale de la technique', *Utopie* (2–3): 147–55.
—— (1970) *La Societé de Consommation*, Paris: Gallimard.
—— (1972) *Pour une Critique de L'Economie du Signe*, Paris: Gallimard. (In translation 1981.)
—— (1973) *Le Mirroir de la Production*, Tournail: Casterman. (In translation 1975.)
—— (1975a) *The Mirror of Production*, St Louis: Telos.
—— (1975b) 'Langages de Masse', *Encylopaedia Universalis*, vol. 17, Paris: Organum, 394–7.
—— (1976) *L'Echange Symbolique et la Mort*, Paris: Gallimard.
—— (1977a) *L'Effet Beaubourg: Implosion et Dissuasion*, Paris: Galilee. (In translation 1982.)
—— (1977b) *Oublier Foucault*, Paris: Galilee. (In translation 1987.)
—— (1978a) *L'Ange de Stuc*, Paris: Galilee.
—— (1978b) *A L'Ombre des Majorities silencieuses, ou la fin du Social*, Fontenay-sous-Bois: Cahiers d'Utopie. (In translation 1983.)
—— (1979) *De La Séduction*, Paris: Denoel-Gonthier. (In translation 1990a.)
—— (1981a) *Simulacres et Simulation*, Paris: Galilee.
—— (1981b) *For a Critique of the Political Economy of the Sign*, St Louis: Telos. (Translation of 1972.)
—— (1981c) 'Beyond the unconscious: the symbolic', *Discouse* 3: 60–87. (Part translation of 1976.)
—— (1981d) 'Fatality or reversible imminence: beyond the uncertainty principle', *Social Research* 49 (2): 272–93. (Part translation of 1983b.)
—— (1982) 'The Beaubourg effect: implosion and deterrence', *October* 20 (Spring): 3–13. (Translation of 1977a.)
—— (1983a) *In the Shadow of the Silent Majorities*, New York: Semiotext(e). (Translation of 1978b.)
—— (1983b) *Les Strategies Fatales*, Paris: Grasset.
—— (1983c) 'What are you doing after the Orgy?' *Artforum* October: 42–6.
—— (1983d) 'Les seductions de Baudrillard (interview)', *Magazine Litteraire* 193: 80–5, March.
—— (1983e) *Please Follow Me* (with Sophie Calle, *Suite Venitienne*), Paris: Editions de L'Etoile.
—— (1983f) *Simulations*, New York: Semiotexte(e). (Part translation of 1981a.)
—— (1984) 'Interview: Game with Vestiges', *On the Beach* 5 (Winter): 19–25.
—— (1984–5) 'Intellectuals, commitment, and political power', *Thesis Eleven*: 10–11, 166–73.

—— (1985a) *La Gauche Divine*, Paris: Grasset.
—— (1985b) 'The masses: the implosion of the social in the media', *New Literary History* 16 (3): 577–89.
—— (1986) *Amerique*, Paris: Grasset. (In translation 1988a.)
—— (1987a) *L'Autre par lui-meme*, Paris: Galilee. (In translation 1988c.)
—— (1987b) *Cool Memories*, Paris: Galilee.
—— (1987c) *Forget Foucault*. New York: Semiotext(e). (Translation of 1977b.)
—— (1987d) *The Evil Demon of Images*, Annandale: Power Institute.
—— (1987e) 'When Bataille attacked the metaphysical principle of economy', *Canadian Journal of Political and Social Theory* 11 (3): 57–62.
—— (1987f) 'Modernity', *Canadian Journal of Political and Social Theory* 11 (3): 63–73.
—— (1987g) 'The year 2000 has already happened', in A. and M. Kroker (eds) *Body Invaders*, London: Macmillan, pp. 35–44.
—— (1988a) *America*, London: Verso. (Translation of 1986.)
—— (1988b) *Jean Baudrillard, Selected Writings*, Cambridge: Polity.
—— (1988c) *The Ecstasy of Communication*, New York: Semiotext(e). (Translation of 1987a.)
—— (1988d) 'Interview: Jean Baudrillard', *Block* 14: 8–10.
—— (1988e) *Please Follow Me* (with Sophie Calle, *Suite Venitienne*), Seattle: Bay Press. (Translation of 1983e.)
—— (1988f) *Xerox to Infinity*, London: Touchepas.
—— (1989a) 'The anorexic ruins', in D. Kamper and C. Wulf (eds) *Looking Back at the End of the World*, New York: Semiotext(e).
—— (1989b) 'The end of production', *Polygraph* 2/3: 5–29. (Part translation of 1976.)
—— (1989c) 'Politics of seduction. Interview with Baudrillard', *Marxism Today* January: 54–5.
—— (1989d) 'Panic Crash!' in A. Kroker, M. Kroker and D. Cook (eds) *Panic Encyclopaedia*, London: Macmillan, pp. 64–7.
—— (1989e) 'An Interview with Jean Baudrillard (Judith Williamson)', *Block* 15: 16–19.
—— (1990a) *Seduction*, London: Macmillan. (Translation of 1979.)
—— (1990b) *La Transparence du Mal*. Essai sur les Phenomenes Extremes; Paris: Galilee.
—— (1990c) *Cool Memories*, London: Verso. (Translation of 1987b.)
—— (1990d) *Cool Memories II*, Paris: Galilee.
—— (1991) 'The Reality Gulf', in *The Guardian*, January 11:25.
Bauman, Z (1986) 'The second disenchantment, review', *Theory, Culture and Society* 5 (4): 738–43.
—— (1987) *Legislators and Interpreters. On Modernity. Post-modernity and Intellectuals*, Cambridge: Polity Press.
—— (1990a) 'From pillars to post', *Marxism Today* February: 20–5.
—— (1990b) 'Dawn of the dead', *Emergency* 5: 48–57.
Benhabib, S. (1984) 'The epistemologies of postmodernism', *New German Critique* 33: 103–26.
Benison, J. (1984) 'Jean Baudrillard on the current state of SF', *Foundation* 32: 25–42.
Benjamin, A. (ed.) (1989) *The Problems of Modernity*, London: Routledge.
Benjamin, W. (1968) *Illuminations*, London: Cape.
—— (1978) 'Surrealism: the last snapshot of the European intelligentsia', *New Left Review* 108: 47–56.
—— (1979) *One Way Street*, London: Verso.
Benton, T. (1984) 'The rise and fall of structural Marxism', London: Macmillan.

Best, S. and Kellner, D. (in press) *Postmodern Theory, Theory and Politics*, London: Macmillan.

Bettelheim, B. (1954) *Symbolic Wounds*, London: Thames & Hudson.

Blanchot, M. (1980) *L'Ecriture du Desastre*, Paris: Gallimard.

—— (1982) *The Space of Literature*, London: University of Nebraska Press.

Blau, J.R. (1989) *The Shape of Culture*. Cambridge: Cambridge University Press.

Bogard, W. (1987) 'Sociology in the absence of the social: the significance of Baudrillard for contemporary thought', *Philosophy and Social Criticism* 13 (3): 227–42.

Borges, J. (1970) *Labyrinths*, Harmondsworth: Penguin.

Bourdieu, P. (1984) *Distinction*, London: Routledge.

Bowie, M. (1978) *Malarme and the Art of Being Difficult*, Cambridge: Cambridge University Press.

Brenner, R. (with Brenner, G.) (1990) *Gambling and Speculation*, Cambridge: Cambridge University Press.

Buhl, P. (1990) 'America: Post-modernity?' *New Left Review* 180: 163–75.

Caillois, R. (1959) *Man and the Sacred*, Glencoe: Free Press.

—— (1962) *Man, Play and Games*, London: Thames & Hudson.

—— (1975) 'The college de sociologie', *Substance* (11–12): 61–4.

Callinicos, A. (1989) *Against Postmodernism, a Marxist Critique*, Cambridge: Polity Press.

Calvino, I. (1959) *The Baron in the Trees*, New York: Harcourt.

—— (1962) *The Nonexistent Knight and the Cloven Viscount*, New York: Harcourt.

Canguilhem, G. (1978) *On the Normal and the Pathological*, London: Reidel.

Cannetti, E. (1978) *The Human Province*, New York: Seabury.

Carrier, D. (1988) 'Baudrillard as philosopher or, the end of abstract painting', *Arts Magazine* 63 (1): 52–60.

Carroll, J. (1974) *Breakout from the Crystal Palace*, London: Routledge & Kegan Paul.

Carter, A. (1979) *The Sadeian Woman*, London: Virago.

Caruso, P. (1969) *Conversazioni con Lévi-Strauss, Foucault, Lacan*, Milan: Mursia.

Certeau, M. de (1984) *The Practice of Everyday Life*, London: University of California Press.

Chamisso, A. von (1979) *Peter Schmihls Wundersame Geschichte*, Berlin: Verlag der Nation.

Chang, B, (1986) 'Mass, media, mass media-tion: Baudrillard's implosive critique of modern mass-mediated culture', *Current Perspectives in Social Theory* 17: 157–81.

Chapman, R. and Rutherford, J. (eds) (1988) *Male Order: Unwrapping Masculinity*, Lawrence & Wishart.

Cheal, D. (1988) 'The postmodern origin of ritual', *Journal for the Theory of Social Behaviour* 18, (37): 269–90.

Chen, K.H. (1987) 'The masses and the media: Baudillard's implosive post-modernism', *Theory, Culture and Society* 4 (1): 71–88.

Cixous, H. and Clement, C. (1987) *The Newly Born Woman*, Manchester: Manchester University Press.

Clifford, J. (1988) *The Predicament of Culture*, London: Harvard University Press.

Cohen, J. (1969) 'The philosophy of Marcuse', *New Left Review*, 57: 35–52.

Connolly, W.E. (1988) *Political Theory and Modernity*, Oxford: Blackwell.

Connor, S. (1989) *Postmodernist Culture*, Oxford: Blackwell.

Cooke, P. (1988) 'Modernity, postmodernity and the city', *Theory, Culture and Society* 5:475–92.

Culler, J. (1975) *Structuralist Poetics*, London: Routledge & Kegan Paul.

D'Amico, R. (1978) 'Desire and the commodity form', *Telos* 35: 88–122.

—— (1981) *Marx and the Philosophy of Culture*, Gainsville: University of Florida Press.

Davis, M. (1985) 'Urban renaissance and the spirit of postmodernism', *New Left Review* 151: 106–13.

Debord, G. (1987) *Society of the Spectacle*, Rebell Press, Aim Publications.

Deleuze, G. (1983) *Nietzsche and Philosophy*, London: Athlone.

Deleuze, G. and Guattari, F. (1977) *Anti-Oedipus*, New York: Viking.

Derrida, J. (1978) *Writing and Difference*, London: Routledge & Kegan Paul.

—— (1981) *Positions*, London: Athlone.

—— (1987) *The Postcard*, London: University of Chicago Press.

Descombes, V. (1980) *Modern French Philosophy*, Cambridge: Cambridge University Press.

Dews, P. (1987) *Logics of Disintegration*, London: Verso.

Dillon, W. (1968) *Gifts and Nations*, Mouton: The Hague.

Donzelot, J. (1988) 'The promotion of the social', *Economy and Society* 17, (3) 395–427.

Dostoyevsky, F. (1972) *Notes from the Underground*, Harmondsworth: Penguin.

Durkheim, E. (1957) *Professional Ethics and Civic Morals*, London: Routledge & Kegan Paul.

—— (1961) *The Elementary Forms of the Religious Life*, New York: Collier.

—— (1963) *Incest, The Nature and Origin of the Taboo*, New York: Lyle Stuart.

—— (1964) *The Division of Labour in Society*, London: Collier-Macmillan.

—— (1972) *Suicide*, London: Routledge & Kegan Paul.

Eagelton, T. (1990) *The Ideology of the Aesthetic*, Oxford: Blackwell.

Eco, U. (1986) *Travels in Hyperreality*, London: Pan.

Elliot, G. (1987) *Althusser: The Detour of Theory*, London: Verso.

Falk, P. (1988) 'The past to come', *Economy and Society* 17 (3): 374–94.

Fekete, J. (ed.) (1984) *The Structural Allegory*, Minneapolis: University of Minneapolis Press.

—— (ed.) (1988) *Life After Postmodernism*, London: Macmillan.

Ferry, L. and Renaut A. (1985) *La Pensee 68*, Paris: Gallimard.

Forrester, J. (1980) 'Michel Foucault and the history of psychoanalysis', *History of Science* 18.

Foster, H. (1985) *Recordings: Art Spectacle, Cultural Politics*, Seattle: Bay Press.

—— (ed.) (1986) *Postmodern Culture*, London: Pluto.

Foucault, M. (1977) *Language, Counter-memory, Practice*, Ithaca: Cornell University Press.

—— (1983) 'Structuralism and post-structuralism: an interview with M. Foucault', *Telos* 55: 195–211, Spring

—— (1989) *Foucault Live (interviews 1966–84)*, New York: Semiotext(e).

Frankovits, A. (ed.) (1984) *Seduced and Abandoned*, Glebe, Australia: Stonemoss Publishers.

Gane, M. (1983a) 'Durkheim: the sacred language', *Economy and Society* 12 (1): 1–47.

Gallop, J. (1988) *Thinking Through the Body*, New York: Columbia University Press.

—— (1983b) 'Durkheim: woman as outsider', *Economy and Society* 12: 227–70.

—— (1983c) 'On the ISAs Episode', *Economy and Society* 12: 431–67.

—— (1984) 'Institutional socialism and the sociological critique of communism (introduction to Durkheim and Mauss)', *Economy and Society* 113 (3): 304–30.

—— (ed.) (1986) *Towards a Critique of Foucault*, London: Routledge.

—— (1988) *On Durkheim's Rules of Sociological Method*, London: Routledge.

—— (ed.) (1989) *Ideological Representation and Power in Social Relations: Literary and Social Theory*, London: Routledge.

—— (1990) 'Ironies of postmodernism: fate of Baudillard's fatalism', *Economy and Society* 19: 314–31.

Giddens, A. and Mackenzie, G. (eds) (1982) *Social Class and the Division of Labour*, Cambridge: Cambridge University Press.

Gillespie, M. and Strong, T. (eds) (1988) *Nietzsche's New Faces*, London: University of Chicago Press.

Giradin, J.–C. (1974) 'Towards a politics of signs: reading Baudrillard', *Telos* 20: 127–37.

Girard, R. (1977) *Violence and the Sacred*, London: Johns Hopkins.

Glucksmann, A. (1972) 'A ventriloquist structuralism', *New Left Review* 72: 68–92.

Goffman, E. (1981) *Forms of Talk*, Oxford: Blackwell.

Gorz. A. (1966) 'Sartre and Marx' *New Left Review* 57: 29–52.

—— (1990) 'The ultimate ideology of work', *Emergency*: 513–21.

Gouldner, A.W. (1979) *The Future of Intellectuals*, London: Macmillan.

—— (1980) *The Two Marxisms*, London: Macmillan.

Griffiths, A.P. (ed.) (1988) *Contemporary French Philosophy*, Cambridge: Cambridge University Press.

Guattari, F. (1984) *Molecular Revolution*, Harmondsworth: Penguin.

Gutting, G. (1989) *Michel Foucault's Archaeology of Scientific Reason*, Cambridge: Cambridge University Press.

Habermas, J. (1981) 'Modernity versus post modernity', *New German Critique* 22: 3–14.

Harvey, D. (1982) *The Limits to Capital*, Oxford: Blackwell.

—— (1985) *Consciousness and the Urban Experience*, Oxford: Blackwell.

—— (1989) *The Condition of Postmodernity*, Oxford: Blackwell.

Hayward, P. (1984) 'Implosive critiques', *Screen* 25: 128–33.

Hebdige, D. (1988) *Hiding in the Light: On Images and Things*, London: Routledge.

Heimonet, J.M. (1984) 'Le College de Sociologie, un gigantesque malentendu', *Esprit* (89): 39–58.

Hirst, P.Q. (1985) *Marxism and Historical Writing*, London: Routledge & Kegan Paul.

Hobsbawn, E. and Ranger, T. (eds) (1984) *The Invention of Tradition*, Cambridge: Cambridge University Press.

Hollier, D. (ed.) (1988) *The College of Sociology 1937–39*, Minneapolis, Minn.: University of Minnesota Press.

Hubert, H. and Mauss, M. (1964) *Sacrifice: Its Nature and Function*, London: Cohen & West.

Humphreys, S. and King, H. (eds) *Morality and Immortality*, London: Academic Press.

Huntington, R. and Metcalf, P. (1979) *Celebrations of Death*, Cambridge: Cambridge University Press.

Hutchinson, L. (1989) *The Politics of Postmodernism*, London: Routledge.

Huyssen, A. (1986) *After the Great Divide: Modernism, Mass Culture and Postmodernism*, London: Macmillan.

Irigaray, L. (1985) *This Sex which is Not One*, Ithaca: Cornell.

Jaccoby, R. (1987) *The Last Intellectuals*, New York: Basic Books.

Jameson, F. (1984a) 'Postmodernism, or the cultural logic of late capitalism', *New Left Review* 146: 53–93.

—— (1984b) 'The politics of theory: ideological positions in the postmodern debate', *New German Critique* 33: 53–65.

Jardine, A. (1985) *Gynesis, Configurations of Woman and Modernity*, Ithaca: Cornell University Press.

Jencks, C. (1980) *Late-Modern Architecture*; New York: Rizzoli.

Johnson, U. (1963) *Speculations about Jakob*, New York: Harcourt, Brace Jovanovitch.

Kafka, F. (1967) *America*, Harmondsworth: Penguin.

—— (1979) *Description of a Struggle*, Harmondsworth: Penguin.

—— (1983) *Stories, 1904–24*, London: MacDonald.

Kaplan, A. and Ross, K. (eds) (1987) *Everyday Life* (Yale French Studies, 73), New Haven: Yale University Press.

Kave, B. (1989) *A Random Walk Through Fractal Dimensions*, Weinheim: VCH.

Kellner, D. (1984) *Herbert Marcuse and the Crisis of Marxism*, London: Macmillan.

—— (1987) 'Baudrillard, semiurgy and death', *Theory, Culture and Society* 4: 125–46.

—— (1988) 'Postmodernism as social theory', *Theory, Culture and Society* 5: 239–69.

—— (1989a) *Jean Baudrillard. From Marxism to Postmodernism and Beyond*, Cambridge: Polity Press.

—— (1989b) *Critical Theory, Marxism and Modernity*, Cambridge: Polity Press.

—— (ed.) (1989c) *Postmodernism, Jameson, Critique*, Washington: Maisonneuve Press.

Kelly, M. (1982) *Modern French Marxism*, Oxford: Blackwell.

Kierkegaard, S. (1971) *Either/Or*, Vol. 1, New Jersey: Princeton University Press.

Kristeva. J. (1980) *Desire in Language*, Oxford: Blackwell.

—— (1986) *The Kristeva Reader* (T. Moi (ed.)), Oxford: Blackwell.

Kroker, A. (1985) 'Baudrillard's Marx', *Theory, Culture and Society* 5 (2–3).

Kroker, A. and Cook, D. (eds) (1988) *The Postmodern Scene: Excremental Culture and Hyper-aesthetics*, London: Macmillan

Kroker, A. and Kroker, M. (eds) (1988) *Body Ivaders, Sexuality and the Postmodern Condition*. London: Macmillan.

Kroker, A., Kroker, M. and Cook, D. (1989) *Panic Encyclopaedia*, London: Macmillan.

La Belle, M. (1980) *Alfred Jarry, Nihilism and the Theatre of the Absurd*, New York: New York University Press.

Lacan, J. (1968) *The Language of the Self*, New York: Dell.

—— *Écrits: A Selection*, London: Tavistock.

—— (1982) *Feminine Sexuality*, London: Macmillan.

Laclau, E. and Mouffe, C. (1985) *Hegemony and Socialist Strategy*, London: Verso.

Lasch, C. (1980) *The Culture of Narcissism*, London: Sphere.

—— (1981) 'The Freudian left and the cultural revolution', *New Left Review* 129: 23–34.

Lash, S. and Urry, J. (1986) 'The dissolution of the social?', in M. Wardell and S. Turner (eds) *Sociological Theory in Transition*, London: Allen & Unwin.

—— (1987) *The End of Organised Capitalism*, Cambridge: Polity Press.

Lecourt, D. (1977) *Proletarian Science? The Case of Lysenko*, London: NLB.

Leenhardt, J. (1986) *The Role of the Intellectual in France*, in ICA Documents 5: 63–5, London: ICA.

Lefebvre, H. (1971) *Everyday Life in the Modern World*, London: Allen Lane.

Levi, C. (1982) *Christ Stopped at Eboli*, Harmondsworth: Penguin.

Levin, C. (1984) 'Baudrillard. Critical Theory and Psychoanalysis', *Canadian Journal of Political and Social Theory*, 8 (1–27): 35–52.

Lévi-Strauss, C. (1969) *Conversations with Claude Lévi-Strauss*, London: Cape.

—— (1972) *The Savage Mind*, London: Weidenfeld & Nicolson.

Lipovetsky, G. (1975) 'Fragments Energetiques apropos du Capitalisme', *Critique*: 379–94.

—— (1983) *L'Ere du Vide*, Paris: Gallimard.

Lukacs, G. (1978) 'On Walter Benjamin', *New Left Review* (110): 83–8.
Lukes, S. (1973) *Emile Durkheim*, Harmondsworth: Penguin.
Lunn, E. (1990) 'Beyond "mass culture" ', *Theory and Society* 19: 63–86.
Lyotard, J.-F. (1984) *The Postmodern Condition: A Report on Knowledge*, Manchester: Manchester University Press.
Macchiocchi, A. (1973) *Letters From Inside the Italian Communist Party to Louis Althusser*, London: NLB.
Macherey, P. (1977) 'An interview with P. Macherey', *Red Letters* 5: 3–9.
MacIntyre, A. (1970) *Marcuse*, London: Fontana.
Macksey, R. and Donato, E. (eds) (1972) *The Structuralist Controversy*, Baltimore: Johns Hopkins.
Major-Poetzl, P. (1983) *Michel Foucault's Archaeology of Western Culture*, Brighton: Harvester Press.
Marcuse, H. (1955) *Eros and Civilization*, New York: Beacon.
—— (1968) *One Dimensional Man*, London: Sphere.
Marin, L. (1976) 'Disneyland: a degenerate utopia', *Glyph* 1 (1): 50–66.
Marx, K. (1963) *Capital*, Vol. 1, Moscow: Progress.
—— *Capital*, Vol. 3, Moscow: Progress.
—— (1968) 'Critique of the Gotha Programme', *Selected Works*, London: Lawrence & Wishart.
—— (1971) *A Contribution to the Critique of Political Economy*, London: Lawrence & Wishart.
—— (1973) *Grundrisse*, Harmondsworth: Penguin.
Mauss, M. (1966) *The Gift*, London: Cohen & West.
—— (1984) 'A sociological assessment of Bolshevism', *Economy and Society* 13 (3): 331–74.
Mauss, M. (and Hubert, H. – this author's name is missing from the English edition) (1972) *A General Theory of Magic*, London: Routledge & Kegan Paul.
McLuhan, M. (1967) *Understanding Media*, London: Sphere.
McRobbie, A. (1986) 'Postmodernism and popular culture', *Journal of Communication Inquiry* 10 (2): 108–16.
Merquior, J. (1986a) *From Prague to Paris*, London: Verso.
—— (1986b) 'Spider and bee: towards a critique of the postmodern ideology', *Postmodernism ICA Documents* 4: 16–18, London: ICA.
Midgley, M. (1984) *Wickedness*, London: Routledge.
Miller, D. (1987) *Material Culture and Mass Consumption*, Oxford: Blackwell.
Miller, J. (1971) *McLuhan*, London: Fontana.
—— (1981) *French Structuralism: A Multi-disciplinary Approach*, New York: Garland.
Morris, M. (1988a) *The Pirate's Fiancée*, London: Verso.
—— (1988b) 'Banality in Cultural Studies', *Block* 14: 15–26.
Murray, D. (ed.) (1989) *Literary Theory and Poetry*, London: Batsford.
Nairn, T. (1988) *The Enchanted Glass*, London: Radius.
Nelson, C. and Grossberg, L. (eds) (1988) *Marxism and the Interpretation of Culture*, London: Macmillan.
Newman, M. (1986) 'Revising modernism, representing postmodernism: critical discourses of the visual arts', *Postmodernism* ICA Documents 4: 32–51.
Niethammer, L. (1989) *Posthistoire. Ist die Geschichte zu End?* Hamburg: Rowohlt.
Nietzsche, F. (1968) *Twilight of the Idols. The Anti-Christ*, Harmondsworth; Penguin.
—— (1969) *On the Genealogy of Morals. Ecce Homo*, New York: Vintage.
Norris, C. (1989) 'Lost in the funhouse: Baudrillard and the politics of postmodernism', *Textual Practice* 3(3): 360–87.
O'Hara, D. (ed.) (1985) *Why Nietzsche Now?* Bloomington: Indiana University Press.

Parsons, T. (1978) *Action Theory and the Human Condition*, Glencoe: Free Press.
Poirier, R. (1989) 'America Deserta', *London Review of Books* 11(47): 3–4.
Popper, K. (1972) *Conjectures and Refutations*, 2nd edn, London: Routledge & Kegan Paul.
Poster, M. (1975) *Existential Marxism in Postwar France: From Sartre to Althusser*, Princeton: Princeton University Press.
—— (1981) 'Technology and culture in Habermas and Baudrillard', *Contemporary Literature* 22(4): 456–76.
—— (1989) *Critical Theory and Poststructuralism*, London: Cornell University Press.
Poulantzas, N. (1967) 'Marxist political theory in Great Britain', *New Left Review* 43: 57–74.
Pribram, E. (cd.) (1988) *Female Spectators*, London: Verso.
Punter, D. (ed.) (1986) *Introduction to Contemporary Cultural Studies*, London: Longman.
Racevskis, K. (1979) 'The theoretical violence of a catastrophical strategy', *Diacritics*, pp. 33–42.
—— (1980) 'The discourse of Michel Foucault', *Humanities and Society* 3(1): 41–53.
Rattansi, A. (ed.) (1989) *Ideology, Method and Marx*, London: Routledge.
Richman, M. (1982) *Reading Georges Bataille*, Baltimore: Johns Hopkins.
Riviere, J. (1986) 'Womanliness as masquerade', in V. Burgin, J. Donald and C. Kaplan, (eds) *Formations of Fantasy*, London: Methuen.
Rojek, C. (1990) 'Baudrillard and leisure', *Leisure Studies* 9: 7–20.
Rundell, J. (1987) *Origins of Modernity*, Cambridge: Polity Press.
Sahlins, M. (1974) *Stone Age Economics*, London: Tavistock.
Sanday, P.R. (1981) *Female Power and Male Dominance*, Cambridge: Cambridge University Press.
Sartre, J.-P. (1963) *The Problem of Method*, London: Methuen.
Schor, N. (1987) *Reading in Detail*, London: Methuen.
Serres, M. (1990) 'Entretien: M. Serres, La Traversee des Savoirs', *Magazine Litteraire* 276: 98–103.
Soper, K. (1981) *On Human Needs*, Brighton: Harvester.
Sprinker, M. (1987) *Imaginary Relations*, London: Verso.
Starobinski, J. (1971) *Les Mots sous Les Mots. Les Anagrammes de Ferdinand de Saussure*, Paris: Gallimard.
Stauth, G. and Turner, B.S. (1988) *Nietzsche's Dance: Resentment, Reciprocity and Resistance in Social Life*, Oxford: Blackwell.
Stearn, G. (ed.) (1968) *McLuhan Hot and Cool*, Harmondsworth: Penguin.
Steiner, G. (1969) *Language and Silence*, Harmondsworth: Penguin.
Stewart, I. (1990) *Does God Play Dice*, Harmondsworth: Penguin.
Styron, W. (1970) *Set This House on Fire*, London: Cape.
Tafuri, H. (1989) *History of Italian Architecture, 1944–85*, London: MIT.
Thomas, K. (1984) *Man and the Natural World*, Harmondsworth: Penguin.
Thompson, J. (1984) *Studies in the Theory of Ideology*, Cambridge: Polity Press.
Tymms, R. (1949) *Doubles in Literary Psychology*, Cambridge: Bowes & Bowes.
Valente, J. (1985) 'Halls of mirrors: Baudrillard on Marx', *Diacritics* Summer: 54–65.
Veblen, T. (1959) *The Theory of the Leisure Class*, New York: Mentor.
Weber, M. (1965) *The Protestant Ethic and the Spirit of Capitalism*, London: Unwin.
Wernick, A. (1984) 'Sign and commodity; aspects of the cultural dynamic of advanced capitalism', *Canadian Journal of Political and Social Theory* 8(1–2): 17–33.

Williams, R. (1961) *Culture and Society*, Harmondsworth: Penguin.
Willis, P. (1990) *Common Culture*, Milton Keynes: Open University Press.
Wollen, P. (1989) 'The situationist international', *New Left Review* 174: 67–95.
Wollheim, R. (1975) 'Psychoanalysis and feminism', *New Left Review* 93: 61–9.
  (See also discussion and reply, in *NLR* (1976), 97: 106–12.)
Zizek, S. (1989) *The Sublime Object of Ideology*, London: Verso.
Zukin, S. (1988) 'The postmodern debate over urban form', *Theory, Culture and Society* 5: 431–46.
Zurbrugg, N. (1988) 'Baudrillard's *Amerique*, and the "Abyss of Modernity"', *Art and Text* 29: 40–63.
Zylberberg, J. (ed.) (1986) *Masses et Postmodernité*, Paris: Meridiens Klincksieck.

Name index

Adorno, T. 4, 6, 226
Althusser, L. 4, 21–8, 38, 86, 91,
    96, 97, 107, 132, 140, 198, 212,
    213
Anderson, P. 19, 22

Baehr, P. 224
Balibar, E. 215
Ballard, J G. 183, 190
Barthes, R. 34–7
Barthel, D. 226
Bataille, G. 4, 5, 7, 37–41, 45, 105,
    212, 222
Bauman, Z. 4
Berthelot, J-M. 132, 215
Benjamin, W. 6, 96, 99
Bettelheim, B. 149
Borges, J.L. 7, 144
Bourdieu, P. 226
Burchill, L. 58–9

Callinicos, A. 47, 55–7
Canguilhem, G. 24, 40, 215
Cannetti, E. 176, 193
Carroll, J. 224
Chang, B. 141
Chen, K. 141
Cohen, J. 217–8
Connor, S. 47

D'Amico, R. 219
Debord, G. 31–4, 35
Deleuze, G. 122, 206, 220, 223
Derrida, J. 37–9, 45, 86, 90, 92, 213,
    222, 223, 226
Descombes, V. 46
Dews, P. 46
Dostoyevsky, F. 7, 69–70, 212

Durkheim, E. 4, 5, 9, 10, 81, 198, 200,
    201, 208, 212, 213, 228

Elliot, G. 214
Enzenberger, H. 139

Foster, H. 46
Foucault, M. 16, 18, 39–41, 120–25,
    199, 214, 223
Freud, S. 11, 115–19, 147, 155,
    194

Gallop, J. 58
Giradin, J-C. 218
Girard, R. 197
Goffman, E. 10
Godelier, M. 101, 103–6
Goux, J-J. 101
Griffith, A.P. 46
Gouldner, A.W. 214, 219
Guattari, F. 222, 223

Harvey, D. 217, 219
Hebdige, D. 47, 216
Hegel, G. 38
Heidegger, M. 20
Holderlin, F. 6, 7, 169, 194–5,
    197
Hirst, P. 23

Irigaray, L. 147

James, W. 19
Jameson, F. 46, 66, 68
Jardine, A. 209
Jarry, A. 50, 225

Kafka, F. 122, 125, 158, 173, 178

Subject index